DISORDERLY MISCONDUCT

Recollections and Reflections of a Military Doctor

SECOND EDITION

Chowdhury Ishraq Uz Zaman

Disorderly Misconduct

tellwell

Tellwell Talent
www.tellwell.ca

ISBN
978-0-2288-4447-1 (Hardcover)
978-0-2288-4446-4 (Paperback)

Dedication

To my beloved wife
Samina Mahmud Zaman,
who gladly journeyed with me
through rain and sunshine

ACKNOWLEDGEMENTS

This narrative has been a work in progress for a good part of the last fifteen years of my life. It took me this long because in the midst of a fairly hectic personal routine over the years, I was able to manage only a few spare moments to be able to gather my thoughts, organize my recollections, compose my reflections – and then put those down on paper. Nevertheless, the urge and the motivation to write this memoir consumed me so overwhelmingly that the act of constantly creating, expanding and amending it turned into a perpetual process made up of innumerable small sessions spread over the years – sessions that I always looked forward to, and which gave me immense pleasure.

Understandably, the contents of this narrative have undergone modifications, extensive at times, since the day I began writing it. What follows, therefore, is the outcome of countless hours of trying to remain honest with myself, true to my conscience and fair to those individuals who played their parts, be those prominent or passing, in my life as a doctor in the armed forces.

In a way, therefore, I am grateful to all such individuals for having created the circumstances, and hence the basis, which kindled the creation of this book. In return, they have been immortalized within these pages for both their words and their deeds, be those either glorious and laudable, or gruesome and lamentable.

Not too many people knew about this undertaking of mine. But I am grateful to those few friends and members of my family who, when told about it, provided encouragement and valuable inputs, or inquired often about its progress. Notable amongst them are Ansar Ahmed, Mansur Hasib, Shabana Siddique, Obaidul Haque, Dr. Mohammad Hannan, Ishtiaque Ali, Mehrab Khandkar and a few others. The list, actually, is much longer. But over the past fifteen years or so – and with perhaps a concomitant failing memory – a good number of those names escape recollection today. To them I apologize, and say, "Thank you".

A few years ago, I began posting short excerpts of my manuscript as my Facebook status, with the intention of getting a feedback from my Facebook friends. And I must admit the response was overwhelming – and which comprised both inspirational remarks and constructive criticisms. I would like to thank all those who took the time and the effort to put in a word or two, the collective outcome of which has certainly improved the quality of this memoir.

Most importantly, however, three individuals have been instrumental in providing feedback and for suggesting modifications, the likes of which can only make a manuscript worthy of publication.

They are Brigadier General Kalam Shahed (Retired), Dr. Shaukat Hassan and Dr. Zulfiquar Sadeq. Proficient and knowledgeable in their own fields, and experienced in publication in their own right, they suggested alterations and additions which have given this manuscript the sparkle and enrichment it needed. I am grateful to them for having given their time, despite their own multifarious personal commitments and involvements. I am grateful, in particular, to Brigadier General Kalam Shahed (Retired), for also having agreed to write the foreword to this book. Having held vital appointments during his illustrious career in the Bangladesh Armed Forces, I felt he would be best placed, not only to be able to appreciate the worth and significance of such a narrative, but also to be able to introduce it appropriately to the prospective reader.

And finally, this memoir would not have possible had it not been for the patient and quiet understanding of my wife, Major Samina Mahmud Zaman (Retired), who so graciously made the space I needed to be able to indulge in such an undertaking. The precious moments outside of our hectic day-to-day life, which were well within her rights to claim to spend together, were thoughtfully and considerately relinquished to accommodate my aspirations. She is the unseen backbone who stands behind this memoir. Nothing I ever do will be sufficient enough to thank my wife for her continued and unwavering support. The least I can do therefore, to express my gratitude, is to dedicate this book to her, with the hope that it can, to some extent, recompense for those few moments of togetherness which were lost in its quest.

AUTHOR'S NOTE ON THE SECOND EDITION

This book was first published in 2017. However, over the months that followed, I found myself going back to it off and on. That was prompted basically by my desire to re-examine and revisit some of the premises, perspectives and assertions I had made in the original book. A fringe benefit of that was also the opportunity of being able to re-inspect a few literary nuggets in the previous edition that were perhaps not as polished as they ought to have been, and to try to refine those a bit more, if possible. It was also my chance to dive into the water again, to try to come up with a few more pearls of my days in the armed forces that I had not fetched earlier.

As a matter of fact, a number of viewpoints that had been expressed in the earlier edition and a few conclusions that were drawn were, more or less, focused on the flawed practices and unfair prejudices of one particular organization only. However, it was a gradual realization over time that it would be remiss to censure one specific entity over such faults and failings. If truth be told, certain patterns of misdeeds, misrules and misdemeanors actually exist across a wide swath of institutions and establishments, and are not necessarily restricted to only one. And more often than not, that happens to be a reflection of the misdeeds of a few bad actors in an establishment, despite the fact that the other players in it could otherwise be entirely rightful and righteous. It is for that very reason that the focus of discussion and certain critical analyses in this edition has been shifted from the whole, to the few – those few who habitually smear and discredit an establishment. My previous assertions, discussions and conclusions have, therefore, been rephrased and readdressed accordingly.

Moreover, in this edition, I have endeavored to make my narration a bit more lucid and vivid to the best of my ability, and therefore I feel that a few nuggets in it, here and there, are now perhaps a bit shinier. I was also able to come up with a few new pearls from the deep, of extraordinary incidents of my years in the armed forces that had earlier escaped my memory. In the process, though this edition is largely a reflection of the previous one, it is perhaps a reflection on a clearer and a somewhat larger mirror.

It is my hope, therefore, that my experiences as a doctor in the armed forces, and my reflections on some of the deeds or misdeeds of a few in it, or their distorting of some of its rules to suit their needs will be able to provide readers with insights into some of the goings-on in any organizational entity.

Major Chowdhury Ishraq Uz Zaman (Retired)

FOREWORD

Major Chowdhury Ishraq Uz Zaman (Retired)'s book recounts his journey, as an officer, through the Army Medical Corps (AMC) which he found difficult, often challenging, and sometimes agonizing. He reconstructs his work environment as a General Duty Medical Officer (GDMO) at a Combined Military Hospital (CMH), at a field ambulance unit, the Armed Forces Medical Institute (AFMI), as a trainee in surgery, a surgical specialist, and finally, as an orthopedic surgeon in the Armed Forces of Bangladesh. He illustrates the contradictions between the ethos and values of the military as well as those of the medical profession, and the actual practices of some senior military doctors, which are driven by their individual concerns of career enhancement and professional rivalries, and which remain rife among the fellow senior doctors and physicians.

Zaman saw the functioning of the AMC quite intimately from the roles that he played as a relatively young, but a bright and rising doctor, and provides a welter of insights; yet, this may only be a partial portrayal of the strategic policy dynamics of the entire administrative syste with its inherent strengths and weaknesses. The AMC is quite a large organization and manages field training of doctors, preparing them to support soldiers in combat and offer specialized training for doctors who would be employed in CMHs across the entire country. Military hospitals offer one of the best medicare in the country, and "non-entitled" senior politicians and civil servants remain keen to avail their services. I do, however, concur with Zaman that CMHs barely have the resources to meet the growing number of non-entitled patients. Nevertheless, some senior officer give priority to these patients for personal, financial or career interests. One complicating issue that Zaman appropriately underscores is the fact that CMHs have to conform to the wishes of the local commanders who, with their rank and seniority, can sometime overrule the decisions of medical administrators.

The author narrates his story in his ornamental style, revealing the gap between his lofty expectations and the realities of everyday life in the AMC. His overall experience was physically and emotionally unnerving and he hints at similar experiences encountered by his wife who was a military paediatrician. He reveals how senior medical administrators and doctors can create unhappy work environment, torment their under-command and hamper professional development. Several sections in his book are laced with emotions as the author felt deeply hurt by an establishment which, in his judgment, remained antiquated and dysfunctional. The debates around the roles of general duty doctors and specialists, the status of doctors and nurses, and the attention given to the rank and stature of patients, rather than to the nature and severity of the medical problems, have continued to haunt the establishment.

The book is not, however, rigidly serious in focus. The text is sprinkled with humor and the lighter aspects of a young military doctor's professional and social milieu. Amidst some apparent senseless preoccupation, he offers glimpses of honest, hardworking and compassionate mid-level officers, who helped foster camaraderie and professional ethics.

Critical reviews of the functioning of any establishment can go a long way to identify problems and take corrective measures. I hope the book will lead to some soul searching and, although many issues raised will be contested with counterarguments by senior policy makers, an objective reassessment of longstanding practices can eventually benefit the organization.

Politicization of military establishments is unfortunate, but this does occur in developing countries. Military is a hierarchical organization; rank and seniority weigh heavily on its morale, integrity and functioning. If the upper echelons of a military hierarchy become corrupt, be it financially, or because of political enticement, the military is likely to develop the traits of a militia force, which seeks self or petty group interests only. I sincerely hope that AMC, with its bright constellation of doctors, administrators and support staff, will continue to offer quality service to the needy patients, and neither the weight of military rank nor political pressure would hinder its professional commitment.

Brigadier General Kalam Shahed (Retired)
Bangladesh Armed Forces

TABLE OF CONTENTS

Chapter 1

A PEEK INSIDE PANDORA'S BOX

The shades of the chameleon

"In reality, hope is the worst of all evils, because it prolongs man's torments." – Friedrich Nietzsche

A book is most often the outcome of an individual's ardent desire to provide immortality to either fiction or fact. Fiction, as we all know, is a matter of telling all that never happened in a way which would make it seem very real. The latter, on the other hand, is fundamentally a matter of digging up and re-examining the past.

Although this book is essentially a factual narration, segments of it may seem to have a somewhat fictional resonance to it. Whether my experiences of an entity which I was thrust into by a run-away cascade of events and circumstances were actually outlandish enough to qualify to be a fiction, or whether my expectations of it were too high compared to what it actually was, I do not know. Nevertheless, one thing is certain: Looking back at all that I encountered and experienced some two to three decades ago not only rankles in my mind as a seemingly 'unreal' reality, it also seems to persist as a distant and, yet, a lasting memory.

Distant memories become lasting when events and experiences have been either rewarding and fulfilling, or disappointing and frustrating. And, at this point, I find myself wondering whether or not, in the final analysis, all this was actually a nightmare dressed up as a dream – a nightmare crafted out of the apparent failures of an institutional system, the inconsistencies of an otherwise esteemed functionary, and the vagaries of some in positions of power.

Do not get me wrong. I am not here to judge the validity or the credibility of some of the traditional and time-honored precepts and principles of any establishment. I am not here to discredit any organization for some of its practices, be those peculiar or prejudicial. It is not within my competence or ability to define or to declare what constitutes the flaws and the failures of any institution. It is also not my place to elaborate what typifies the fallibilities of a person, or the frailties of a personality. And I certainly do not seek to validate or predicate my views and opinions either, regarding certain institutional norms – be those preposterous or painful. I leave all that up to my readers to deduce and to decide, after having gone through the pages that follow. I am here only as an individual who has once had to travel down the intricate and sometimes confusing labyrinths of an institutional arrangement – either reveling in its glory or suffering its consequences. This is merely a narrative of that journey, sprinkled with suggested remedial measures, regardless of whether or not those seem logical or acceptable to those who guide and govern.

So therefore, as much as this book is an endeavor at expressing my feeling of pride and glory in once being part of a mighty and colossal establishment, and as much as it is an attempt at providing immortality to a few of my personal triumphs and accomplishments, it is equally an effort at weighing those against some of the distorted principles, devious practices and peculiar personalities inherent in almost any establishment. But, above everything else, this book is a testament to the heart-rending emptiness of a few unfulfilled hopes, dreams and aspirations of one individual – which, I am sure, could also be said of many in a similar setting and situation. In fact, it is a story so collectively familiar and so outrageously commonplace that I feel it is only fair that it be told. And equally importantly, this book is also my very personal tribute dedicated to those unsung heroes who have always had to endure more than their share of certain institutional insolences and injustices, but have always had the grace and the elegance of having done so with sensible silence and noble forbearance.

For every human who has ever walked on this planet, a chronicle of events follow their footsteps from the moment of their birth to the last breathe they take. And as harsh as it may sound, only a pitiful few of such journeys are ever remembered. In fact, most are never even noticed – their arrival being as silent and disregarded as their departure. The sound of their footsteps disappear over the horizon, ignored by humans and unheard by humanity. Their footprints get erased by the winds of a worldly race for prestige, prominence and pompous positions, never to be seen again, and lost forever.

But sadly, this also erases stories – little insignificant stories that are like little stitches in the mighty fabric of the Human chronicle, which are lamentably lost in a one-way trip in Time. Whether this augments or diminishes the worth of Humankind is debatable. What is not debatable, however, is that even though most of these insignificant and inconsequential stitches seem to go missing in the annals of human history, they somehow create a vague and mysterious force somewhere within the vast and timeless epic of the human journey, and which helps to hold that mighty fabric together.

Because, just as it was an imperfection of cosmic proportions that has left this Universe with a diversity beyond comprehension and a beauty beyond description, the imperfections resulting from those missing and forgotten stitches have also given the human saga its distinctive character, and the human chronicle its divine value. In reality, those unseen, forgotten and mysterious stitches hold the human saga together, in much the same way the unseen and all-pervading Dark Matter holds our entire Universe together.

This book is an attempt at taking a closer look at one of those stitches – lest it gets unfairly forgotten in the haste of Humanity.

It is not very often, or very easily, that one takes up a pen to begin to recount events in one's life – which, distinctly, is true in my case. Even so, I chose to undertake this fairly overwhelming task to be able to share moments, incidents, situations and experiences which were at times perplexing, and at other times outrageous. This is also an attempt at examining certain behaviors which were not always righteous or conscientious. But above everything else, this is an effort at putting to rest a conscience which is considerably – and quite rightly – perturbed, and the reasons for which, I hope, will gradually unfold as the pages go by. This is my endeavor to share the story of a segment of my life as it happened, and which I feel is significant enough for me to want to preserve within these pages.

I am not a writer, and never intended to be one. Obviously, the exceptional and extraordinary nature of events of this particular segment of my life has, quite strangely, brought out the writer in me. Though the literary quality of this book may not be quite as rich or as engrossing as of an accomplished writer, it will nevertheless be interesting enough for the readers to want to take a closer look – if not for anything else but to experience how good sense and good governance can sometimes be pushed to the very brink of existence, and then very casually tipped over its edge into oblivion. I write this book to share with my readers a dream which was meticulously institutionalized, and then – in my case at least – quite craftily turned into something akin to a nightmare.

For me, it all began at a crucial crossroad in life, the essence and embodiment of which had an implication similar to the dawn of a new day. It was a moment when I was emboldened by Life's early freshness to strike out and make the most of what lay ahead for me. It was a moment when I paused briefly, only to consider the consequences of my past and the sequences of my future – and a nascent star took birth within the cosmic particles of new hopes and aspirations.

Following my graduation from medical school, I stood at a fork in the forest, where one path led to service with the civil administration, and the other to the armed forces. I chose the latter, perhaps because I could see a bright light at the end of the tunnel. In reality, however, as one heads down towards such bright lights, it can very well begin to flicker at some point, and sometimes even get extinguished. And since the way is then lost in the darkness, turning around gets difficult. All that one can do at that point is grope around blindly and hope for the best – betrayed by Fate, and bent over under the burden of decisions made. This memoir is my recollection of both the good fortune and the misfortune of having traveled down such a tunnel once.

The pages that follow relate to events and experiences of my life as a doctor in the armed forces of Bangladesh, which I could not bring myself to lock up in a corner of my mind and forget about – for two reasons. Firstly, if I did that, I would have failed to have preserved the stories of personal triumphs and accomplishments of a certain chapter of my life, however trifling and insignificant those might have been. And secondly, it would have amounted to being unfair to my own conscience for having disregarded my sense of morality and dignity in the context of my interactions with certain practices and personalities of an institutional existence. Moreover, it is also an obligation I feel I owe to those who are yet to pass through the vaunted and celebrated gates of any institution, and who therefore need to know some of their quirks and quandaries, as much as they long to revel in their glory and greatness.

By and large, the fundamental attributes of any disciplined institution is decidedly underscored by fairness, integrity, neutrality, and an orderly conduct. But, unfortunately, there are also times when a certain degree of prejudice, intolerance and unfairness exists in certain isolated segments of any such establishment. Though, in all fairness, this should not to be interpreted as a comprehensive representation of the establishment in question, or assumed to be its modus operandi, it nonetheless tarnishes its bona fide image, which some of the other members so tirelessly toil to uphold.

The so-called 'pernicious worms' in an otherwise perfect apple are a few impoverished souls, sometimes surprisingly high in any hierarchy, who seem to be living within a self-centered domain of petty self-interests. For them, it is a world of created self-importance meticulously orchestrated to bolster their egos, and mindlessly motivated to serve certain vested interests. And, in the process, they convert the establishment they belong to, into an apparatus which neglects the prescription for healthy institutional growth, and ignores the principles of fair institutional practice. They dispatch their establishment to the wilderness of inefficacy through misplaced priorities, and damn it to dormancy under a burden of archaic practices.

But that is not the tragedy.

The real tragedy is that such individuals – thus ensconced within their self-created and prejudiced world of self-seeking and self-gratifying selfishness –do not seem to have either the perception to realize their impropriety or the ability or the inclination to look beyond the borders of their self-centered egotism. Tragically too, they do not seem to have the time or the temperament to even consider where the establishment was going because of them.

Sadly, such improprieties are made even worse when certain intuitional norms and practices are left out in the open by the trusted guardians of the establishment, to be ravaged and ruined by the exponents of decadence and deception. Whether this is through indifference or by design, I do not know. But, unfortunately, this is where any establishment – or more specifically, a part of it –goes horribly wrong.

A case in point is where some people distort the otherwise universally accepted relationship between *action* and *destiny*. Understandably, there has always been a perpetual debate as to whether or not the former actually influenced the latter. And interestingly, there has never been a shortage of proponents belonging to either side of this argument which, of course, helped to keep the debate alive.

In my opinion, *action* and *destiny* are similar to the duality of the *yin* and the *yang*. The state of harmony and equilibrium between the two is the outcome of the influence of one on the other – more specifically that of *action* on *destiny*. I, along with a sizeable segment of the world community, would like to believe that *action* directed diligently and judiciously is well capable to altering the *destiny* of any individual to a great measure under a variety of circumstances. As a testament to that fact, we have billionaires making it from rags to riches, and inventors, writers, entrepreneurs and entertainers alike, making a name for themselves against all odds.

Unfortunately, a handful few always seem somewhat averse to such a paradigm – and which is obvious from the fact that hard work and sincerity do not always produce the desired or expected results. And, that is because certain 'powers', by virtue of being placed high in an organizational hierarchy alter the destinies of its denizens as they please. It does not seem to matter that diligence and devotion are unreservedly delivered by some. The equation is never complete, it seems, unless it fulfills the goals and the game-plans of the proverbial 'worms' in the apple. And in the process, it always dooms a person into being what "others" want him or her to be, rather than what that person actually wanted to be, or had the potential to be.

Ranks, designations and appointments within any organization are created for the efficient functioning of its various components. But unfortunately, a coterie of self-serving individuals in any organization seems to think that those are also meant to meet their individual needs and demands. And not surprisingly, therefore, the responsibility and the sanctity of the ranks and appointments placed on them are often casually brushed out of sight under the disreputable carpet of personal interests, egotistic attitudes, and a mode of governance geared to a self-serving agenda. It hardly matters, sometimes, that you happen to get in the way. You mostly get brushed under as well – and forgotten forever. But, it pains and disappoints me to see that the conscientious and virtuous segments of such establishments hardly ever take those misappropriations into cognizance, or bother to do anything about it. This often results in the loss of not only the good name of an establishment, but also the eventual and inevitable premature loss of many of its meritorious personnel.

In the context of a military organization in particular, whatever some of such presumptuous individuals achieve, is done largely through the clever and rampant use – or rather, abuse – of words and phrases contained in the judicial manuals, and which seems to give whatever they say or do, a semblance of legitimacy and of wonderful authority. They seem to overlook the fact that such judicial manuals exist in any institution to actually provide proper direction and uphold immaculate discipline. But, distorted, deviant and aberrant implications and interpretations of words and phrases like "lawful command", "disorderly conduct" and "behavior unbecoming of an officer" and so on, are often used by certain such individuals with unprecedented passion and with disconcerting frequency to help fulfill their agendas for personal gains and inglorious schemes. It is as if the voluminous judicial manuals, which otherwise stand like a bastion of justice and fairness behind the functional consummations of any establishment, are also the great neutralizer and equalizer for all institutional misdemeanors perpetrated by them. And since this keeps them assured that they are right, and that they have all the impunity they need, to impose and to execute their whims and wants, it obviously and frequently leads to the random, and sometimes whimsical, application of the codes. And the fact that all such codes have come out of a book which is often credited with years of successful 'judicial deliverance', it seems to assure such individuals, therefore, that they are right.

Structuring an organization rigidly by rank is an excellent example of a successful functionary. It is a system which requires no explanation, and moves forward on the indisputable authority of its own momentum and genuineness. In actuality, the very concept of rank, designation, status and appointment had originally germinated from a basic and well-intentioned attempt at successful governance. Regrettably however, these are also synonymous with Power which, in the wrong hands, can very well turn into a double-edged sword. And when welded by someone inclined to carving out opportunities for oneself, and not clearing the way for an establishment to forge ahead, it is likely to adversely affect the immediate and long-term role and repute of the establishment itself. That is when the credibility of any institution – however mighty or majestic – is always at a significant risk of ruination beyond repair. References to this will be made in the pages which follow while examining and discussing situations where these have been shown to have the potential of either making or breaking an institution.

Furthermore, the power and pomposity of an elevated rank and appointment, particularly in the context of individuals inclined to 'institutional misdemeanors' if you will, often instills in them a disposition contrary to the solemn purpose behind their creation. Such a disposition often results in the loss of an establishment's standing as an institution of fairness and neutrality in situations where the so-called 'power' of ranks and appointments are, at times, employed as a means of fulfilling demands, returning favors, denying justice, depriving rights, expressing displeasure and, in some instances, as an instrument for revenge, retribution and retaliation – particularly where it concerns promotions and postings. Suffice it to say that such practices are particularly prevalent in institutions where the checks and balances for containing such imperious belligerence and self-gratifying egotism are non-existent.

It was interesting to observe, moreover, that in the context of the establishment in question, some of such belligerence and intemperate egotism was often exercised by some with unrestrained liberty on the medical institution – with the resultant and obvious subjugation of its hierarchy, suppression of its true potential and the thoughtless desecration of its dignity. But what disheartened me actually was that the medical hierarchy seemed to repeatedly surrender subserviently to such outrageous and inconsiderate conducts without the slightest dissention. Was such a demeanor perhaps the natural outcome of a fear of losing coveted rank and status which some in the medical hierarchy wanted to cling on to even at the expense of their own dignity and self-respect? I do not know.

Furthermore, in certain instances and in certain establishments, it is seen that ranks and appointments – regardless of how some of those may have been acquired or been bestowed upon – provide a perfect pretext for some to relegate certain relevant qualities and qualifications of others to worthless insignificance. It is beyond any comprehension as to the useful purpose it serves to assess a person's worth merely by rank and not by any other valid measurable yardstick – a topic that I shall discuss at length in a later chapter. Perhaps, in the hunting grounds for competitive survival, it reconfigures the playing field to one which favors a certain group over another and provides a perfectly legitimate basis for ignoring and relegating merit and qualification with surgical precision and surprising convenience. It is the same as curbing the running prowess of a deer, so the cheetahs could have a field day.

In that regard, I always failed to comprehend the norms which compelled me to assume a posture of obscure lowliness at an official gathering where, perhaps, a classmate of mine from high school would be wallowing in the pomp, prominence, and splendor of his elevated rank and appointment. Obviously, the critical line of demarcation was the fact that he had more brasses on his shoulders than I did. To me, it seemed as if the two years he spent learning military science was perhaps somewhat more momentous and meaningful than me having spent five years learning medical science. No effort, it seemed, was ever exerted to ensure minimum parity in terms of rank and seniority between someone who had attended medical school and another who had been to the military academy. It was as if the five years of academic hardship and arduous hours devoted to attaining intellectual excellence in medicine were not quite enough to be given much credit.

Do not get me wrong. This is not an attempt at taking anything away from anyone or any institution. I fully respect the virtues and values of any educational establishment, whatever be its course and curriculum. But I will still insist that this was where the fundamental basis of reasonable practice fell short in terms of sense and sensibility. The equivalence in rank and seniority drawn between a doctor in the armed forces and a member of the arms and other services in the context of their respective academic background and experience seemed somewhat lopsided, and perhaps designed to favor one over the other. Because even with an antedated seniority, doctors always fell short by anywhere between three to five years, in terms of seniority, of their high school classmates who were now in the arms and other services. Besides being a trifle embarrassing under certain circumstances, this was taking place in an organization where even half a day of seniority had far-reaching consequences.

Younger brothers of three of my high school classmates, who were about two to three years junior to me at the same school, became my senior when they joined the armed forces. It was infinitely gracious of them to have indicated, through subtle hints and cues, that they preferred not to be addressed as 'sir' by me. But unfortunately, not everyone was a younger brother of a friend; nor was everyone from the same high school.

This was perhaps the price and the penalty one had to pay for having decided to pursue a career in medical science and for having brought over its values and assets for the services of such an establishment.

The chapters that follow are a narration of events – some glorious, and some ghastly – which unfolded in my career with painful slowness, and the deductions from which I shall leave to the judgment of my readers. I have tried my best to recapitulate events and experiences spanning more than fifteen years of my service as a doctor in the military, and naturally, only the most memorable, significant and relevant, have found a place in this book. Predictably most, if not all, relate to the corps that I belonged to.

I have taken the liberty of mentioning some of the people I had come across during the period of my service, both within and outside the establishment, who left a mark in my life – be those auspicious or adverse – and whose names, pseudonyms or appointments were therefore indelible enough not to be mentioned. I apologize for not having taken the permission of those individuals, either because after all these years most cannot be reached, or I have no idea where they are now. But I know that they, as well as those I am still in touch with, will accept their inclusion sportingly and in good spirit.

My readers may notice the conspicuous absence of a timeline while going through this narrative. This, along with the fact that individuals have not been named while discussing certain sensitive issues, has been done out of respect, and for privacy and confidentiality.

Nevertheless, a good number of my ex-colleagues reading this book may be able to make an educated, and perhaps even a fairly accurate guess. However, it is not the objective of this book that they should be able to, because I am not here to lay any blame on anyone. This is my story, and it really cannot be helped if certain individuals somehow got involved in it by way of situations, circumstances and Destiny. This story simply recalls what such individuals chose to do, or not to do, under certain circumstances, and the ways in which those affected my career and the course of my future, be it favorably or adversely. Whether they were right or wrong is something I shall leave to the judgment of my readers. Nevertheless, should any of those unnamed individuals happen to be reading this narrative, and should they be able to guess that they have had some sort of an adverse role to play, I hope they will put up with their inclusion with humility, tolerance and forbearance – qualities I hope they, by now, have been able to acquire.

Understandably, some of the unnamed individuals, of whom I have been rather critical at times, have neither had the opportunity of defending themselves, nor have they been given a chance for justifying their actions. However, from a pragmatic perspective, a narrative as concise as this cannot conceivably be expected to entertain a discourse of monolithic proportions capable of weighing all sides of any given argument. In all fairness therefore, if they wish to, and if it makes them happy, the individuals who have been critiqued are at complete liberty of considering this memoir as nothing more than a diatribe of speculative conjectures – and, I will understand.

Nevertheless, like everything else in life, there are always two sides to every story, and this is my side of it – a side I remember rather distinctly. Every incident narrated in this memoir was factual enough for me to have had the audacity of having included those in these pages. And every conclusion arrived at was made with a clear conscience and with morality, dignity and fairness in mind. Therefore, any outright disapproval and denunciation of my personal observations would mean being unfair to me as well. I only wish I had the inputs from the so-called 'other side' as well, on the basis of which to deliver a universally acceptable verdict. But, then again, I would also like to be shown a verdict delivered since the dawn of Mankind, which has been unanimously and universally accepted. By and large, therefore, though I am frankly and honestly open to the fact that there may be some who may not want to entirely agree with the contents of this narrative, I would like to hope that it will be received with tolerance, humility, good spirit and fair judgment by those who have been either acclaimed or critiqued.

I have this firm conviction that my readers will agree with what Winston Churchill had once said – that *"Criticism may not be agreeable, but it is necessary. It fulfills the same function as pain in the human body; it calls attention to the development of an unhealthy state of things. If it is heeded in time, danger may be averted; if it is suppressed, a fatal distemper may develop."* And that is something I think every nation, race, group, establishment and individual ought to always bear in mind and accept with dignity, courage and confidence in order to be able to establish a better world and ensure a better tomorrow.

In the words of Norman Vincent Peale, a renowned motivational author, *"The trouble with most of us is that we'd rather be ruined by praise than be saved by criticism."*

And at this point, I would like my readers to understand that my views and opinions – be those complimentary or critical – of some of the men, the machinery and the machinations of an institutional entity are my very own and personal. And should anyone like to profess on the other hand that those cannot be construed as being conclusively accurate, nor assumed to be universally shared and accepted, that would be their prerogative.

And finally, I say this with utmost sincerity that all that have been discussed and revealed in this book are not intended to demean, defame or dishonor the reputation or worth of any individual, group, class, profession, qualification, institution, establishment or organization.

This, then, is my story … … …

Chapter 2
A RUDE AWAKENING
Joining the army: Days at CMH Savar

"One half of knowing what you want is knowing what you must give up before you get it." – Sidney Howard

The curtain rose on a cold February morning.

My wife, Samina, and I departed from the capital city of Dhaka, where we lived, to join a military hospital about thirty kilometers away, close to a small town called Savar.

This hospital was one of the installations of the military Cantonment located in the outskirts of that town. A Cantonment is the equivalent of a Garrison or a Fort – a nomenclature left behind by the British colonials when they left. The military hospital at Savar was known as CMH Savar – CMH being the acronym for Combined Military Hospital. The word "Combined" signified the fact that the hospital was meant for the treatment of personnel from all three branches of the armed forces – the army, the navy and the air force. In fact, every military hospital anywhere in the country was called a CMH, followed by the name of the city or town it was located in.

The military cantonment at Savar had been around for quite some time now, but basically as one of the smaller ones with very little logistic significance. Moreover, with the very core of Bangladesh Army, and with it, the largest military cantonment sitting only a little over forty minutes to the south, Savar Cantonment was always doomed to irrelevance and perpetual insignificance – but only up to the day that the National Memorial Monument was built at Savar.

This was a memorial dedicated to the thousands of Bangladeshi civilians, freedom fighters and soldiers who were either killed, had gone missing, or had died fighting, during the course of the war that led to the creation of Bangladesh. Also known as the *Jatiyo Smriti Shoudho* – which translates to the *National Memorial Monument* – it immediately thrust the previously little-known town of Savar into the limelight of national attention, activity and interest. Along with that, it gave Savar Cantonment a new-found military status and significance.

And CMH Savar was our very first place of posting on signing up with the Bangladesh Armed Forces.

Having graduated from Dhaka Medical College, my wife and I were at the end of our one-year period of internships at the Dhaka Medical College & Hospital, when the Bangladesh Army advertised in the newspapers that it needed medical graduates for the Army Medical Corps. To us, this presented itself as a very attractive and timely proposition for a few reasons.

Following the completion of our internships, we were both staring at postings to remote rural health centers. It was certainly not the remoteness that was unappealing to us, because neither of us would ever shirk from providing our services to the ailing, regardless of location. But what made it unattractive was the fact that such rural health centers had little or no medical facilities in terms of equipment, instruments or even medications. An added absurdity was the fact that any initiative to have that situation resolved was either going to be brazenly and callously ignored or even misconstrued, as has often been the case.

Moreover, doctors at such rural health centers have, more often than not, had to deal with the wishes and demands of local political heavyweights who, after being done with their deadly and sometimes fatal political confrontations, wanted the medical authorities to clean up their mess on paper – or otherwise face grievous consequences. To be very honest, this was something we were not at all familiar with, and neither were we mentally equipped to deal with such conducts. But more importantly, we were not the least interested in getting involved in the fray of local politics. This is not to say, however, that there weren't any amongst our colleagues who thought otherwise – and we felt that such a practice was better left to them.

As if all this was not enough, the Ministry of Health then decided that ours would be the first batch of medical graduates required to sit for the Bangladesh Civil Service Examinations in order to qualify for a posting to any of the rural health centers. I would not like to go into the debate of whether this was right or wrong – because that is not the purpose of this book. But, besides the fact that a rural health center was not our preferred career destination for the above reasons, we also felt that we had already had our fair share of having to write examinations while in medical school, and were not quite willing to go through any more of it.

But perhaps the most compelling reason which finally convinced us that the civil service was perhaps not for us, came as a 'revelation', so to speak. I call it a revelation because it opened our eyes to a rather reprehensible practice, apparently rampant, which we had little or no knowledge of, or no previous experience with, and which we were therefore ill-equipped to handle. It all stemmed from an incident which took place right after Samina and I had graduated, and we were waiting for an official posting to Dhaka Medical College & Hospital as interns. It was for the purpose of some official paperwork in that regard that we were at the Ministry of Health & Population Control one day.

It was always in the interest of fresh graduates that internships begin as soon as possible following graduation, because that determined service seniority which, understandably, had long-term implications. And this was where the clerks at the ministry wielded a big stick. Posting as an intern could either be enhanced or delayed by them, depending on whether or not they had been adequately gratified financially. And right there, in front of our very eyes, Samina and I witnessed the execution of that abhorrent practice, as one of our friends who had graduated with us ensured an undeserved quicker passage for himself. If this was what it was going take to get a posting, I decided that the civil service was just about the last place we wanted to be in. And if such a despicable practice was being encouraged at the beginning of one's career, it was beyond comprehension as to what lay ahead as one progressed.

Besides all this, however, there was one final motivating factor which made the armed forces more attractive than the other. Whether or not one would like to admit, this particular matter always has an overwhelming influence on the decision-making process when it comes to seeking a job – and that is the pay. The salary in the armed forces was going to be at least three times that in the civil service. And however much one may want to downplay this aspect of an employment, it will always figure prominently in anyone's preference for a job.

All who endorse the fact that life is probably a proverbial bed of roses, will also have to contend with the thorns of the other imperfect half of it. For what might seem to be full of promise, hope and opportunity can also have its dismal and disappointing aspects. Life has a way of offering us choices at crucial crossroads, none of which are often particularly watertight in terms of promise and potential. Basically therefore, it is a matter of weighing options for the future and embracing any decision made, along with its flaws and failures – content in the realization that life could have been worse.

And so it was, with our choice of joining the armed forces and not the civil service. Unfortunately, both had their good sides and bad, with perhaps the armed forces holding a slight edge over the other in terms of promise and potential – or so we thought. Because, over the following fifteen years or so, however much we looked around for a ray of reassurance that we had made the right choice, or however deep we dived with the hope of finding one perfect pearl, we mostly came up empty-handed.

And so, here we were, approaching CMH Savar about an hour later.

Looking out the window of the car we were greeted by the view of prim gardens splashed in all the splendor of winter blossom. Rows of barracks looking smart and purposeful with their sloping tin roofs glistening under the late morning sun soon came into view. It was almost a case of love at first sight, and I seemed convinced that perhaps, at length, we had come to the right place. However, I was soon to learn that one had to be a bit more careful while arriving at such hasty conclusions, and not get so easily carried away by blissful blossoms and smart barracks with sloping tin roofs.

We were stopped at the gates of the hospital by a smartly turned-out sentry in combat fatigues, who, after inquiring into the purpose of our visit, let us through.

Upon reaching the hospital we were informed that the Commanding Officer was busy, and so were ushered into an adjacent room to wait for him.

The words 'Conference Room' were neatly painted above the door. Inside, surprisingly, it looked more like a living room, with comfortable chairs, couches, sofas and coffee tables. The reason for this, I discovered later, was because this room played the primary role of a tea-room, where the officers of the hospital gathered for their mid-morning tea and snacks. But, that was perhaps not to be expressed in as many words, and my initial hunch for the reason for that was somewhat confirmed later on during my career. There seemed to be this general notion all around – vague, yet running rather deep – that in a hospital situation, one was not supposed to leave one's work and spend time in a room having tea – more so, if one happened to be a junior medical officer. That would perhaps be very much 'contrary to good order and discipline', and would portray a lack of commitment to one's work.

Indeed, there have been times later on, especially during the initial years of my career while, during a tea break, I have had this queasy feeling within the deepest recesses of my sense of responsibility, for being where I was, and not in the ward. Whether this was the result of an intuitive concern for my patients or the outcome of an institutional inculcation, I do not know. But, what I do know is that this hospital somehow got away with the designation of 'Conference Room' – where I never saw a conference take place for as long as I was at CMH Savar.

But it turned out to be an ingenious guise because it gave any visitor the impression of important meetings going on within – while the accompanying act of food consumption was made to look like an ancillary activity only!

I may be wrong, but I have always had this feeling that there was, perhaps, a prevalent sentiment among some in the non-medical segments that the scenario of doctors having food and sipping tea while their patients allegedly suffered in the ward was being willfully negligent. Here was a phrase – willful negligence – very neatly and conveniently tucked within the pages of the judicial manuals, which could readily be used whenever required, for reasons ranging from the most justified to the most superfluous and bizarre.

It was perhaps a matter of a deeply ingrained notion which automatically took for granted the instant availability of a doctor, and a perpetual accessibility to them. It was as if everyone here possessed a magic lamp, which all they needed to do was rub, and out would emerge the genie of a doctor, ready to resolve all medical complaints at any time of the day or night, regardless of whether or not those were actually warranted. I am certainly not saying that a doctor shouldn't be available or accessible, regardless of the time of the day. But, when the need for medical attention is blown out of proportion to the actual health issue, as it often was, and the treating physician unnecessarily under duress to deliver, the matter seemed to test the boundary between genuine need on one the hand, and 'exploitation' on the other. One of the reasons that I can think of, for this tendency of 'rubbing the lamp' practically at the drop of a hat was that this so-called 'genie', and its accompanying accoutrements came free of cost – a matter that will be discussed in-depth in a later chapter.

But, for now, as I strode into this 'Conference Room', I immediately proceeded to make the first of a long series of 'mistakes' in my career. As I blissfully sank into the most comfortable couch I could find, I was instinctively drawn to the almost painful expression of apprehension on the face of the soldier who had ushered us in. To my inquiring look he muttered that the sofa I was sprawled upon was meant for none other than the Commanding Officer. Ah, a throne! I quickly ejected myself from the couch – not as much out of any reverence for it, as it was for putting a quick end to the expression of distress and agony on the face of the tormented soldier.

Being around mid-morning, it was time for the so-called 'tea break'. Very soon medical officers of all levels of seniority working in the hospital began filtering in and taking their rightful places around the room in order of their rank and seniority. At length, a smart fellow in uniform, with a stick tucked under his arm and a small leather box hanging by his side from a strap going across his chest, marched up to the door. He stomped on the floor with thunderous might, saluted, and inquired if all were present, so the Commanding Officer could make his grand entrance.

This individual, I later discovered, was the Commanding Officer's 'stickman', a sort of a sidekick. Or better yet, a corporeal insignia of the Commanding Officer's 'authority', who accompanied him everywhere he went, and was always at his beck and call. The leather box by his side, I was told, represented a time when messages from a Commanding Officer, placed in that box, would be delivered by this person, riding on a horse, it to its destination regardless of distance. Looking at that leather box, I kept wondering where his sword, crossbow and spear were hidden! To be honest, there were times I was very tempted to call this person aside and give him something a bit more useful to do for the nation.

At length, the Commanding Officer, after having made sure all in his 'fiefdom' were present in the Conference Room, made his pompous entrance. Everyone, including myself and my wife, stood up as a sign of respect. To my untrained eyes I noticed that the others in the room stiffened their upper bodies with a jerky movement, as they thrust both hands back like a pair of bamboo sticks.

I realized later that when not wearing a 'headgear' – that is, either a cap or a helmet – this was a form of showing respect to seniors. With the headgear on, however, one needed to salute in the traditional manner. But, whatever the mode of greeting or of showing respect it was usually accompanied, in an informal setting, by a concomitant loud utterance of *"Slaam, sir!"* – Where "Slaam" was an extreme short form of the traditional Islamic greeting, "as-salaam-wa-alaikum" meaning "peace be upon you". Though the phrase *"Slaam, sir!"* was linguistically meaningless, as long as the intent was adequately demonstrated, it was quite acceptable in the form it was being delivered.

I was very amused, over the years of my service, to observe that the physical expression of respect for a senior, as well as a senior's demand for it, was often very strictly adhered to. Sometimes it seemed to turn into a superfluous, bothersome, time consuming and, worst of all, a distracting preoccupation. This was more so in a hospital situation, where the need to pay attention to the sick and the ailing, including those requiring intensive care, was clearly more important than the need to pay attention to brasses hovering in the vicinity. But sadly, that did not seem to sit well with some! To be honest, there were times I felt that very little got achieved around here besides everyone being busy saluting everyone else. All this stemmed from the fact that repercussions and retributions for a salute not made often proved not only costly, but grisly as well. Territories of rank and seniority were not only marked out quite sharply, they were defended rather ruthlessly as well.

Suffice it to say that a physical demonstration of respect remains a demonstration only, where respect may not exist. Respect is to be earned, and not demanded. And in situations where it has been adequately earned, it will be forthcoming rather spontaneously, be it in or out of uniform, or with or without the brasses. Understandably, my standpoint does not include ceremonial situations. But, neither is every situation ceremonial, nor is every salute a representation of respect.

We were cordially greeted by the Commanding Officer, who welcomed us to the medical corps with words of encouragement, briefly attempting to draw an attractive picture of the world we were about to enter which, obviously, made both Samina and me quite happy.

Snacks were then served by butlers (called mess-waiters) dressed in immaculate white. And that was when I learned that timing one's culinary proceeding with that of the senior's was of vital importance in the armed forces, and that it constituted a fine point of military etiquette. It helped further if one could also nod enthusiastically to every comment and opinion of a commanding officer, whether or not one agreed. One also needed to be able to get into the 'herd behavior' at times, of guffawing with the rest, as the commanding officer reeled off his so-called witty jokes and quips – however morbid, sordid or mundane those might be.

The indoctrination

> *"In our nature, however, there is a provision, alike marvelous and merciful, that the sufferer should never know the intensity of what he endures by its present torture, but chiefly by the pang that rankles after it." – Nathaniel Hawthorne, "The Scarlet Letter"*

All necessary paper-work related to our joining the Army Medical Corps was completed after the tea-break, and which took place in the Commanding Officer's plush office.

I was instructed that from the following day onwards I was to shadow a senior officer, Lieutenant Colonel Matlub, around the hospital. Besides imparting vital information on the mode of treatment as practiced in the armed forces, he was also to familiarize me with the various military customs and etiquettes – including the intricacies of saluting, the complexities involved in demonstrating respect to a senior officer, and the absurdities of culinary practices, amongst others.

The matter of 'quartering', as it was commonly known in military language, came next. This was the provision of accommodation for an officer and his family. And so, right after having signed all official documents related to our joining the Armed Forces, we were ushered into the room of the Quartermaster of the unit. Here was Major Hakim from the Infantry, a quiet and ever-smiling officer who, over the years, had risen up the ranks from being a Non-Commissioned Officer (NCO), to a Junior Commissioned Officer (JCO), and finally to where he was today.

In terms of status and service privileges, a JCO is sandwiched between a Regular Commissioned Officer and an NCO. Occasionally, some JCOs are given Regular Commission on the basis of seniority, length of service and service performance. However, they hardly ever rise beyond the rank of Lieutenant Colonel. Major Hakim was one such officer.

Coming back to the matter of accommodation, regulations required that if a male officer was single, he would have to be accommodated in the Officers' Mess. And when a single female officer or one unaccompanied by her family arrived at a cantonment either on posting or on temporary duty, that officer would have to be accommodated in the AFNS (Armed Forces Nursing Service) Mess, which was a mess for single female nurses. Incidentally, only the Army Medical Corps had female officers at that point in time.

However, with Samina and me comprising a family, we needed to be accommodated either in the Officers' Mess or in a 'family accommodation' – called the 'Officers Quarters' – if those were available. 'Officers' Quarters' were housing complexes located in certain designated areas within a cantonment, and large enough to be able to accommodate a complete family.

And since the matter has come up, allow me to deviate momentarily at this juncture, as I attempt to make some sense of the Armed Forces Nursing Service (AFNS) and its officers.

The AFNS Officers were the female nurses of the Army Medical Corps. They were given ranks similar to that of the Regular Commissioned Officers – as evidenced by the brasses displayed on their shoulders – but were not given the same status. In other words, though they wore the exact same brasses and ranks as the Regular Commissioned Officers, the senior-most AFNS Officer was never senior to, or given more privileges than, the junior-most Regular Commissioned

Officer. Consequently, a Lieutenant Colonel of the nursing service, for example, could be heard addressing someone as junior as a Second Lieutenant of the Regular Commission as 'sir'. But surprisingly, there was nothing on the shoulder of the nursing officer to suggest as to why she should be doing so. Clearly, she had the same brass ranks as a Regular Commissioned Officer. Yet, somehow, she was not a Regular Commissioned Officer!

In reality, and in terms of status and privileges, the cadre of nursing service was carefully interposed between the Regular Commissioned Officers and the Junior Commissioned Officers (JCOs) – but leaning heavily towards the optical resemblance to that of the regular commission. This was perhaps done with the intent of enhancing the nurses' worth and eminence. Why, I do not know. But, unfortunately, it succeeded only in adding to the confusion.

There is no denying the fact that nurses are an essential and an integral part of the system which delivers patient care. But, it is equally important that their placement in the overall scheme of status and functionality be commensurate with both the level of their qualification and the nature of their work.

Moreover, the armed forces is a complex set-up comprised of multiple well-defined, well-knit and carefully-placed groups of individuals with their own distinct class, status and seniority and, yet, functionally inter-linked within a chain of command in order to be able to perform like a well-oiled machine. It is therefore imperative that the brasses, badges, insignias and stripes which define and categorize the various groups and individuals, be explicitly representative. And this is where the decision-makers, particularly of the medical establishment, ought to have been a little more diligent in selecting both the status and the insignia of the nursing personnel so as not to leave any room for doubt and confusion and, at times, embarrassment.

Needless to say, such a move must have been orchestrated by the luminous minds of the corps who had conceived its administrative setup during its infancy. Though rumors are rife as to the real reason behind such a decision, I do not subscribe to it on grounds that it constitutes a biased and unfair deduction on the basis of hearsay. But, whatever may have been the context, I find it astonishing that the so-called 'founding fathers' of the medical corps would have displayed such a lack of foresight and fortitude in not having considered the consequences of such a move.

Those in favor of the nurses wearing the same kind of ranks as the regular commissioned officers might argue that the uniform worn by the nurses was visibly different from that worn by the Regular Commissioned Officers, and that that was what set the two categories apart. In that case, I would like to remind them that in the real world, particularly in any military organization, it is the brass on the shoulder which counts, and that the uniform is immaterial. It is the rank which confers the status and earns the salutes. A soldier and a general mostly wear the same kind of a uniform, but it does not take a genius to figure out why a general gets all the salutes, and a soldier doesn't.

All said and done, such an arrangement often led to situations of awkwardness and confusion within the chain of command of the armed forces. Sadly, the custodians of the medical corps either couldn't see the confusion they had created, or chose to overlook it. Or maybe they simply didn't care. And, why should they? In a setting of incontestable unilateral prerogatives, they were the undisputed masters of their quirks and cravings.

Returning to the matter of accommodations again, the Officers' Quarters which Samina and I qualified for, usually were rows of two-bedroom tin-roof houses called *Rupsa* – which was an acronym for "Repatriated Unemployed Person's Single Accommodation". These were accommodations put together rather hurriedly for those officers of the armed forces and their families who were returning from Pakistan following the liberation of Bangladesh. Interestingly, about three or four such accommodations in a row, and all under one sloping tin roof, resembled a soldiers' barracks more than anything else. And groups of such barrack-looking accommodations were clustered together in certain areas of the cantonment. These were known as the Officers' Quarters. Surprisingly though, despite the fact that these three-room accommodations were exceedingly small, they were rather comfortable to live in, particularly for smaller families. And it is rather amusing that pretty soon the *Rupsa*, by way of phonetic convenience, began to be called "Rupsha" which, in Bengali, means "impeccable beauty"!

However, the construction of modern multi-storied apartment complexes, which were eventually to replace the *Rupsas*, was already underway at most places. Nevertheless, the *Rupsas* had not yet been totally phased out of service, and were therefore still to be found in most cantonments.

Samina and I, being a 'family', naturally qualified for either a *Rupsa* or one of the newer apartments. However, there were times that family accommodations were not readily available, and so officers and their families had to be put up in the officers' mess temporarily. And, with neither a *Rupsa* nor an apartment available at the time we joined CMH Savar, we too were destined for an officers' mess.

The one in which we were accommodated was the less glamorous of the two in the cantonment, but was preferred, since it was only a couple of minutes walk from the CMH. It was a four-storied building, old by any standard, with rows of single rooms on each floor, and all opening on to a long common verandah in front. For us, it was life in one room with a bed, a couple of chairs, a table, and an attached bathroom.

It is customary for officers residing in an officers' mess to have their meals in the dining hall. However, the mess we were residing in was rather antiquated, and therefore, did not have one. The other officers' mess in the cantonment, being big and more recently built, came complete with a huge dining hall as well. But unfortunately, it was at quite a distance from the one we were residing in. Going over to that mess during every meal was obviously going to be a hassle for us, more so since we didn't have any transportation of our own. Therefore, the only other option was to have the meals brought over from that mess to our room by a 'batman', who would be carrying our meals in what is known as a 'tiffin carrier'.

Being rather common in South Asia, a 'tiffin carrier' is actually 4-5 round aluminum containers stacked one on top of the other, and held together by a latching mechanism. However, some vastly improved versions of the tiffin carrier are available these days – ones which would make those from our time look like Lilienthal's glider on display at the Smithsonian Institute!

More importantly though, this is where I feel a brief description of a batman, and the rather indispensable role played by them in the armed forces is warranted, particularly for those not conversant with the army way of life.

Far from being the well-known comic superhero, 'batman' is a term which was originally used to refer to the orderly of an officer of the British army. And true to tradition, this term has been carried forward by the armies in the Indian sub-continent, including that of Bangladesh. Wikipedia defines 'batman' as "a soldier assigned to a commissioned officer as a personal servant" – which he exactly is. Traditionally, the duties of a batman are usually assigned to one of the junior-most of the junior soldiers of the unit who has to be at the beck and call of the officer he is assigned to. This includes, amongst other things, having the officer's uniform readied for the next day, including polishing the brass ranks and shining the officer's pair of boots. Also included are running errands – big or small, difficult or easy – for the officer. As it turns out, most batmen usually performed all those tasks to excellence. In fact, when it came to my batman, I never was able to figure out how he could ever get the brass ranks on my shoulders to shine like the brightest of stars, and get the toes of my boots to shine to a point where one could almost make out the teeth of a grinning face on it!

However, the armies of the sub-continent, at various points in time, decided not to have soldiers, but civilians, employed as an officer's batman. This individual was to be anyone selected by the officer from a source and arrangement of his choice. Moreover, it was left up to the officer to arrange to have that person trained to be a good batman. The batman's salary too, was to come out of the officer's pocket. Eventually, and thankfully, the role of training this individual was – by an unwritten understanding – taken over by the junior soldiers of the unit or by the 'senior' batmen belonging to the other officers.

Within only a few hours of joining CMH Savar, we were faced with the question of whether or not we wanted a batman. Although, at that point, we had a vague idea of what was being implied, the term 'batman' was nonetheless fairly new to us. But, when the plethora of responsibilities undertaken by a batman was eventually explained to us, we knew right away that such a person was an absolute necessity.

The very next day, a quiet and lanky kid in his mid-teens was standing in front of us, as the Havildar who brought him over provided us with his background details, while explaining to him at the same time, his roles and responsibilities. For the added benefit of our new batman, the Havildar also drew a rather vivid picture of the dire consequences he would face if not able to live up to our expectations. After the matter of his salary was finally settled, and we agreed to recruit him, our batman went on to receive an adequate 'behind-the-scene' indoctrination and training from unit personnel and the other batmen.

Zamir Ali was our dependable and trusted batman for a number of years thereafter, and I cannot think of a single occasion which required us to complain about him. And it was Zamir Ali who would punctually and unfailingly bring our meals over from the kitchen of the main mess to our room – besides polishing our ranks and my boots till they shone brighter than the sun! And besides running other errands, the little thoughtful things he did for us time and again won our hearts.

The only other couple besides us, who resided in our mess building, was Lieutenant Reza and his wife. The rest were junior bachelor officers belonging to the arms and other services. Reza was a dentist who was posted to CMH Savar, and like us, was waiting to be shifted to a family accommodation whenever available. We would make social calls to each other's room on some evenings. At other times, Reza and I would try our hand at playing lawn tennis on a cement court which was situated right across the road from our mess. I will not say we were particularly adept at that game, but we nevertheless derived a certain degree of satisfaction hitting a ball with a racket – however wayward our shots might have been.

Besides, Samina and I also interacted socially with the other junior bachelor officers residing in the same mess. On some evenings, we would pull chairs out on to the verandah in front of our rooms and have a delightful time sharing stories or just gossiping. Some days we would also sit around a cassette player and listen to *ghazals* playing on it.

A *ghazal* is a slow melodious song in Urdu (the language spoken mainly in Pakistan and in northern India) which is extremely rich in its literary quality, and mostly conveys sentiments centered around rejection in love. Some of these songs, written by accomplished and well-known Urdu poets have been able to enchant the minds and capture the hearts of listeners through time immemorial.

Having grown up in Bangladesh, and therefore having no knowledge or understanding of Urdu, I could hardly comprehend or appreciate the passion and the sentiments that were embedded and ingrained within the lyrics of the *ghazals*. And this was where Samina came in.

Samina had grown up in West Pakistan (as the western wing of Pakistan was known before East Pakistan broke away to become Bangladesh) because her father, being an officer in the Pakistan Air Force, was posted to air bases in Pakistan throughout most of his career. Urdu therefore always came more naturally to Samina than did her mother-tongue Bengali – though, by now, she is equally proficient in both.

Obviously therefore, Samina would have to explain most of the words and lines of the *ghazals* that we often listened to together – and that was how I actually got totally immersed in the magic of its melodious tune and the passion and sentiment of its overwhelming lyrics. Nevertheless, my knowledge of Urdu had always remained rather rudimentary and every so often I would have to have Samina explain to me the more difficult lines of the *ghazals*.

It was from watching the way the young officers, sitting around the cassette player, listening to the *ghazals* with their eyes shut and swaying their heads as if in a trance, that I had this wretched feeling that I must be the only one in the entire group who was not being able to fully gauge the sentimental enormity of the songs that were playing. It was only after Samina, rather voluntarily, began to extol and explain the richness and the splendor of some of the lyrics to the apparently enchanted group that I realized that none actually had a clue to most of what was being sung in the songs – but had decided to sway their heads and go into a trance anyways! Samina soon, and quite understandably, became a favorite – and a rather indispensable – member of the group that gathered in the verandah for an 'evening of *ghazals*'.

On the second or the third day of joining CMH Savar it was suggested to me by both the Commanding Officer and the Quartermaster that I go down to the Station Headquarters of Savar Cantonment as soon as possible to have my name entered in the list of those waiting for an accommodation in the Officers' Quarters. The reason for the rush was simple. Accommodations were allotted on the basis of the order in which an officer had reported to the Station Headquarters. I was to meet the SSO or the Station Staff Officer, since he was the person who dealt with officers' accommodations.

The Station Headquarters was roughly a little over two kilometers from CMH Savar, and though our unit's vehicles quite regularly went that way, I was told that getting there was something I would have to arrange myself. And not having any transportation of my own, I set out on foot the very next day, for the Station Headquarters.

That was something I strongly feel I should not have been made to do. And, as I shall soon explain, it led to a considerable conflict of conscience on my part, and a significant desecration of military decorum. Bear in mind that that was within only a few days of my joining the service. That means that I have not had any sort of military training till then, but was already wearing the uniform, with ranks on my shoulders. It was not as if my Commanding Officer, the custodians of the corps or the lofty offices had not foreseen the consequences of such a venture. But, what actually bothered me more was the fact that the upper echelons simply didn't seem to care – perhaps because it was all about a solitary officer and that too, from the medical corps. Perhaps, therefore, none seem particularly bothered.

This is where I feel I need to take a step back and delve into another pertinent matter and discuss its dire consequences: It is about the doctors freshly inducted into the Army Medical Corps having to put on the military uniform within only a couple of days of having joined the forces.

Let me begin by saying that for the AMC Officers, putting on the military uniform with ranks on the shoulders took place without any prior formal indoctrination in the code of military conduct. This, in my opinion, was most irresponsible of the authorities because it clearly indicated that they were willfully ignoring the ramifications of such an inconsiderate and reckless practice, be those shamefully embarrassing or painfully awkward.

In reality, the moment one puts on a military uniform with ranks on the shoulders, that person becomes morally and ethically responsible for upholding the worth and status that that uniform signifies. But understandably, without proper military training and with no tutoring in the code of conduct in the armed forces, a person is not expected to be suddenly endowed overnight with the morals, ethics, etiquettes and responsibilities that come with putting on a military uniform. I did not even know how to put on the military uniform the day before

I joined the armed forces. And for the authorities to expect that I should be able to uphold its worth the day after, was not only a clear example of an indifference to the worth of its medical personnel, but also an indication of an woeful institutional practice.

Quite understandably, I was so ignorant of military etiquettes at the time of my joining the armed forces that I was addressing senior officers as 'Bhai' (brother) instead of 'sir'. And, on the day of my arrival at CMH Savar, I remember having walked into Major Hakim's room, and addressing him as 'Hakim Shaheb' (Mr. Hakim). I had to be gently reminded that senior officers in the armed forces were to be addressed as 'sir', and not as 'Bhai' or 'Shaheb'. Though I felt somewhat embarrassed at my own ignorance in this regard, in all fairness, it was hardly my fault. This would never have happened had I been formally instructed in military etiquettes before joining a military unit. And stories were already making their rounds as to how the newly-commissioned AMC Officers were making an apparent fool of themselves all over the place – and by virtue of which they had, sadly, become an institutional laughing-stock.

I do not blame the newly-commissioned AMC Officers for any of this, for in the absence of any formal instruction or training, they were only doing what they thought was right and proper. Rather, I blame the shortsightedness and the failings of the authorities, which lay shamelessly and ruthlessly exposed by all this.

My trek to the Station Headquarters that day, therefore, was indeed painful – both physically and psychologically.

It was physically painful because this was only the third or the fourth day of my life in the armed forces and, expectedly, I came up pitifully and awkwardly short in terms of physical fitness. And so, by the time I was only a little more than halfway to my destination, both my calf muscles had gone rather numb, and were starting to lose control over my feet. And, by the time I was walking into the room of the SSO, my feet were actually flopping to the ground at every step, much like that of a scuba diver coming out of the water with flippers on. Thereafter I made every effort at prolonging my stay with the SSO, so the circulation to my leg muscles would return in time for my dreaded trip back.

The other painful aspect of the trek to the Station Headquarters was my conscience, which was troubled by the fact that with no training in military customs or codes of conduct, I was perhaps not doing justice to the innumerable salutes and salutations being directed at me during the trip.

If my Commanding Officer was perchance thinking that that was the way to introduce a newly-commissioned officer to the army way of life, that would have to be a clear indication of a lack of maturity and sensibleness. I may have been the joker on the road that day, but in reality, my Commanding Officer was the actual joker – occupying the limelight on the center stage, from where he revealed his ignorance, imprudence and lack of critical perception. The greatest misfortune of this abject drama, however, was the fact that none of what transpired as a result, was even remotely comprehensible to either my Commanding Officer or to the higher offices. Or perhaps they never wanted to be bothered by something such trifling as this. Who knows?

Ideally, and in my opinion, the very first place all doctors joining the Army Medical Corps ought to have been sent off was to the center for basic military training, with the formal commissioning coming only after the training was over. That way, the brass would be sitting on the shoulders of a physically well-trained individual well-versed in military customs, etiquettes and practices. And thereby, neither the muscles of the legs would need to go numb, nor would the psyche need to suffer.

Receiving a Regular Commission in the armed forces is undeniably a matter of great pride and honor for any individual. It is a momentous event and a life-changing milestone. Small wonder, therefore, that such an event is routinely and traditionally associated with an impressive passing-out ceremony, followed by enthusiastic celebrations – as is the practice in most military academies around the world, including the Bangladesh Military Academy.

In sharp contrast, doctors joining the Army Medical Corps were to be found putting on their own ranks in the quiet, obscure and lackluster environment of their rooms in the messes. Or their batmen were putting it on for them. There was no passing-out parade or any subsequent celebration. And why should there be? The authorities probably never felt inspired enough to put ranks on the shoulders of a bunch of individuals who were still untrained and untutored in the military way of life, and were still practically a civilian.

My brass ranks were attached on to the epaulets of my uniform by my batman, which he then brought over to me, and which I put on with my wife as the sole audience. That was how I received my commission in the armed forces. That was how a potentially glorious moment of my life was denied me through the unfortunate failings of a system.

And then I strode out of the mess and started to walk towards the CMH. I remember walking a bit awkwardly, because I was in a pair of boots, the likes of which I had never worn in my life before. And I was also literally flooded by salutes from uniformed personnel on the road, to all of which I nodded a solemn acknowledgement in a most civilian style, not knowing how to return a salute properly!

Despite all that, life at CMH Savar continued, as Lieutenant Colonel Matlub went through his daily hospital activities, with me in tow. Here was a giant of a man, very affable and jovial, who gave me innumerable important and relevant tips and pointers pertaining to military rules, behavior and conduct.

Lieutenant Colonel Matlub was the medical officer in charge of the MI (Medical Inspection) Room, and incidentally, the only medical officer there. An MI Room at a CMH functions as the initial point for sorting patients who report to the hospital, where it is decided whether a patient can be treated in the MI Room itself, or needs to be referred to a specialist. In a sense, therefore, it could be considered an emergency cum triage station of sorts.

But what struck me as strange was that Lieutenant Colonel Matlub was actually a pathologist – which left me wondering as to what, in Heaven's name, was he doing attending to patients in the MI Room. This, I was told later, was how things worked around here. It did not really matter that an individual was a specialist. When instructed, he had to spend his time and waste his expertise being something else, and not what he was trained to be. Since this had been the practice all along without the walls of this establishment crumbling into a worthless heap, I inferred it must be notoriously efficient. What I hadn't realized at that time was that the walls already had a few fatal cracks here and there, but were being constantly plastered over very cleverly and expertly in an effort to make a flawed structure look flawless.

Lieutenant Colonel Matlub and I spent about six to seven hours in the MI Room every morning, processing patients with everything from fever to foot-drop and constipation to cancer. We provided treatment for the most basic ailments, and those we could not treat or rather were not allowed to treat, we sent to the specialists concerned.

Here is another matter which I shall delve into deeper in a later chapter. But, for now, I was left feeling a trifle inadequate for not being allowed to prescribe anything beyond pain-killers and antacids, or requesting the most basic investigative tests, despite being a medical graduate.

Why were my medical knowledge and abilities restricted to requesting only Blood for Complete Picture (CP), Urine for Routine Examination (RE) and Stool for RE? I am certainly not implying that, sitting in the MI Room, we ought to have been requesting a chromosomal analysis, an endoscopic examination or an echo-cardiogram. But being a medical graduate, why wasn't I considered capable of requesting basic microbiology if I suspected an infection, or a most straightforward x-ray if I suspected a disorder of the skeletal system, or an insanely simple ECG if I suspected a pathology of the heart? I am no one to question anyone's wisdom, but I would certainly be interested to hear the answers to those.

Meanwhile, the good Lieutenant Colonel taught me to always walk a step behind him. This, he explained, was a demonstration of respect for an accompanying senior officer, adding *"You also have to stay to my left"* – which was perhaps a physical requirement for the ample room needed to return the countless salutes directed at him. Interspersed too, were timely and handy reminders like *"You don't have to salute him when you are walking with me! I am senior to him even though we wear the same rank!"*

That was when I learned too that when two officers wore the same rank, it was important to determine who was senior, so that the rituals of saluting, salutations and appropriate demeanor could be displayed accordingly. Interestingly too given an ante-dated seniority that was nowhere near to what it ideally ought to have been, we – the doctors from the medical corps – often found ourselves having to salute and revere officers of the arms and other services who were clearly a few years junior to us academically.

And while we were out walking together, Lieutenant Colonel Matlub also suggested *"...if you can, could you also please try to match your steps with mine?"* This was a trifle difficult for me to catch on at first. Quite frequently, therefore, I found myself executing a comical combination of short and long steps as I strutted beside the large frame of my mentor, trying to keep up with him in both speed and rhythm.

My Commanding Officer soon decided that since I was to go for my basic military training very shortly, I needed to be toughened up while still in his unit. This was perhaps prompted by the fact that the tell-tale evidence of my past sedentary lifestyle and a somewhat unbridled food habit shone like a lighthouse beacon from miles away. I was therefore instructed to start running with the troops early every morning – which I did, with great enthusiasm and even greater respiratory distress. At the same time, however, I was greatly relieved to see that no other officer from my unit, including our quartermaster – presumably a tough nail from the Infantry – ever joined in on this run to witness my early morning predicament. Thankfully, this worked out well for me as I gasped through two grueling miles in the near-darkness of dawn with my vocal cords emanating a language of their own!

At around the same time, my Commanding Officer also desired that I undergo an ultra-condensed version of the basic military training at the unit. By having me go through it, he was perhaps trying to make up for the unrealistic practice of having the medical officers put on ranks and uniforms before their basic military training. But I knew that despite all my best efforts and my Commanding Officer's well-meant intentions, this would be like trying to hide an elephant under a scarf. The elephant was bound to show – and unfortunately, it did. Nevertheless, there was no shortage of eagerness on my part since I realized that till such time that I received my formal military training at the AMC Center, this was all I was going to get in order to survive the mounting pressures for a demonstrable ritualistic military behavior.

A Havildar-Major was detailed to conduct my condensed training. A Havildar-Major is the rough equivalent of a Sergeant-Major, and is typically the senior-most Havildar of a unit. For about a week, an hour or so was set aside every morning for me to train in a few of the basic and ritualistic military moves and stances. This included coming to an attention, of standing at-ease, of turning right and left at one spot, and marching. And yes, saluting, of course – the very life-blood of existence around here!

The mini-training was conducted at a spot tucked away beside the tin-roofed structure which housed the main administrative wing of the hospital. This spot was strategically out of sight of passing human traffic – and this bit of privacy suited me well. Nevertheless, I knew the odds were still stacked quite heavily against me under the circumstances. Firstly, this Havildar-Major was not exactly a qualified instructor. So, despite his most sincere and dedicated efforts he was probably not going to be able to instruct me in the manner and to the preciseness it ought to be done. And secondly, only a week of his training was certainly not going to be enough to impart any lasting abilities in me, and nor was it expected to instill any appreciable self-confidence in my own competency. Despite all that, my eagerness knew no bounds. And so, by the end of a week or so, a wide area of the ground where I trained was bereft of any grass and left looking very brown – all as the result of my enthusiastic stomping.

What my Commanding Officer had in store for me next reinforced my conviction that here was a person who was literally brimming with ideas for the newly-joined medical officers. Whether or not those were an outcome of genuine good intent or were designed out of pure jest, I will never know. He probably wanted those who served under him to take away lingering memories of him – be those good or bad. And the fact I am writing about this even after thirty-two years is proof enough of the fact that his strategy was a resounding success. Now, whether those lingering memories were worth cherishing or forgotten about isn't for me to decide. Potentates in plush offices didn't really care whether or not the serfs suffered from the effects of whimsical and pompous decisions made either on the pretence of able and lawful command or as a result of their veiled attempts at self-advertisement.

And so, towards the end of my three-month tenure at CMH Savar, I was instructed by my Commanding Officer to join a grueling 20-mile Route March in which all the units of the brigade were participating. A Route March is where unit personnel walk twenty miles in full battle gear as part of an annual activity to prove the unit's battle-worthiness.

Though I will not attempt to analyze any of the confounding implications of such a decision, it is my assumption that my Commanding Officer felt that making someone who has not had even a day of formal military training plod through a grueling and physically demanding hike such as this – a hike which even seasoned military personnel found exacting – would add an extra feather to his cap of achievements and his ability of command. I say this because I realized only much later that a good part of my Commanding Officer's decision had been prompted by his efforts at being noticed by those who mattered to him. My role in it, sadly, was that of a pawn being marched and prodded around on some sort of a giant chessboard. And with 'sacrificial pawns' such as myself being in abundant supply, the knights in shining armor felt very safe in their private and cozy little corners, since they had the merchandise at their disposal with which to appease their 'kings'.

On the day of the Route March, under the gray sky of dawn, and in full battle gear, I trudged into a parade ground where about a hundred soldiers stood in silence. High-pitched drill commands floated to my ears from a distance. Still trying to shake off the effects of a delightful slumber, I half-heartedly joined the troops, and stood abreast some other officers from adjoining non-medical units. The officers stood facing the rows and columns of troops, at the head of their own units, because they were to deliver the commands which would set their respective units off on the route march. And as the officer representing CMH Savar, I too had to take my place at the head of my unit, and facing it.

I have to admit that at that point, with no formal military training, I had no idea how to deliver a military command, except that it needed to be screamed, short of the vocal cords getting torn to bits and pieces. Though I was fairly confident I could somehow come reasonably close to the required decibel level of the scream – perhaps at the expense of a hernia – I kept wondering *what* to scream. Nevertheless, I was sure of one thing: That the other units would be starting the route march before ours, since medical units always came lower down in order of priority in anything that the military did. I was therefore banking on being able to catch on to a bit of whatever the other officers had howled at their own units to set them off on the route march. I felt that as long as I could come reasonably close to what had been howled, I would somehow be able to get away with it. After all, where it concerns howling and screaming, the diction need not be entirely intelligible. A fairly close approximation is usually expected to suffice.

Fortunately, the Havildar-Major of our unit, who was with the troops, seemed capable of assessing the situation, as well as my predicament, better than my Commanding Officer ever could. He came up to me and, in a tone that was almost-apologetic and as humble as he could make it sound, requested me to turn around and stand facing the other way, and not face the troops, while he would deliver the marching order on my behalf. This was heaven-sent! But, if truth be told, my feeling of relief was in no way greater than my feeling of embarrassment and of wretched incompetence at that point. It felt like I was a useless appendage in uniform, thrown mindlessly, needlessly, and rather forcibly, into a situation which I had neither foreseen, and nor was I prepared for. It felt like I was an egg being fried on a pan without the stove having been turned on.

All this made me wonder whether my Commanding Officer had foreseen any of this by thrusting me into the midst of such a predictable predicament. And, I was convinced he had. Perhaps at that very moment, in the privacy of his cozy surroundings, he was relishing the outcome of his momentous decision and deriving some sort of a sadistic pleasure out of it. He was probably basking in the potential for personal glory that my participation in the Route March promised, while I suffered in the dilemma and the perplexity of ignorance and confusion.

On quite a regular basis, during weekends, Samina and I would go to Dhaka to meet and to spend time with family and friends. We would make the thirty-some kilometer trip by bus which came from the north, went through Savar, and then all the way to Dhaka. Quite often, however, there would be an ambulance going to CMH Dhaka carrying a patient from CMH Savar, and an officer or two would hitch a ride in it. We didn't know about it until the day we too were offered a ride by one of the officers going to Dhaka in that same ambulance. It seemed like a fairly convenient arrangement, and I remember having made a trip or two in it to Dhaka thereafter, although we always made sure that we were not getting in the way of the patient's safety and comfort. At times though, it did seem to me that the ambulance was perhaps carrying patients to CMH Dhaka a bit more often than it needed to, particularly on weekends. However, the matter of patient transfer was always the prerogative of the specialists, and not being one myself, I never felt I was in a position to draw any speculative conclusions.

After about three months at this hospital I was called up for my basic military training at the Army Medical Corps Center situated in Rajshahi, a district to the north of the country.

I will admit that as far as I was concerned, those three months at CMH Savar were packed with unforeseen experiences, unaccustomed practices and unexpected revelations. Nevertheless, I kept my spirits up on the premise that all this was perhaps only a passing experience and that the apparent chaos and confusion around me, which was just beginning to take shape, was only transitory. I firmly believed that my on-going activities as a soldier were only a prelude to the real role I was soon to play as a doctor in the armed forces. I truly believed that this institution would actually serve as a catalyst, transporting me into a climactic world of academic excellence and professional achievements. I kept my spirits up since I had faith in my dream that Pinocchio would indeed come to life; that the goose would one day lay the golden egg, and that Sleeping Beauty would eventually awaken.

I wish I had known then, that Sleeping Beauty had long since been poisoned in her sleep and that the goose laid its proverbial golden egg for only a fortunate few. I hardly realized at that point that ***the die had been cast*** for transforming me into what a system wanted to make out of me, rather than what I wanted to make out of my life.

Chapter 3
THE DIE IS CAST
Transformations at the AMC Training Center

"Fate is like a strange, unpopular restaurant, filled with odd waiters who bring you things you never asked for, and don't always like." - Lemony Snicket

With the gradual passage of time it became painfully clear that I was not actually on a road to the Future. I was, in fact, in a narrow tunnel which got narrower the further I went – a tunnel which seemed to be headed nowhere. And by the time I considered getting out of it, that tunnel had become so narrow that I couldn't even look back over my shoulder, let alone turn around. The effect was downright claustrophobic as I groped around in the suffocating and oppressive darkness, pondering my predicament and the circumstances that had delivered me there. My future, apparently, had already been planned and charted – by someone else.

Growing pains

"Growing up is losing some illusions in order to acquire others." – Virginia Woolf

Down this tunnel into my future, I headed out for my basic military training at the Army Medical Corps Center situated in the outskirts of Rajshahi, a district to the north of the country.

In anticipation of my departure for the training course, the authorities made arrangements to have Samina transferred to CMH Dhaka for the duration of my course. Since I would be away for a while, they assumed it would be more convenient for her to be in Dhaka, where her parents also lived. However, Samina's transfer to Dhaka took place on the day I left for the Route March in the dark and early hours of the morning, bidding her farewell in full battle gear. Though this, of course, was of no worthwhile consequence, especially where official transfers were concerned, the reality for me was returning to our room from the Route March with every muscle and sinew of my body screaming with pain – not to mention the emptiness I felt, with Samina not being there when I returned. I left for Dhaka three days later.

For the purpose of my basic military training at the Army Medical Corps Center in Rajshahi, I needed to be in Dhaka for a couple of days to procure items and personal belongings which would be required during the course. Moreover, the bus which would eventually take me to Rajshahi, departed from Dhaka. The added benefit of being in Dhaka for those couple of days before departing for Rajshahi for the sixteen-week course was the precious time I would be able to spend with Samina. More so because eight months into our marriage, this was the first time we were to be separated for any length of time.

I made the trip with a colleague of mine, Barendra Chakravarty, who was selected for the same course from 11 Field Ambulance – a field medical unit also located in Savar Cantonment, and close to CMH Savar. Barendra was my classmate from medical school, and so, with the bond of friendship having already been formed between us years earlier, our trip together to Rajshahi was that much more enjoyable. It was an eight hour journey by bus, and I still remember Barendra and I being so engrossed in conversation during the entire trip, and so excited to be going for our basic military training, that those eight hours literally flew by. Finally, we arrived at our destination – exhausted, but exhilarated. We completed the remainder of the trip, from the bus station to the training center, perched along with our bags and baggage, atop a cycle rickshaw.

As we approached the Center I was rather disappointed to see that this military installation did not share the pristine look of the unit I had come from. This was more of a sprawling complex, with more grounds, fields and terrains than edifices. The clear and instant message conveyed by such a topography was of an establishment more concerned with outdoor activities than indoors which, given the fact that this was where we were supposed to be toughened up physically, was certainly understandable.

We were stopped at the gates by a sentry who inquired into the purpose of our visit. When we informed him of who we were, and why we were there, I thought I caught the faintest hint of a smile playing across his lips as he saluted us smartly, trying his best at the same time, to put on a somber façade. At that very moment I was not quite sure if it was a smile of welcome or of sympathy. I was soon to find out that it was the latter!

At the training center we were instructed to report to the Quartermaster, who would allot us our rooms. It was a pure stroke of luck that Barendra and I were allotted the same room, along with another trainee officer. That, for us, was literally heaven-sent because, at that point, we needed each other the most, being in new surroundings and soon to be in the midst of new and unknown faces. Incidentally, Barendra and I were one of the first few Trainee Officers to have arrived at the center. And while we unpacked and were in the process of gradually settling in, the rest of our course mates slowly arrived over the day. The remainder of our time was spent in acquainting and familiarizing ourselves with the twenty one other officers who had arrived from medical units across the country for the same course.

The Army Medical Corps (AMC)
Training Center in Rajshahi
(Right: Officers' accommodation. Extreme left: Married Officers' accommodation. Middle lower structure: Dining Hall and Recreation Room)

That evening, we were ordered to gather in front of the Officers' Mess and made to sit on chairs set out on the front lawn. Half a dozen barbers were then let loose on our heads which, till then, had a verdant crop – some very flamboyantly styled. Not a great deal of finesse was displayed as the barbers went about their business in a most casual and dispassionate manner. In fact, they appeared rather happy and content that a job couldn't have been easier or more straightforward than this! Not much time was spent in eventually getting rid of everything except for a pitiful tuft on top of our heads. And after it was all over, I couldn't help but openly chuckle and smirk at the altered countenance of my friends, not quite realizing that I too was as much a cause for their jive and laughter as they were for me!

Our basic military training, in fact, couldn't have been at a worse place and at a worse time. It spanned the months of May and June – which was the height of summer. And this was Rajshahi – one of the hottest places in the country. A worse combination than this couldn't possibly have been put together, except perhaps by the 'gods of misery', and that too out of pure jest. At that point, none of the twenty three unsuspecting, out-of-shape, crew-cut trainees could even begin to fathom what was in store for them.

We were instructed to gather the next morning in front of our accommodations at 5 a.m.

That, we knew, was going to be somewhat difficult, but certainly not impossible, and therefore we didn't let it bother us much. Rather, we were excited to be out in the grey light of dawn the next day, perhaps doing some free-hand exercises and jogging around the huge field we had seen on our way in. It surely couldn't get any worse than that, we thought. Our minds were still in the mode of making new acquaintances, as we all retired to bed that first night – looking forward to a new kind of an experience that awaited us as the sun rose the next morning. Little did we realize then, that this was not going to be just *an* experience for us, but rather *the* experience, which would finally and irreversibly affect our lives. While silence finally descended upon the AMC Center, with us drifting off to blissful sleep one after the other, the 'gods of physical fitness', sitting atop dark and sinister nocturnal clouds, must have been chuckling.

We had hardly shut our eyes, when the incessant, piercing whistle of the drill sergeants tore our eardrums to pieces and shattered the world around us, as if announcing the arrival of Doomsday. It was a kind pandemonium which would have made even the dead sit bolt upright in their graves – let alone us. Naturally therefore, we were on our feet like catapults of an invading medieval army. Peering out the window through bleary and sleepy eyes, we saw it was still as dark outside as it was when we had gone to bed just a few seconds ago. Some of us were mumbling that perhaps the drill sergeants wanted to make another announcement before we retired for the night. And then we looked at our clocks.

The time: 4 am!

This was one of those moments when one is convinced that something must be wrong with all the clocks and watches in the world. But, once we eventually came to terms with the heart-wrenching fact that they were all in perfect working order, we were distraught by the fact that we had been aroused that early. We were starting to curse our drill sergeants, when the wisdom of such an early start began to finally sink in. With four trainee officers from two adjacent rooms sharing a common toilet, waking up at 4 am actually didn't seem quite early enough!

We were soon dressed in the traditional 'whites' of our morning activity – white shorts, white vest, white socks and white sneakers – and were assembled on the concrete roadway in front of our accommodations, standing eight abreast and three rows deep. Three sun-baked drill sergeants with chiseled features, and looking like God's hand-picked re-incarnation of Devils from Hell, confronted us. Their ice-cold stares literally ripped our guts out, leaving us standing like empty shells.

We were to learn later that they were Havildar Sikander, Naik Shamsu and Naik Amjad. The fourth drill sergeant, not present that morning, but whom we got to know later, was Lance Naik Najmul.

Havildar Sikander, being the senior-most of the three, seemed to be at the helm of the proceedings. If truth be told, he also looked the meanest. Naiks Shamsu and Amjad, though not coming across as quite as threatening as Havildar Sikander, could nonetheless get rather stern when they wanted to, as we later found out. Lance Naik Najmul, being the junior-most drill sergeant, mostly hovered on the sidelines during our field training sessions, from where he would offer helpful hints whenever he felt those were needed. However, any time that it was necessary to demonstrate anything that had to do with proper marching, including illustrating the various types of marching and the intricacies involved in those, Lance Naik Najmul would be drafted in from the sidelines. Frankly, I am yet to see someone march as confidently, effortlessly and gracefully as Lance Naik Najmul did. It was a challenge for us to be able to achieve even fifty percent of his level of execution, but when even that much was achieved by us, we would feel it was enough for us to rest on our laurels.

In the meantime, Havildar Sikander was howling and screaming his instructions in the direction of our befuddled and petrified assemblage under the grey early morning sky. His venomous and malignant shrieks sounded like huge globs of verbal spit smacking our faces and slapping our cheeks. And we heard through his screams that, amongst other things, we were to address them – the drill sergeants – as "staff", that our physical capabilities would be tested to their limits, and that anything and everything we did which the "staff" did not like, would constitute a punishable offence.

At the same time, however, we were somewhat taken aback as we found ourselves – apparently lowly creatures assembled for the purpose of physical vilification – being addressed as 'sir'. The reason for that was simple. Unlike officers of the arms and other services who were trained at the military academy, and who received commission only upon completion of their course, we arrived here with commissioned ranks already on our shoulders. The implication of this was apparently well-understood by the drill sergeants. Nevertheless, this did not stop them from hurling threats and admonitions at us whenever needed, except that their venomous and almost-insulting phrases unfailingly ended with a 'sir'.

The shrieking introductions over, our whole group was then made to run, with one of the 'doomsday devils' leading from the front, and the others bringing up the rear. After about five minutes of running, we arrived at a huge ground where the drill sergeants resumed their shrieking from where they had left off. Nevertheless, at that point, I felt pretty satisfied with the way my just-concluded morning run had gone, since I was still breathing quite effortlessly. I presumed we would be doing some free-hand exercises now which, undoubtedly, should be a walk in the park. I was starting to think that perhaps, after all, this basic military training was not going to be as difficult as I had feared.

And then, when I was not quite expecting it, one of the Devils screamed that we should start running again – and, of course, we complied. Our group made its way out of the ground and soon we were jogging down the road beside the training center. I assumed, therefore, that we would be running along this road which actually went around the perimeter of the center. This, I knew, was going to be quite a bit of a distance, since this facility was somewhat huge and sprawling. Even so, I felt it was something well within the limits of human capability and endurance, and that I would be able to survive it – more so, since I was not breathing too hard as yet.

But very soon my legs started to ache and my breathing got somewhat labored. Yet I was comforted by the fact that the perimeter of the training center was a closed loop, and therefore, the road going around it couldn't possibly go on forever. A spark of hope soon ignited within me as a bend on the road came into view up ahead and beyond which, it seemed, was the home stretch back to the training ground from where we had started. I perceived a collective sense of relief around me as we approached the bend, because by now, besides the thumping of twenty-three pairs of tired feet, the sound of twenty-three pairs of rasping lungs also filled the air. We were just about preparing to lean our bodies into the turn back to the grounds when, quite astonishingly, the Devil leading from the front kept going straight! It was heart-breaking to watch the alluring bend go by, as we jogged past it. At that point, I believe I was not the only one in the group who was starting to panic.

Soon we were all pounding along the streets of the little township adjacent to the training center. Strangely, the very few early risers there did not seem to have the least bit of interest in the men in white gasping, groaning and grunting through their streets. And that was perhaps because, over the years, they had seen it all.

Personally, I lost all reference to time and place as the run continued interminably down the many winding streets within the town. By now, my legs had gone almost numb, my lungs were literally bursting out of my chest, my ears were ringing, and my bleary eyes were on the verge of popping out of their sockets. And in the humid heat of May, sweat was pouring out of me like the Niagara Falls. People kept falling out of step and slowing down, but were promptly brought back to their places against all laws of physics and physiology by the bone-chilling shrieks of the two Devils behind us.

To make matters worse, I had the added burden of having to deal with the rather bothersome accumulation of fat around my middle, which had gathered over many sedentary years, and which now seemed to bounce to a rhythm of its own with every step as I ran. I could hardly focus on anything that was on or beside the streets that we ran through. The world seemed like a surreal tunnel with fuzzy walls. The only object in focus was the sweaty and gasping figure of my course-mate in front, who seemed busy fighting his personal war with gravity.

By the time we eventually arrived back at the huge training ground, it seemed as if almost a year had gone by. The distance we had just run seemed much more than just 2 miles. Maybe it was 3 miles – or perhaps even 4! Who knows? Did we ever measure it? It must have been measured by one of the Doomsday Devils! No wonder it seemed endless!

As we all dragged ourselves back into the training ground, our group must have looked like the remnants of General Custer's army after their last stand at Little Bighorn. The sight of a cluster of people as dazed, flustered, frazzled and exhausted as us, as we re-assembled on the training ground, must have been a sight to behold! At the same time, it was somewhat disconcerting to observe that the two Doomsday Devils, after all this, were breathing as if they had just walked down the aisle of a movie theater! Some free-hand exercises followed thereafter which, to be very honest, was comparable to swatting a fly after having wrestled Godzilla to the ground. Nevertheless, the fact that Godzilla would have to be wrestled to the ground every morning for the next twelve weeks was a matter of great foreboding and dread at that moment.

Our gait, stance and groans as we all gathered again for the morning exercises and the 2-mile run the next morning clearly indicated the genuine need for walking sticks and wheelchairs amongst the gathered collection of broken and battered individuals. Though the drill sergeants still continued to breathe fire and spit venom,

I did detect a hint of amusement in their eyes at the pathetic sight of the ragtag assemblage. They must have seen it all over the years, and sure as hell, they knew how to take care of it.

With a voice as thunderous as the loudest thunderclap, one of the drill sergeants informed us that our pains would have to be dealt with, guess what – more pain! He went on to scream that this pain would have to be 'killed' – in his words – at the very first opportunity, failing which it would make a home in our bodies. Thereupon we were informed that the golden opportunity of 'killing pain with pain', if you will, was right then and right there, through another infamous morning run! We were convinced that for some reason, yet unknown to us, God must have decided that our Day of Judgment had arrived, and that our time in Hell was to begin here and now – at the AMC Training Center! Assuming that the severity of punishment in Hell is usually proportional to the degree of immorality, we had to be at the very top of God's list of all-time sinners!

No mercy was shown during the 2-mile run that second morning, as our loud and unbridled groans, grunts and grumbles reverberated again through the township we ran through, perhaps also waking up a few residents in the process. Surprisingly however, our debilitating aches and pains weren't as horrific at the end of it, and by the third or the fourth day, we had almost forgotten about it.

This was the beginning of Officers' Basic Course – 12 (also known as OBC-12). It was a grueling course aimed at converting us into tough and tenacious individuals within a short span of sixteen weeks. It was a phase in our lives which shall forever remain etched in our collective memories as a significant milestone. There were moments of success and moments of failure, of hope alternating with despair, and of elation interspersed with anguish. There were moments when our physique all but gave in to the stress of relentless training, but was propped up in the nick of time either by the bellowing of the drill sergeants or by the gradually maturing character of our inner self. And with each storm that lashed us, our grit and resolve got stronger, and the bonds of comradeship and camaraderie between us grew from an acorn to an oak. And 'Godzilla' kept getting smaller and weaker!

Officers of OBC-12 posing at the end
of a morning training session
(The author is kneeling on the
extreme right, middle row)

Besides the intense physical training, we were also taught subjects I never dreamed I would ever need to learn as a doctor – subjects related to military administration and military law. We were taught how to conduct a Court of Inquiry (commonly referred to as a 'C of I'), distribute rations (also known as 'rat') amongst the troops, handle unit funds, maintain unit vehicles (called a 'veh') and take care of ordnance ('ord') stores and so on – the knowledge of which, of course, was fundamentally essential to running the affairs of any typical military unit.

However, at that point, what bothered me much more than the content of the curriculum was the passion and fervor with which those subjects were being taught by instructors who were – brace yourselves – graduates of medical schools!

I am not saying that doctors couldn't either learn or teach subjects like military administration or military law. Anyone can learn any subject, given proper education and instructions. But, the one question which instantly came to my mind was: Why? Why was it necessary for doctors to be teaching these military-related subjects when there was certainly no shortage of officers from the ASC (Army Services Corps) or the JAG (Judge Adjutant General) Branch who were easily available for this job and who, more importantly, were supposedly more proficient in those subjects?

Even more importantly, what was the whole point in going through five grueling years of medical school, if one had to end up teaching military law and military administration? In my opinion, a doctor conducting such classes was a thoughtless waste of knowledge and resources – something similar to an engineer conducting classes on accounting, for example. Do not get me wrong. It is certainly not my intent to demean any subject or profession by saying this. I am merely emphasizing on the fact that two subjects, both equal in value and credibility, could be poles apart in terms of concept and content, as medical is, compared to the military. My bone of contention is merely to underscore the wastage of abilities and resources in this kind of an arrangement and exercise.

Allow me to step back slightly at this point, to try to provide a bit of a background which may explain the circumstances leading to doctors teaching military law and military administration, and the premise on which it could have been based.

There are two kinds of doctors in the medical corps.

The first is groomed primarily to run the administration of a hospital, and are known as General Duty Medical Officers or GDMOs.

They are the ones who are required to be knowledgeable in military administration and military law, given the kind of duties they have to perform and the responsibilities they have to shoulder. They are the ones who become the accounts officer, the transport officer, the quartermaster, the second-in-command, or sometimes even the commanding officer of a medical unit. In other words, they are the ones who do everything else – everything, besides what they had, for five long and grueling years, learned to do: Which was to treat patients.

I always wondered whether the matter of administration – be that of a hospital – couldn't have been better, and more logically, left to those whose profession it actually was. Officers from the ASC would perhaps have been a better choice for the job. And should anyone, at this point, ask what the ASC officers knew of medical science that would make them a better choice to run a hospital, the answer would be simple: Nothing.

But, here's the catch: The ASC officers know military administration and the proper delivery of services like the back of their hands. And that is what matters here. There is certainly a huge difference between pursuing a subject which one has mastered versus pursuing one in which a person is not officially qualified. Would an ASC Officer ever venture to treat a patient? No? Why then, does a doctor venture into the realm of military administration and military law?

The bottom-line is this: An AMC officer joins the corps primarily as a doctor, and not as an administrator. So obviously, a doctor's role in the organization should be to treat the patients, and not be caught up with administering a hospital. And insofar as an ASC officer running a hospital is concerned, I assume that matters related to everything in the hospital – everything besides the treatment of patients – could have been taken care of by them quite adequately. Any decision which required specialized medical opinion or guidance could always, and quite easily, be made with the consultation of the relevant specialists. After all, the bulk of the activities at any hospital are administrative in nature. Anyone in the medical corps who has ever commanded a military hospital can easily relate to what I am talking about here.

Nevertheless, if the GDMOs felt that being a military administrator rather than a doctor was a fair trade-off, then that was certainly their choice. But, personally speaking, and assuredly not with the intention of belittling the worth of any particular class, group or profession, I always felt that doctors administering a hospital was the rough equivalent of building an airplane and then driving it along the city streets. But that, of course, is my opinion, with which some may differ – and which is entirely fair and acceptable.

I am given to understand that GDMOs these days are required to be a Master in Public Health (MPH) to be promoted to the rank of Lieutenant Colonel and above, and to be able to administer a hospital. That certainly seems to be a more logical approach. Nonetheless, in my opinion, a core competency in a subject like Hospital Administration perhaps, through obtaining an MHA (Master of Hospital Administration) could also have been an option – and possibly a better one. After all, a worldwide requirement these days, in order to be considered a hospital administrator, is a degree in Hospital Administration. This would certainly ensure a more knowledgeable, proficient and efficient running of a hospital.

The other kind of doctor in the Army Medical Corps is given an education on various medical subjects, a good number of whom go on to complete post-graduate training and courses on various medical specialties. They are the Specialists. They are the ones who provide treatment to the patients.

In reality, however, the GDMOs and the Specialists have always been like the two sides of the same coin – intimately attached, yet facing the opposite way. Their activities and viewpoints were not only diverse, but also discordant to the point that they often transformed routine hospital activities into an exercise in which their pursuits and philosophies went around in futile circles. Consequently, they were either bumping into one another or totally missing the point, much like a bumper car ride at an amusement park. Neither were generally able to emerge from their own confines of prejudices and preconceptions to which they were perennially bound, and therefore, not usually able to find a common ground or a mutually agreeable working formula. This, in my opinion, was one of the reasons military hospitals were losing credibility, not only with those who solicited their services, but also with those who worked in it.

I must admit, however, that I have also had the good fortune of having served with GDMOs who knew exactly what their and the specialists' respective roles were, and conducted themselves accordingly. Those remain as some of the bright segments of my service, and which I look back at with fondness and with gratefulness.

Back at the Army Medical Corps Center, it was my intrinsic hunger for knowledge and my singular determination to excel in whatever I did which kept me engrossed in all the new and strange subjects I was being compelled to learn. So, while I spent my days either in the classroom acquiring supposedly indispensable military knowledge, or stomped around on the grounds learning how to march properly, my non-military medical colleagues were either gaining valuable experience in a clinical setting, or preparing for their post-graduate courses and examinations.

And by the time I was done with learning about veh, rat, ord and C of I, and had completed the mandatory period of military activities before being deemed fit to engage in medical matters, I discovered to my great dismay, that I was miles behind my civilian counterparts in terms of medical knowledge and academic progression. More than the fact that this caused me to cringe and lament deep within my subconscious awareness of agony and anguish, I was disturbed, and to some extent disgusted, to realize that none in the upper echelons seemed the least bit concerned by what they were actually making out of a doctor. They either did not realize or did not seem to be troubled by the fact that this imposed 'over-indulgence' in non-medical indoctrination of medical graduates actually amounted to transforming a well-prepared dish into a dog's breakfast. And as if all this was not enough, the ominous dictum *"You're a soldier first and then a doctor"* was also barked at me more often than once during the formative years of my service – and then sprinkled most generously over the rest of it.

This aspect of a medical graduate's career in the armed forces has been discussed to a greater detail in a later chapter, where I have also attempted to provide a viable and a sensible solution to this apparently senseless practice.

The one person entrusted with the solemn responsibility of ensuring that we be transformed into the all-time epitome of a perfect soldier was our Training Adjutant, who was an officer from the Infantry. He was a stolid and stocky package of an officer who supervised every activity of ours on the field – from the early morning runs to the parades, from the drills to the obstacle courses, and from weapons training to the countless push-ups meant to convince us that he was not quite satisfied with our efforts, or our enterprise. Our Training Adjutant hardly ever talked and never ever smiled. When he did open his mouth, however, it was intended solely to emanate a deafening holler, sometimes instructive, and at other times abusive. His supervision of our training was also frequently and conspicuously highlighted by generous helpings of both verbal and physical admonishments.

But as the weeks went by, and we all gradually got leaner, tougher and meaner, our Training Adjutant seemed to get friendlier, but by measured and imperceptible degrees, and by only as much as his disposition and his appointment would allow. And very soon we discovered that under that rough and tough veneer was actually a man of a fairly gentle nature – and with a pair of very asthmatic lungs. And that, unfortunately for him, turned out to be his Achilles heel. The painful memories of the endless sufferings and miseries handed out to us during our early days of training were still fresh in our minds.

Weeks of hard training had now made us all lithe and nimble. Heaven-sent days were those when, prior to our morning 2-mile run, we got a whiff of the fact that our Training Adjutant's lungs were not quite up to the mark. That was when we took off like a drove of hares.

By now, the township we usually ran through had become like a second home to us. Even some of its residents had become known faces. But, most importantly, we were now breezing through its streets most effortlessly during our morning run, without a single grunt or groan. And particularly, on a day like this, when there was a particular 'mission' to be accomplished, we ran as if the world record for the 2-mile run needed to be broken. The gratifying scene of our Training Adjutant gradually falling away from the front of the pack with his mouth wide open, sucking air in like a vacuum cleaner and trying desperately to replenish his depleted lungs, was always considered a reasonably satisfactory way to begin the day's business. Crowning and glorious moments were those when his raspy, whining commands to slow down, so he could catch up with us, could be heard floating to our ears from somewhere far, far behind.

One of the things which greatly amused me during my training and later on during my career as well was the existence and use of a strange and bizarre language. It was English, yet not quite used the way it was supposed to be. The words and phrases sounded like English of course, but would be totally incomprehensible to the untrained listener. It is my understanding that such words and phrases probably took birth from the need and desire to exercise command, control and perhaps even manipulation, with overpowering emphasis and authority. Moreover, I am also convinced that a large part of it was also a legacy of the army from our colonial past.

The first such word which vilified my ear-drums was "bullshit". It was not as if I had never heard that word before, or that I didn't know what it implied, both literally and figuratively. But the number of times I had heard it used in a single day here was perhaps more than the total number of times I had heard it used in my entire lifetime. I was flabbergasted by the way this word was being thrown around most casually by some around me. And every time I heard it being used, it felt like someone was slamming a pair of cymbals with full ferocity – with my head in-between.

When preceded by the word "Don't", as it most often was, it meant "Don't mess with me" or "Don't make up stories" or thereabouts. And the phrase "That's bullshit" meant that whatever was being told was being considered totally false and fabricated. All of this, of course, begged the question of what the implication of that word ever had to do with the excrement of the animal being referred to. Over the course of my career, however, I got used to it being used rather indiscriminately, although the image of the abhorrent lump unfailingly leaped out at me each time. And that, in a way, was rather disconcerting.

I was also very fascinated by the universal assumption that there was blood all over this place, as I noticed an irrepressible urge in most to add the word "bloody" to almost any and every available noun, verb and adjective in the dictionary. Whether this implied a more emphatic and spiteful reference to the object or action in question, I knew not. I only knew that in the eyes of propriety, everything in this world did not necessarily have to be smeared in blood.

But, combining the words "bloody" and "bullshit" was pure genius. The resulting product was a purely demonic and devilishly effective witch's brew – almost a weapon of mass destruction. And when delivered with the right amount of venom in the voice and spite in the stare, it was like acquiring the Black Belt in the art of malicious and demeaning admonitions. And the one person who had mastered that art to perfection was our Training Adjutant. That phrase could often be heard reverberating across our training grounds, having emanated from his vocal cords with full-throated ferocity. He used it liberally while expressing his dissatisfaction with our performance, or while implying that our displayed exhaustion was a most flimsy excuse for earning undeserved reprieve. "It's all bloody bullshit! Go, join the rest!"

Nonetheless, I commend the attempts by some around me, at communicating in English – just for the effort itself – though, oftentimes and unfortunately, it turned out to be a haphazard conglomeration of disjointed words and phrases thrown in at random. That is quite understandable though, since English isn't our mother-tongue. But what actually amazed me was the attitude and flair with which it was regularly being delivered, combined with an air of certainty that that was all there was to the language. Somewhere along the way, some people must have missed out on the true richness, splendor and appeal of the English language, as I simply stood aside and witnessed a glorious language being dispatched confidently and remorselessly to martyrdom.

This is not to say, nonetheless, that there weren't any around me who didn't know how English was to be spoken and written in a most proper manner. In fact, I have had the good fortune of having come across some officers, the medical corps included, whose expressions and articulations in English were most admirable, and worthy of emulation. But, sad to say, the number of such individuals was pitifully few.

Our basic military training also, was a way of instructing us on the various nuances involved in sanctioned culinary practices. One had to be spot on in the observance of its assorted rituals, failing which we were either likely to be reprimanded by the instructors, or ridiculed by fellow officers.

For dinner, we would have to enter the mess hall most properly dressed – in white shirts, black pants, black neck-ties and dress shoes. Lunch, on the other hand, was rather informal, when we were allowed into the mess hall wearing our combat fatigues, since our field training sessions continued all the way up to lunch time.

But, be it lunch or dinner, the timing of the act of food consumption, the proper and silent use of the cutlery, and the quality, volume and topic of table conversation had to be correct and by-the-book. Over time – albeit some embarrassing blunders and awkward moments notwithstanding – we were able to get all of it down to the tee. We were soon so acclimatized to the ritualistic mode of having a meal in the mess hall that the slightest tinkle from our tableware or any wayward table manner or conversation would either evoke startled stares from fellow officers, or their good-humored taunts thereafter.

With Captain Samina, in the dining hall of the AMC Center

Chairs would be laid out some evenings in front of the dining hall where, before we headed in for dinner, we would have to attend what was called a 'mess meeting' – which, in fact, was an instructional class. During it, we were lectured on the various customs and etiquettes associated with military table manners by Colonel (later Brigadier General) Manzoor Mollah, the Deputy Commandant of the training center and its Chief Instructor. He was the epitome of a perfect military officer who looked as fit as a fiddle, spoke impeccable English and seemed to know everything there was to know about military service. I do not know about the others, but personally, I always looked up to him, and often caught myself imitating him without even realizing it.

Coming back to the grounds, our training also included an obstacle course that had to be completed within a specified time, and on which we had to train and practice almost every morning. I do not quite remember the order in which the obstacles were placed, but I do remember the obstacles rather clearly because they were all fairly difficult to deal with.

One was a ditch, six feet wide, which we had to jump across. On the face of it, six feet didn't seem like much. Nevertheless, with a loaded haversack on our back, and a steel helmet sitting on our head, defying gravity proved to be a challenge. We would run up to the ditch at breakneck speed, hoping against hope that the Lord Almighty would somehow endow us with the ability of flight by the time we reached its edge. But realizing at the very last instant that no such miracles happened these days, we were left with no option but to take the leap of faith with our arms flailing like a pair of windmills and our legs crazily pedaling the air – as if doing so would help. Most of the time we made it – though barely. At other times, we landed inside the ditch. Things got a bit messy, though, if it had rained the night before and the ditch was filled with muddy and murky water.

Another obstacle was a six feet wall, and as its name implies, it was six feet in height, about two feet thick, and made of brick and cement. Standing beside it for the first time ever, with the wall itself being a few inches taller than us, we were convinced there was no way we were going to be able to go over it in full battle gear.

The drill sergeant then demonstrated how it was to be done, and in his words 'quite easily'. But, one needs to understand that that was *his* point of view, not ours. He ran up to the wall, placed the toe of one of his boots about one-thirds of the way up its vertical face for leverage, launched himself, latched on to the far edge at the top, and then quite effortlessly pulled himself up on to the top of the thick wall. It did look fairly easy from an observer's point of view. But, what we hadn't realized at that point was that all this was being demonstrated by a qualified instructor who must have gone over that wall so many times that, if he wanted to, he could probably have done it with one arm tied behind him. Sadly, that was not the kind of credentials we came with!

It took quite a few practice runs for us to be able to somehow clamber up that wall – but not before the immediate vicinity reverberated with the sound of bones hitting brick, and with our arms, elbows and knees bearing the evidence of a rather abrasive effort in the form of bumps, bruises, scratches and cuts. There were times one of us would somehow latch on to the far edge at the top, but then get stuck there, unable to pull up the rest of the way – looking much like a stuck frame of a Spiderman movie – in which the movie had decided to get jammed with Spiderman in an embarrassingly ungainly pose. This always infuriated the drill sergeants, who would let out a blood-curling scream, race up like an angry rhinoceros, grab Officer Spiderman by his projecting rump and literally toss him over the top.

A most terrifying obstacle was 'the rope', which was about as thick as the wrist, strung between two posts about twenty feet apart, and stretched out at a height of about ten to twelve feet above the ground. Close to the upright posts at either end, the rest of the rope hung vertically, almost to the ground – and this was the way up to and down from the horizontal part. The routine consisted of climbing up the vertical rope, crossing along on the horizontal portion, and then descending down the other free-hanging vertical end.

Confronted by something like this, we seemed convinced that humans would perhaps have been better off had their evolutionary process been arrested at the stage of the tree-dwelling primates! There was, however, a definite technique to dealing with this obstacle, particularly in climbing up the vertical portion, which appeared to be the most difficult, and which was demonstrated to us by the drill sergeants. Nevertheless, when we tried the same, it looked much like a wrestling match between a human and a rope, where one was trying to knock the other out, but getting nowhere. Eventually, and after much practice, we managed to put together a decent-enough act, as we grappled, grunted, flailed, swung and swore across this obstacle.

Crawling through a tunnel in full battle gear was yet another obstacle. This tunnel was nothing more than several large oil drums cut vertically into two halves, with the halves placed end to end to form a tunnel. The degree of difficulty – and of misery – was enhanced by having barbed wires going over the top for several feet at one end of the tunnel. Interestingly, these barbed wires were intentionally placed at such a height that it would ensnare the haversacks on our backs even if we so much as lifted our chins!

There was a definite technique too, to traversing the tunnel, in which the elbows, knees and the tummy took over the function of locomotion. The entire exercise was made even more difficult by the fact that we also had to carry with us a cumbersome rifle as we traversed it. So, the only way of getting through this cramped tunnel was to push the rifle ahead and follow it. Having a full haversack on the back made it even worse because there was hardly enough room left at the top. So one had to literally hug the ground as one crawled. More often than not, and predictably, our haversacks would get entangled in the barbed wires as we either entered or emerged from the tunnel, whereupon the drill sergeants would have to get busy 'untangling' us, in much the same way a hunter would free a trapped and wounded animal.

Emerging from the tunnel of the obstacle course (The author [right] accompanied by Captain Aftab [left] and Captain Barendra)

Incidentally, these tunnels were also a favorite resting place for nocturnal creatures, including foxes, which frequently dumped their overnight excrement within, to greet us the next morning. The drill sergeants, standing at the exiting end, and waiting to holler at anyone who took a bit longer to negotiate the tunnel than was permitted, would often witness fox excrement emerging ahead of a trainee, as we pushed the offensive-smelling lump in front of us with the butts of our rifles. This was certainly better than crawling all over the foul-smelling lump on our chests and bellies.

Other obstacles included the Burma Bridge, which was a bridge made of rope which had a tendency to swing notoriously as one crossed over it, as if it had a mind of its own; a vertical net about fifteen feet high, on which we went up one side, and then down the other; the monkey swing, where one swung over a ditch, hanging on to a rope; and the 'zigzag', which was a zigzagging wooden plank hardly four inches wide, and about two to three feet above the ground, and which got higher as one walked from one end to the other.

Though difficult and sometimes dreadful, I will admit that the obstacle course certainly helped to enhance our physical abilities, improve our reflexes, and boost our self-confidence. And so, however much the drill sergeants hollered and swore at us as we struggled to negotiate the obstacles in a most clumsy and ungraceful manner, I am grateful to them for having guided us through those most masterfully.

Besides, our curriculum also included a few classes on camouflaging techniques. These classes were held during our morning outdoor sessions.

The outdoor classes were conducted under the shade of a huge tree, with benches laid out for the trainees, and a blackboard for the instructor. There were a couple of designated spots for such classes, most of which were conducted by a member of the Staff. A class under the shade at that hour of the day, and at that time of the year, with the heat and the humidity competing to outdo the other, was considered time in Heaven!

Our classes on camouflaging techniques were conducted in one such spot – one set in the midst of lush green foliage and bushes. During our first class, we were given a thorough introduction to what camouflaging was all about, its various techniques, its advantages, and situations where it might be useful. And then, at one point, the Staff said, "Sirs, this is what I mean."

And just then, to our shock and bewilderment, the bushes around us began to move – and some bushes also stood up on two legs! The element of surprise was so sudden, and of fright so overwhelming, that some of us had to genuinely curb an instinctive and overpowering urge to bolt from there! To think that we were sitting only about an arm's length from these camouflaged soldiers all this while, without even realizing it, was enough to give us goose bumps! And that was enough to convince us how effective camouflaging could be.

Being able to carry away a wounded comrade away from a flashpoint of conflict to a relatively safer location is obviously expected of every soldier. And to be able to do that easily and effectively, we were taught a technique known as "fireman's lift". Obviously, this technique was in use by firemen to get injured or weakened victims to safety in the event of a fire, and hence the name.

The drill sergeants taught us the technique by having us lift one of our course-mates and carry that person a distance of about fifty meters, before putting him down. The technique was to bend down in front of the person to be carried, pass one arm between his legs and wrap it around one of his thighs. And then grabbing the person's arm on the same side with the lifter's other arm, the lifter would straighten up. This way, the person just lifted would now be on the back of the person lifting him up in much the same way a scarf would be wrapped around one's upper back with two of its ends being held in front of the chest of the lifter – with those two ends being one arm and one leg of the lifted person.

While getting into position for lifting up the other person was fairly straightforward for the lifter, straightening up with that person sprawled across the upper back was quite another story. Most unfortunately, the drill sergeants never seemed to pay attention to the respective weights of the lifter and the one being lifted – which, at times, was painfully disproportionate. Objectively speaking, however, the drill sergeants were right in doing so. Injury in battle would certainly not be decided on the basis of the weights of the lifter and the lifted.

About five or six of us would be selected at a time to carry out and practice the fireman's lift. Gross disproportions in weights would routinely result in noisy grunts, groans and grumbles from lifters who were smaller, thinner or lighter than the person being lifted. It was not surprising, therefore, that those with smaller body frames and weights were in great demand for this particular training.

One other art of military engagement that we were trained in was bayonet fighting. However, not much time was wasted in training us in this particular art. A leading reason for that was obviously because bayonets, in the context of modern warfare, are close to becoming obsolete, and are used only as a last resort during a battle. Another reason could have been the fact that the chances of medical personnel getting involved in a bayonet encounter during a battle were either slim or close to none, obviously because they would be more involved in the background treating the wounded. Yet, we were being given some training in it, however rudimentary, just in case.

The rifles we used for this training had an arrangement at the end of its barrel on to which a bayonet could be affixed in no time. Needless to say, the bayonets on our rifles were blunt dummies. We had to imagine there was an enemy standing in front and had to go through a set of martial moves comprised of hops, leaps and blood-curling screams, ending in a huge lunge with the bayonet at an imaginary adversary. All that was expected to wound the enemy – mortally or otherwise – or at least instill such fear in their hearts that would have them either on their knees begging for mercy or running with their lives.

Frankly speaking, from what we did, and the way we did it, I had serious doubts about the efficacy of our bayonet fighting technique and training. And that was because we conveniently assumed that the enemy would be standing there like a statue and allowing us to have it our way. If anything, he too would be hopping, screaming and lunging, trying to make minced meat out of us, as much as we would be trying to make a plate of Russian salad out of them. It would probably have made more sense and would perhaps have been a better use of our time and efforts if we were, even for a few sessions, allowed a sparring partner to practice with, and to hone our skills. If anything, that would have at least infused some sort of exuberance and excitement into our bayonet training sessions. But sadly, at the end of the day, all that we learned was how to hop, scream and lunge with a glorified stick in hand.

The author with the drill sergeants
(From left to right: Naik Amjad, the author, Havildar Sikandar, Naik Shamsu)

And then came the month of Ramadan – the period of compulsory fasting by all Muslims – and we all decided to fast. I will admit, however, that our decision to do so in the midst of such a rigorous course was more an attempt at extracting concessions in our physical routine on the premise of our fast, than an overly religious sentiment or a sense of religious obligation on our part. So, on the very first day of the month of Ramadan, our morning

2-mile run was not as feisty, our drills and parades not quite as sharp, and our groans and grunts that much louder.

Our Training Adjutant, however, was quick to spot this radical change in our behavior and performance, and promptly came up with a most ingenious fix to our clever attempt at exploiting this religious ritual. He declared that there would be no concessions made as far as the intensity of our training was concerned because, as he put it, training, like fasting, was a form of *ibadat* or prayer, and therefore carried equal significance. So, however much we groaned, whined, whimpered or feigned exhaustion, our training continued with unabated intensity. And, under such circumstances, most of us felt that at the end of the day, it wasn't worth it. And, from then onwards, not too many of us were seen waking up before sunrise for the pre-fast meal.

In the meantime, the friendship and companionship between some of us were steadily growing. We would seek out the company of each other and enjoy spending time together during our spare moments. It was a common practice to gather in one of our rooms, and the stories, chuckles and laughter we shared during those occasions went a long way in allaying the exhaustion of the course, both mental and physical. As mentioned earlier, Captain Barendra and I were sharing a room. And every so often, some of our course-mates like Captains Shahjahan, Ghani, Habib, Baset, Mujib and some others would assemble in our room. And the few moments we spent together at those times rejuvenated us. It gave us hope and renewed our faith in ourselves. It is with a heavy heart, however, that I have to mention here that Captains Baset and Mujib passed away a number of years ago.

Gift of Gratefulness

Halfway into our course we decided it would be a fine gesture of appreciation on our part to present the training center with a gift on behalf of all officers of OBC-12. Added to our intention of presenting the training center with a useful memento was also our desire to leave behind a mark as a reminder to those who came after us, that we were there. Understandably therefore, we wanted it to be permanent – or as close as it could possibly get to being permanent.

After much deliberation it was unanimously decided that that gift would be a chandelier for the main hall-room at the Centre, which also functioned as a recreation room. We had noticed that the single source of light hanging from the ceiling was not only insufficient, but rather decrepit and antiquated. That was why we felt a chandelier would be the perfect gift.

We next needed to decide who would go to Dhaka to purchase the chandelier. I found myself wondering about the excitement the officer chosen, would be overcome with. This welcome break from the daily grind of physical exhaustion and educational torment would not only be like a cool refreshing shower on a hot and humid afternoon, it would be the epitome of wallowing in a pool of liberty and freedom with carefree abandon. And just so no one felt justice was not done, it was decided that the officers would cast their votes to choose the one they felt was best suited for the job.

It would hardly be an exaggeration to say that I was fancying my chances too, to be elected – though why, I have no idea. Perhaps it was this intrinsic urge in me to be the one to get a job done, especially one as significant as this. Every Human has a dream and a desire to be part of something pioneering or momentous – like being on the deck of Starship Enterprise exploring 'strange new worlds' or scoring for the nation in a stadium filled with cheering fanatic supporters. Moreover, besides being a welcome break from the mundane routine, it also held the more alluring prospect of being with Samina, whom I had not seen for almost two months now.

At the end however, it turned out to be more of a selection than an election. Whether my course-mates felt I was more suited for the job or whether it was their graciousness to have given me this break, I do not know. All I know is that I was literally over the moon for having been chosen to go to Dhaka to procure the chandelier.

I reached Dhaka a couple of days later with the collective contributions of my course-mates – an amount we felt would be quite enough for a decent chandelier.

As I was climbing up the stairs of the apartment where my wife lived, someone known to me and living in the same apartment crossed me on his way down, and didn't even greet me. Though I found this a bit strange, I didn't give it much thought as I hurried up the steps. When I rang the bell, Samina opened the door. She looked at me without the slightest hint of recognition for almost five painful seconds. She was perhaps on the verge of asking me what I wanted, when her face suddenly – and finally – lit up. A piercing shriek, the likes of which I had never heard before, greeted me.

The last several weeks of harsh and incessant physical training had apparently converted me from being a relatively fair-skinned, moderately long-haired, and an awkwardly burly individual to a lean, close-cropped, and sun-baked dark specter. That was when the reason why I had not been recognized by the person going down the stairs finally dawned on me. This radical transformation had actually taken place right under my nose, and I hadn't even realized it! And that was perhaps because I was seeing myself in the mirror every day, and the change had been subtle and gradual enough to escape notice.

Over the next couple of days, Samina accompanied me as I went shopping for the chandelier, and helped me choose one which we both felt was fairly adequate and attractive. She even suggested that it be engraved with the inscription "OBC 12", which was done, and which my course-mates back at the center felt was an exquisite idea.

The chandelier that was presented to the
AMC Center by the officers of OBC-12

The Ladies Come to Town

It was during the last four weeks of the course at Rajshahi that five lady officers, along with Samina, joined OBC-12. Four of them, including Samina, were the wives of officers already in the course. And so following their arrival, the four couples, Samina and I included, were shifted to slightly larger family accommodations in an adjacent building. Although it separated the four married male officers from the rest, this 'separation' was only as far as accommodation was concerned. The deep bonds of comradeship and camaraderie that had grown and blossomed between these four married male officers and the rest, continued unabated.

The five lady officers of OBC-12 with Naik Shamsu (one of the drill sergeants)

With Captain Samina, in the Recreation Room of the AMC Center

The author and Captain Samina relaxing
in the Recreation Room of the AMC Center
with some OBC-12 course-mates

Having been reunited again after so many weeks, Samina and I therefore, and understandably, frequently gave in to urges for adventure.

One such 'urge' was to be constantly on the lookout for an opportunity to sneak out of the training center after sundown, to have a quiet dinner in the nearby town center. Being towards the end of the course, we somehow felt – either rightly or wrongly – that we had the license for such escapades. Nevertheless, we always endeavored to seek out a restaurant as obscure as possible, both in terms of locale and visibility, in order to avoid being spotted by an official from the training center.

In one such exploit of ours, just when Samina and I thought we were seated at a perfectly dark corner in a perfectly obscure Chinese restaurant, I turned my head to catch the unmistakable silhouette of our Training Adjutant hunched over his plate at a table we had just crossed to get to ours! Despite the fact that he seemed to be studiously looking down at his plate, he must have witnessed our entire act, from our arrival to us being seated. I would imagine he was having a most difficult time showing he had not noticed, and would rather have been more in his elements howling his infamous training-ground expletives at us for having left the training center without permission, and after sundown.

We soon found ourselves seriously debating the best course of action under the circumstances. Part intuition and part indoctrination told us that it would only be fair, proper and honorable – at least for me – to go up to our Training Adjutant and greet him. Yet, my instinct for survival held me back, screaming that I was perhaps better off walking out of that restaurant alive, than walking the plank. Nevertheless, in spite of all my intuitive warnings, I decided to be a man. And so, tearing myself from my chair, I went up to our Training Adjutant on unwilling legs, and greeted him.

He looked up as if he had seen me for the first time, forced a wry smile, and asked, "Well, what are you doing here?" While I was mentally groping for a conceivable reason, besides having a meal, that would bring a person to a restaurant, I mumbled a response which must have sounded something like a cross between the croak of a toad and the quack of a duck. The phrase, "Well, enjoy your meal" which finally floated to my ears in the midst of my incoherent cacophony was the equivalent of a pardon for a death row inmate. I don't quite remember my mode of retreat, but I must have looked like a wounded animal desperate in putting as much distance as possible between itself and a hunter, as I wildly scampered back to the sanctuary of my seat, almost on all fours!

Have Gun, Will Fire

Part of our training was to learn the use of small arms. This comprised a few initial demonstration and practice lessons at the training center, on the aspects of handling and firing pistols and rifles, including their disassembly and assembly – sometimes even blindfolded, just to make things more interesting.

A few lessons later, all twenty three of us departed for a firing range some 40 kilometers away in the outskirts of a town called Bogra, to bang away at targets to our hearts' content. We made the trip on the back of a huge army truck, usually referred to as a "3-ton", and called so presumably because those were capable of carrying a cargo of up to that weight.

The mood in the back of the truck was positively upbeat as the twenty three trainee officers in full battle gear were in a rather boisterous and jovial mood at the prospects of the 'adventure' awaiting them. However, during the trip, it was not very reassuring to learn that none of my course-mates had ever fired a small arm of any kind before, let alone a deadly rifle used in war – which we were to be firing soon! I therefore contemplated, and not without good reason, that once the firing started I couldn't afford to keep my sights on the targets alone, and that the absence of a Kevlar vest would have to be adequately compensated for by sheer vigilance and an instinct for survival.

At length our group arrived at the firing range. Brimming with confidence and overflowing with inexperience, we immediately went about converting everything around us into a world of confused mayhem. This was accompanied by the howling and screaming of our drill sergeants trying to give the entire exercise some semblance of order and sanity. Needless to say, they were being tested to the limit of their patience and tolerance!

We were to start with rifle firing first, which was a Chinese 7.62 caliber army-issue rifle. This was the same rifle we had been carrying around all these weeks during our parades and drill practices. This was the same rifle we lugged on our shoulders during the 2-mile runs and 16-kilometer walks, and by the end of which it felt as if it weighed a ton. This was the same rifle we pushed fox excrement with, inside the tunnels. And this was also the same rifle we had assembled and disassembled countless number of times, preparing for this moment.

We were to have a total of three sessions, and were given fifteen bullets each – five bullets to be fired in each session. Seven of us were to take firing positions at a time on a raised ridge on the ground, lying prone, to fire at respective targets boards, four feet by four feet, a hundred yards away, with a bulls-eye in the center.

Havildar Sikander, the senior drill sergeant, who was conducting the firing session then provided detailed instructions regarding the firing protocol, stressing on the importance of starting to fire only after the 'firing order' had been given, and not a moment before. Right there in front of him were seven prone figures in full battle gear, lying spread-eagle, staring down their barrels, about to take a life-changing step.

For those of us lying flat on our bellies, with our elbows on the ground and our hands supporting the rifle pointing down at the targets far away, this was a defining moment. This was a moment with the promise and the potential of finally transforming us into the 'soldier' we were preparing to be. This was a moment beyond which, for the rest of our lives, the act of having fired a gun would become a glorifying qualification of ours. It would amount to a sharp and decisive demarcation between being an innocuous and harmless novice in uniform versus a true soldier capable of being in a battlefield.

One hand supported the cold metal barrel, while the index finger of the other lay lightly curled around the trigger. Our heads were tilted over the rifle, with the open eye trained on the gun-sight, trying to line it up with the little targets a hundred yards away. Butterflies took wings in our stomachs while the instructions of the drill sergeant reached our ears from somewhere above us. We tried to concentrate, but if truth be told, the intensity and the excitability of the moment made the instructions of the drill sergeant sound like the monotonous drone of an irrigation pump. We were visibly excited, and raring to go.

The firing instructions were soon over. Havildar Sikander then paused briefly to finally deliver his firing order. And all it took was for him to open his mouth to inflate his lungs, preparing to howl the firing order – when we somehow decided to take matters into our own hands.

Suddenly, and without any warning, all hell broke loose. If hell didn't exist before, it was being created right here, at this firing range. Scores of rifles went off almost at once, mercilessly drowning whatever was beginning to take shape within Havildar Sikander's lungs. While some projectiles whistled high above their targets and tumbled onto nearby unsuspecting villages, others ricocheted off the ground only yards from us, amid clouds of dust and clumps of flying grass. Results were considered to be within limits of respectability if one could somehow manage to land at least one bullet on his own target board – and it didn't matter where. Because, considering the quality of the proceedings, the bulls-eye was totally irrelevant at that point. It didn't count, however, if someone decided to riddle the next person's target with his own bullets, which seemed like an unfair rule, given that that was what frequently happened.

In the midst of this bedlam of smoke, dust, flying grass and wayward bullets, some of us were to be seen cantering back from our firing positions with an expression of supreme satisfaction, but with unused bullets still left over within the rifle magazine! The expression on the faces of the drill sergeants could hardly conceal their confusion as to whether they were still a part of the armed forces or had just joined a circus. I am convinced that throughout this pandemonium, and despite their screaming and swearing, the drill sergeants were very studiously watching their own backs, and given time, would probably have grown eyes at the backs of their heads too – just in case that was needed – and which, in this case, seemed rather necessary!

To my own great surprise and satisfaction, I felt not the least bit flustered by the immensity of the situation when my turn finally came. Once I lay prone on the ground with the loaded rifle in my hands, I seemed to have subconsciously gone into a shell of intense focus. It was as if, at that moment, nothing else in this world mattered or anything else even existed, except for the gun-sight on my rifle and the target at a distance. I remember telling myself not to rush the proceedings, and to space myself between one bullet and the next, because, at that moment, time was on my side. And then, with the final factor of Providence coming into play, which guided my head, heart and hand, I most calmly sent five bullets off, one after the other, toward the target – and they all landed within an area only 4½ inches across!

This, in military language, is known as 'grouping', which is the area within which one can land five bullets. The smaller the number, the more exalted and admired the person. It is something like a personal trophy to be toted around, in which, if the number happens to be enviably small, its disclosure usually leads to considerable *'oohs'* and *'ahhs'*. Every conversation concerning firing, therefore, invariably boiled down to one final question: "What is your grouping?" The smallest number I have ever come across is 2 inches. Compared to that, 4½ inches wasn't too bad either, and it showed on the faces of those who inquired.

But to this day, I cannot explain how that could ever have happened. The only firing experience I have had prior to this was a friend's almost toy-like .22-bore rifle which fired pellets, smaller than peas, one at a time. The target too, was ample and generous, being the window pane of one of our neighbors whom we weren't particularly fond of, and which was invitingly located across a pond right behind our house.

But, what had just happened here on this firing range was totally different. In my hand was an army-issue rifle used in real battle, and capable of killing humans. And out there in the distance was a target so far away that it could easily hide behind my thumb. I believe that each time I was about to pull the trigger, two things had happened simultaneously. The first was probably a state of asphyxiation, resulting from my breathing being held in complete abeyance out of pure fright. And the other was probably an 'adrenaline rush' experienced during states of stress, but which leads to an enhanced physical ability. These two must have led to the kind of immobility seen only in statues made of rock or metal, and which adorn the promenades and city intersections.

That, incidentally, turned out to be the perfect recipe for a 4½ inch grouping!

Senior officers present at the firing range, including a few from nearby Infantry units, were so impressed by my performance that they called me to their tent to inquire if I have had any previous experience with firing a rifle. And when I replied in the negative, they were visibly surprised. "How then, do you fire so well?" asked one of them, to which I preferred to remain silent. I guess they had no idea of what a state of deathly asphyxiation, combined with a tsunami of adrenaline, were capable of achieving! And, of course, I had no intention of boring them with the stories about my neighbor and his windows!

Though my groupings were a trifle larger in the remaining two sessions, I am thankful that none took a trip to a nearby village, dug up the ground in front, or added a few extra holes in another target board!

But, to be very honest, I have always had a nagging feeling at the back of my mind since then, as to whether the ability which I had demonstrated at the firing range in Bogra was a fluke, or whether it was truly an ability of mine. My conscience finally rested easy some years later.

While we were posted to CMH Chittagong – about which I have stories aplenty to share with my readers in a later chapter – Samina and I, along with two other friends of ours and their families, made a pleasure trip to a tea garden in Sylhet, which our family owned. We were lounging on the verandah of the bungalow one morning, enjoying the silence and the serenity around us, when one of my friends, who had brought along with him a hunting rifle, suggested we have some fun with it. He then produced a match box, clambered up a tree next to the bungalow, and placed it pretty high up on it. We were to try to knock that match box out of there with our shots, from a distance of about fifty yards from the tree.

My friends went first and fired. But the match box remained where it was. When my turn came I seemed overtaken again by that same 'state of stillness', and which, unfortunately, boded ill for the match box. It was promptly blown out from where it was. My friends instantly claimed it was all a fluke, and decided we should go at it again. It was the same result the second time too – and the third time!

And I silently heaved a huge sigh of relief deep within my inner conscience at the final realization that whatever had transpired at the firing range in Bogra some years ago was not a fluke after all, and good enough to write home about. It was something I could truly be proud of!

However, my crowning moment at the Bogra range was yet to come.

With the rifle firing over, and after a break, we proceeded to pistol firing. The target, in this case, was a life-size human cut-out figure made of thin hardwood, about forty or fifty feet away. We were to fire five bullets at a bulls-eye drawn on the chest of the cut-out figure, where the heart usually is.

Before everything else, our Training Adjutant demonstrated how the firing was to be carried out. We were to stand with our body at a slight angle to the target and with the legs slightly apart for better balance. The hand holding the pistol would have to be held straight out at the target, and the other hand, made into a fist, would have to be tucked behind, with the fist resting on the small of the back. Five trainee officers were to take turns at a time, and as in the case of rifle firing, there was no time limit within which to fire the five rounds. So, there was no pressure.

Basking in my most recent success, I proceeded with the task with a sense of complete relaxation. More importantly, there was absolutely no pressure on me now. I had already made a statement with the rifle, and that statement was rather 'bang on', in a manner of speaking! So, I stood there with my legs spread as instructed, and pumped out five rounds from my pistol. No sooner had the smoke cleared, our Training Adjutant, as usual, was off at a sprint toward the targets to see the results.

I was extremely disappointed when I heard him announce that only four of my five bullets had actually found their mark. And as I most reluctantly, and rather disappointedly, ambled up to him, I was a bit surprised to see that our Training Adjutant was still staring at my target and a wee bit more intently than I would have expected him to. He then turned and looked at me with a most weird expression on his face, and it seemed as if his lower jaw was not entirely under his control. What then emanated was something between a stammer and a mumbo-jumbo, and it took me a while to decipher from his almost-unintelligible diction that the bullet declared "missing" by him had actually made its way almost cleanly through the hole of one of the preceding ones! I would give myself to believe that, yet again, a combination of asphyxiated stillness, and the 'adrenaline factory' that I had turned into by now, had guided my hand!

One of the most rewarding benefits of the training for me was the disappearance of a substantial portion of unwanted weight and an expanding middle, most of which had been accumulated over years of sedentary habits, particularly while in medical school, not to mention frequent wayward dietary deviations. To this day I squirm uneasily as I look back to that first evening at the training center when we were being 'weighed in', and which took place right after the barbers had mercilessly decimated the meticulously groomed hair on our heads. This weighing-in was to record our baseline weight, so that the progress made by each, in terms of physical fitness, could be tracked and additional measures, whether dietary or physical, taken.

That day, my turn came with all my new-found friends and acquaintances gathered around the weighing scale. I was intentionally drifting at the fringes of the circle of trainee officers, hoping against hope that I would somehow be overlooked and forgotten, and not have to stand on the weighing scale. But, most unfortunately, my name was on that list, and eventually it got called out. I found myself literally willing the machine to come up with some sort of a mechanical problem which would force this embarrassing session to be postponed. But that weighing scale, unfortunately, was one of a generation built to withstand the worst of heavy weather. As I most gingerly stepped onto it, trying to be as light-footed as possible – as if that would help – the dial took off like a terrified steed in a fright-night movie, and settled at an excruciating 180 pounds!

That I was in deep trouble was plainly obvious from the expressions of concern all around. Some of my course-mates even came up to me to express how worried they were about me. They offered me their earnest and sincere best wishes in anticipation of what might transpire once the rigorous training started.

That, however, did not daunt my determination and enthusiasm as I simply refused to succumb to the fathomless hardships and the exhausting harshness of the training. I must admit, however, that I started off quite badly as compared to many of my leaner and more athletic course-mates. But about halfway into the course, and purely through raw grit and dedicated perseverance, I was actually ahead of most of them, much to their surprise. *"If Ishraq sir can do it, so can you"* soon became a very popular phrase with our drill sergeants, and one which could often be heard being yelled with unbridled fervor.

Officers of OBC – 12 before their passing
out from the AMC Training Center
(The author is standing back row, extreme right)

The most prized compliment, however, came during the farewell dinner, when the Commandant of the Training Center remarked, while referring to me, that "*Captain Ishraq came in as the fattest, but he is leaving as the fittest.*" I was not afraid of standing on a weighing scale any more. I weighed a willowy 148 pounds that night!

Immensely pleased as I was with the way my military training had gone, and the satisfying way that my physique had shaped up during the last twelve weeks, I seemed oblivious of the grim fact that that also marked the beginning of the end of my career – that that installation in Rajshahi was, in fact, a portal of entry ***into a maze***.

Chapter 4

INTO THE MAZE

Hectic days at 61 Field Ambulance

"Reality is merely an illusion, albeit a very persistent one." – Albert Einstein

The largely physical part of our basic military training was over at Rajshahi. Our entire group then had to move to Dhaka Cantonment for the remaining four weeks of the course, to be conducted at the Armed Forces Medical Institute (also known as the AFMI). This second part of our training was referred to as the 'Phase-2' of the Officers' Basic Course.

Our trip back from Rajshahi was in sharp contrast to the one which Barendra and I had made to the training center some twelve weeks ago, sitting atop a cycle rickshaw. Looking back, twelve weeks now seemed like twelve months, probably because the physical hardships, the mental pressures, the educational torments, the various indoctrinations, and the fathomless fatigue had somehow slowed down the clock. It was something similar to the impression we get of the hands of a clock moving around its face at a snail's pace when we actually want time to pass quicker. Nevertheless, we were all going back with a feeling of pride and accomplishment. Our mettle had been tested, and we had been assayed in fire – and we seemed to have emerged from it with more grit and character than what we possessed when we had arrived at the training center.

But finally, after twelve long and laborious weeks, we were leaving the training center for the last time.

We were leaving behind the huge training grounds on which we ran, marched, played, crawled and toiled – and the soil of which now bore the salt of our sweat.

We were leaving behind the bellowing of our drill sergeants, the profanities of our Training Adjutant and the lectures of our instructors, all delivered to make us what we were.

We were leaving behind the mess hall where we ate like famished scavengers, and where we also learned the fine art of culinary etiquettes.

We were leaving behind the rifles we lugged on our shoulders, pushed fox excrement with, and which we fired at almost everything else besides our own target boards.

We were leaving behind the beds on which our exhausted and shattered bodies slept like babies.

And we were also leaving behind a chandelier which would announce, for years to come, that "OBC-12" was there.

But, most importantly, we were leaving behind a chapter of our lives, the lessons from which would help to shape our futures, and the memories of which would remain with us forever.

The AMC Center chartered a bus to take us all back to the AFMI in Dhaka. We were all packed and ready at the crack of dawn on the day of our departure. Our spirits were visibly and understandably high, as we waited for our bus to arrive. And after a wait which seemed like ages, it finally lumbered up to our accommodations.

As we were boarding the bus, we spotted our drill sergeants, all four of them, approaching us from a distance. As they got closer, we noticed that for some reason, they didn't look like God's hand-picked re-incarnation of the Devil anymore. After twelve weeks at the Center we, the trainee officers, now seemed to be appreciative of the sincere and dedicated intent behind the drill sergeants' screaming and swearing, as much as the drill sergeants themselves were perhaps pleased by our earnest efforts in trying to live up to their demands and expectations. And this had created between us a feeling of mutual respect, and which led to a special bonding between us. Obviously, the drill sergeants were here to say farewell, and I can say with firm conviction that every one of us were equally pleased to see them.

But the drill sergeants were there for yet another reason – and which truly warmed our hearts. They had come to also atone for their harsh treatment of us during our training, and to express their regrets for their liberal use of expletives. But we all seemed to know the reason and the intent behind those, and what those had achieved. And as the trainee officers and the drill sergeants exchanged farewell greetings and embraced each other under the early morning sky, there were tears in many an eye. The salutes we received from our drill sergeants as our bus rolled out of the premises of the AMC Training Center, was the smartest – and the sincerest – I have ever seen or received in my life.

> *It is with a heavy heart that I would like my readers to know that sadly, Havildar Sikander recently passed away. Though he does not walk on this Earth today, Havildar Sikander has left behind scores of medical corps officers with the qualities of perseverance and tenacity, and the physical and mental toughness to never give up or to give in.*

The journey from Rajshahi to Dhaka was usually anywhere between seven to eight hours in duration, depending on the traffic and the road conditions. This also included a ferry trip, the duration of which varied between three to four hours, depending on how fast or slow the ferry sailed, and whether or not it was going for or against the current. Though quite decrepit and rather antiquated, this ferry nonetheless, was fairly large, with a dining area on the second floor, which was open on all sides – perhaps more through default than by design.

During the ferry ride, Samina and I, along with some of our colleagues, were having lunch in that dining area, when she pointed to a glass of lemonade a guest sitting at a nearby table was having, indicating that she too wanted one of the same. I was about to call a waiter to order a glass of lemonade for her when my eyes strayed over to the open kitchen area nearby. That was when I noticed one of the kitchen-helps throwing a pail over the side of the ferry, and into the river. When he proceeded to pour out its contents into drinking glasses lined up on the table in front of him, I realized that the 'lemonade' Samina was referring to was actually the murky river water the guests were being served to drink! That effectively put an end to our drinking anything further on that ferry, unless it came enclosed in a natural protective barrier!

We finally reached Dhaka late in the evening, and were put up in *Rupsa*-like tin-roofed officers' accommodations within walking distance of the AFMI.

The AFMI was the educational institution of the Army Medical Corps which, besides conducting the last four weeks of the Officers' Basic Course, also dealt with training the army doctors in various specialties, as well as the periodic publication of the Armed Forces Medical Journal. This phase of our training involved educating us on ways the army dealt with diseases, and instructing us on the administrative aspects of dealing with patients. The Commandant of the institute,

Colonel (later Brigadier General) Shahjahan Hafiz, a larger-than-life personality with chiseled features and a somber countenance, talked very little. But when he did, it seemed to make sense, unlike most of similar rank in equally elevated positions.

This phase of the training did not, however, exonerate us from the compulsory early morning physical exercises or the two-mile run. But, that did not quite bother us any more, especially after what we had been through over the past twelve weeks. Most importantly, this 2-mile run did not have the infamous Devil from Hell at our heels, screaming expletives at the slightest hint of tiredness. Nor was there the devil leading from the front as if we were a column of human battering ram bent on tearing down the door of a medieval castle. And the free-hand exercises which followed the 2-mile morning run were comparable to the Chicken Dance on a Saturday night at a seniors' bingo club. All this, added to the fact that we were to concentrate on subjects that were medical, and not military, in nature, made our life at the AFMI seem like a paid vacation.

Perhaps the only sticking point for most of us during this phase was an extempore speech which had to be delivered by us on the very last day of the course, as part of the curriculum, on geopolitics, current world affairs and issues of national importance. To make matters worse, it was to be delivered in the presence of none other than the Commandant of AFMI himself, who would be presiding over the proceedings. This, obviously, made this exercise all the more unnerving since, by the end of the course, we had come to the undeniable conclusion that the Commandant's knowledge of English was impeccable, and that his ability of public speaking truly commendable. And he, of all people, would be judging our capacity to speak in public!

The AFMI, however, in an effort to make matters a bit easier for us, provided a list of topics we were to speak on. The twenty eight officers (including the five lady officers) were given twenty eight topics to prepare on. None, however, knew the topic he or she would be speaking on, because that was to be randomly decided by a lottery as a speaker went up to the lectern to speak. For us therefore, it meant preparing twenty eight different topics, unless one was willing to perform hara-kiri in front of twenty seven spectators – twenty nine to be exact, counting the Commandant and his Adjutant.

Understandably therefore, during the last few days of the course, we were all literally consumed in our efforts to prepare the topics provided. To be fairly honest, preparing to speak on twenty-eight different topics was no small task. Obviously, we burned the midnight candle in our efforts to cover as much as possible, with most of our spare time also being taken up discussing and educating ourselves in world affairs, geopolitics, and issues of national importance.

On the day of the frightful event, with all the officers of OBC-12 gathered in the small auditorium at the AFMI, and with the Commandant sitting stern-faced beside the lectern, we all felt like little sacrificial lambs herded into a pen as an offering to the 'god of public speaking'. My course-mates sitting on either side could probably hear my heart pounding, and I was also convinced that if they looked down, they could also see my legs turning to jelly. Nevertheless, it was also a huge relief and consolation to observe that they too were no less flustered than I was.

The speeches soon began.

Nothing that any of my course-mates said while standing in front of the gathered audience even registered in my head, as I tried my best to keep calm, and not show that I was actually shaking like a leaf. But as time went by and the parade of people to and from the front of the room continued, I seemed to calm down. Because, from where I was, I witnessed an assortment of wide-eyed terrified stares and awkward spastic gestures from behind the lectern. The quivering voices, frequent stammers and inadvertent whines and whimpers made as little sense to me as it probably did to the speakers themselves. This seemed to usher in a great deal of self-confidence, as I took comfort and courage from the fact that since I now knew what could happen to someone standing behind the lectern, I would try my best not to repeat the same when my turn eventually came. At the same time too, I was trying my best to recollect and recapitulate the points I would be speaking on, on the various topics I had prepared over the past few days – and nights.

It is a well-known fact that anyone can get frozen in fright quicker than the blink of an eye at the prospect of any impending doom and disaster. But never in my wildest dreams had I expected that I would experience it first-hand. My world and my life took a sudden apocalyptic turn when the Commandant finally called out my name. His voice sounded like a wave which, quite effortlessly and rather mercilessly, washed away the sandcastle of courage I had built while sitting in the audience, watching and listening to the others speak. From the moment that I left my seat, till I reached the front of the auditorium, I probably looked like a zombie from the "Night of the Living Dead". To me, the world seemed like a silent movie from the early 1900s. I saw my course-mates clapping and the lips of our Commandant moving, all in slow motion – but heard nothing. And, when I finally reached the front of the room, the Commandant indicated that I pull out of the bucket sitting on his table, one of the folded pieces of lottery paper for the topic of my extempore speech.

Looking in, I could see that not many were left, since I was one of the last few speakers. I said a silent prayer, dug in, and pulled one out. I unfolded it – and stood there as if hit by lightning. I heard a ringing in my ears, while darkness descended around me as if this was some sort of a doomsday event. I felt like dropping to my knees, beating my chest with both fists, and singing the saddest song ever written in the history of mankind at the top of my voice!

Written on the wretched piece of paper which I had just pulled out was the topic "The Education System in Bangladesh" – the only topic out of a total of twenty eight that I had NOT prepared!

The 'gods of misfortune and of mischief' must have joined hands in enticing me to pull out of the bucket the only topic I knew absolutely nothing about! If ever was Murphy's Law, which says "anything that can go wrong will go wrong", represented in its most authentic, yet most vicious and malicious of versions, then this had to be it. I doubt if ever in the entire history of mankind was Murphy's Law so harsh, unkind or cruel to a human being!

I then began walking towards the lectern. I can assure you that rarely in my life had I ever walked slower than that, trying my best to extract as many extra seconds as I could between the lottery jar and the lectern. At the same time too, my mind was racing faster than a bullet, straining and striving to gather some – any – pertinent facts on the topic.

What did I know of the education system in Bangladesh? Absolutely nothing!

I was a part of that system all my life, but had I ever stepped out of the jungle to look at the forest? Never!

One is always so wrapped up in getting through the intricacies and struggles inherent in a system that there is hardly the time or the opportunity of looking at it in its entirety.

So no, I had absolutely no clue as to what to say.

Yet I began to speak, because I had to say something. Salutations and opening greetings and remarks were easy, as I took a deep breath and got into it with a slowness I hoped would convert into the impression of a confident speaker, and not a pathetic know-nothing. And then I picked my way carefully through the speech with deliberate slowness. I generalized my own experiences with the system, making intermittent forays into the good and the bad of it, while attempting to provide my own – rather concocted – solutions at the same time. And throughout this excruciating exercise, my mind had to be at least a step ahead of my mouth, failing which I knew I would perish. Eventually I was able to wrap it all up without any major disaster I believe, because while summing up our performances the Commandant said, "There are people who know absolutely nothing about a topic, and yet will present it in a way which gives the impression they are adequately knowledgeable about it."

My suspicion that I was somehow, and eventually, able to put together a pretty laudable performance overall, in this second phase of the course, was reflected in the 'Alpha-Outstanding' grade I received at the end.

Into the Hall of Induction

With our basic military training completed, I was posted as a GDMO (General Duty Medical Officer) to 61 Field Ambulance, which was a field medical unit located in Dhaka Cantonment. At the same time Samina was posted as a GDMO at CMH Dhaka, which was about a twenty-minute walk from my unit. Understandably, my posting to 61 Field Ambulance now came with an expectation vastly different from what it had been when I had joined CMH Savar. Because, having now completed my basic military training, I was expected by all to typify the ideal military officer, both in words and in deeds.

A loose connotation of a GDMO is a "one size fits all" kind of a doctor, or a 'handyman' of sorts who could be called upon to undertake a plethora of responsibilities in a medical unit. And, as mentioned earlier, this ranged from being anything from a medical officer to a garden officer, a duty officer to a transport officer, a DQ to a quartermaster or an adjutant to an accounts officer. But of course, one could also climb up the ladder to become the Second-in-Command or even the Commanding Officer of a unit, provided one had enough seniority and no adverse comments in the officer's Annual Confidential Report (ACR) sent in yearly to the headquarters by the unit commanding officer.

For a lady officer, on the other hand, being a GDMO meant being a medical officer at a CMH, looking after patients under the guidance of a specialist, unless of course, she was senior and qualified enough to be the in-charge of the Family Ward (where the soldiers' wives were admitted), the Officers Family Ward (where the wives of officers were admitted) or the CWC (Child Welfare Center). Lady Officers were never posted to a field medical unit.

In the meantime, Samina and I were offered an accommodation at 57 Shaheed Badiuzzaman Road in Dhaka Cantonment, which was roughly a ten-minute ride on a motorbike, from our respective units. This accommodation, we were told, was temporary and 'not proper', and that we could choose to live in it till such time that a proper accommodation in an apartment complex was available. We were given the choice of either accepting it or waiting our turn for a proper accommodation. We decided to accept it because getting to work early every morning while staying somewhere else, possibly outside the cantonment, was obviously going to be a tall order.

The reason this accommodation was branded 'not proper' was simply because it was actually not proper. It had been a bachelor officers' mess at some point in the past, accommodating four bachelor officers in four bachelor units. Each unit, comprising one large room, an adjoining smaller room – which probably served as a utility-cum-storage space – and a toilet, were placed one beside the other, making up a single one-storied building. Understandably, therefore, all the larger rooms were the same size, as were the smaller rooms and toilets. The front of the building had one long verandah, with doors from the larger room of each unit opening on to it.

But over the years, as newer and better bachelor officers' accommodations were gradually constructed, this building was on the verge of being abandoned. But then, a bright bulb in someone's head suddenly lit up, and the building was converted into a family accommodation. Doors were inserted in the walls separating the four units, and a kitchen was put in. Therefore, with the four units now being interconnected, and with a kitchen in there, this could now be considered a single, and a fairly large, family accommodation.

When Samina and I went to inspect the house – if one could call it so – we were immediately perplexed and baffled by how convoluted the layout was since, in getting from one end of the house to the other, one had to go through a maze of eight rooms. Interestingly, and quite understandably, this house also had four toilets, which could easily be considered the ultimate in luxury – especially with only two of us living there!

However, the one thing about this accommodation which impressed us, and was perhaps a deciding factor was this: That, unlike the barrack-like *Rupsas* on either side of it, this accommodation was within a private compound, complete with a perimeter wall, a fairly large lawn in front, and a decent backyard behind. So, after all the necessary paper-work was completed, we finally moved into 57 Shaheed Badiuzzaman Road, where Samina and I lived most contentedly over the next ten years or so!

Residence at 57 Shaheed Badiuzzaman Road

Of the four large rooms, we decided to use the one at one end as our bedroom, with the other three functioning as the dining, living and guest rooms, in that order, with the guest room being the farthest away. Of the four toilets at our disposal, we decided to use the ones not attached to our bedroom or to the guest room, as storage rooms. Understandably therefore, we ended up with an abundance of storage space as well!

But, despite its rather antiquated state and its convoluted layout, Samina and I soon converted this house into a home. The convolutions didn't matter after a while, as we soon got used to it. But, we hadn't realized how much we had actually gotten used to this apparent 'inconvenience' until the day that an elderly uncle of mine visited us, and wanted to use the toilet. So I took him through the maze of rooms to the toilet adjoining the guest room which, as I had mentioned, was at the farthest end of the house. And, just before entering the toilet, my uncle looked at me and said, "You stay right here and wait for me. I need to be able to get back to where I came from"!

Considering the abundance of area in front of and behind the house, Samina had all the space in the world she ever needed, to do her gardening to her heart's content – which ranged from beautiful and exotic flowers to the most varied and healthy vegetables. There was also a jackfruit tree at one end of the front lawn, and it bore the sweetest jackfruits I have ever tasted in my life! And during pleasant winter evenings, we would pull chairs out on to the front lawn and have an enjoyable time with either friends or family, or listen to songs playing on a cassette player.

The one sticking point in this house, however, was that the door from our bedroom to the front verandah, which was kept permanently closed, was one of the most ill-fitting doors I had ever come across. There was such a large gap between the wooden door and the frame around it that if one tilted one's head to a certain sweet angle, one could make out a sliver of daylight coming in through the gap! And this was a problem during winter nights, when the cold wind blew in through that gap like the Roaring Forties! My innovative solution to that inconvenience was to fold up pages of newspapers into long strips and inserting those into the gaps. And it took quite a few newspapers to have the job done properly!

Samina and I lived at 57 Shaheed Badiuzaaman Road for ten long years. In the meantime, however, we were repeatedly offered accommodations in the most attractive and the most recently-built apartments at Dhaka Cantonment – all of which we refused. We refused because we had soon realized that the virtues of this house far outweighed its shortcomings. But, above all, we refused because we had somehow fallen in love with this house, had made it our 'home', and had given it our hearts.

The Blight of Blindness

> *"The only thing worse than being blind, is having sight, but no vision." – Helen Keller*

My unit, 61 Field Ambulance, catered to the medical needs of an entire Infantry Division (including its ancillary brigades and their arms and services), the headquarters of the three forces (the army, the navy and the air force), and other civilian supplementary establishments. This unit's commitments therefore, besides being burdensome, were also multifarious and diverse.

Moreover, this field medical unit, like any other medical unit, was also severely under-staffed, and therefore stretched to its absolute limit trying to cope with its innumerable obligations and responsibilities. And being the junior-most officer at such a unit, particularly having come fresh out of military training, I somehow seemed to be the solution to a great deal of the burden of responsibilities constantly nagging it and was, therefore, in special demand! And as an obvious and expected outcome, I felt that much more than my normal share of duties were being delegated to me on a notoriously regular basis. And at a certain point, as a result, I lost all track of time and all sense of purpose.

To begin with, I was entrusted with the responsibility of looking after several scattered out-patient clinics called MI (Medical Inspection) Rooms every morning, which were under the unit's jurisdiction. These had to be attended to in turn, over the week, where I would be driven over in a rather rickety WW II Russian-made *UAZ* ambulance, which looked more like an elongated metal soap-case, and a rode much like a bullock-cart. For ease of pronunciation, and not knowing the Russian pronunciation of "*UAZ*", we called this haphazard conglomeration of metal "YAZ". No one really looked forward to a ride in it, not even as a passenger, let alone as a patient, because vehicles such as these were bound to make Henry Ford repent his invention.

The out-patient clinics which I looked after were usually so overflowing with patients that comparing the assembled crowd to a country fair would have been a fairly accurate description, both in terms of the human volume and the prevailing mood. It didn't take me long to realize that a substantial number of those waiting for me wouldn't have been there at all, had this not been a free consultation. Though the matter of entitlement to free medical consultation and treatment in the armed forces has been dealt with in greater detail in a later chapter, for now, it made me apprehensive as to whether, in giving my time to everyone gathered at the MI Room, I was really doing justice to those who genuinely required my undivided attention.

Besides being perplexed and overwhelmed by this, I was further frustrated by the fact that the authorities, despite their knowledge of the situation, chose to let the matter continue unabated. It was definitely not a case of simple oversight because there had been instances when the authorities had sorted out matters much less significant than this, almost overnight. So, the only possible explanation would have to be the fact that perhaps a handful few at the top were in no mood of falling out of favor with the lower tiers by implementing a system where only those who genuinely required medical attention be allowed to gather. So anyone and everyone who wanted to abuse the system were welcome.

In fact, none in authority seemed the least concerned as to why so many patients were reporting to not only the out-lying MI Rooms of the field medical unit, but also to the MI Rooms and Out-Patient Departments (OPD) of the military hospitals, and the various CWCs (Child Welfare Centers). Besides those genuinely requiring medical attention, there were also the malingering soldiers looking to extract a few days of rest, as were their wives, with or without their children, looking to pick up some free medications on the pretext of the most trivial of physical discomforts.

Oddly enough, from the perspective of those who ran the show, such reasons for reporting to a doctor didn't seem to be of any concern at all. Of over-riding importance was the fact that since a patient had reported, he or she would have to be sent off with some sort of a *medication* – and not necessarily a *treatment*. And in order to endorse and enforce such a practice, a brilliant word was pulled out of the dictionary and put to use – Disposal. Fittingly enough, it sounded sharp, definitive and decisive, and denoted an adequate and a fulfilled medical response. In other words, anyone and everyone reporting to a doctor would have to be sent off with a 'disposal'.

Astonishingly, it seemed immaterial to the authorities that the real reason for reporting to the MI Rooms may not have been entirely genuine, or even warranted. Nevertheless, the actual reason was so plainly obvious that I am pretty sure the authorities noticed, but chose to turn a blind eye. On the contrary, certain individuals in certain exalted offices appeared to be implicitly supporting this senseless distribution and wastage of medical resources resulting from such a reckless and mindless practice. They opted to ignore the fact that some of the medicines, however expensive, which were being dispensed free of cost were sometimes being unnecessarily wasted in the process. Rather, the only commodity, it seemed, which could not be wasted at any cost was an exhibition of the fact that some sort of a medical response – however ineffective, inappropriate or unethical – was being ensured by the lofty offices for all and sundry.

If the true objective and essential obligation of a treating institution is perfunctorily cast aside to cater to the wishes of a handful few at the top, then the very spirit with which a medical establishment serves humanity is seriously undermined. Here was a reality the powers-that-be either failed to comprehend or refused to admit. The desires of the mighty few – be those illogical or injudicious – always seemed to be at the forefront, thereby depriving some of the real patients of their real needs.

Study Periods were frequently conducted by the local brigade or logistic area during the evenings, where matters pertaining to military strategy and military history were presented, and then discussed in considerable detail. Insofar as any routine military activity is concerned, that was perfectly fine – but only up to the point where the doctors were not only made to attend such study periods compulsorily, but also expected to actively engage in the proceedings. And to ensure that that happened, I still remember instances where some senior officers of the arms and other services sitting at the head of the gathered audience turning around, before the start of the presentation, and declaring, "The doctors will also have to participate and ask questions."

However, I am pretty sure they knew, as much as anyone with an intellect a notch above that of a chimpanzee, that where it concerned military history and strategy, doctors would obviously be lacking in knowledge – as much as they themselves would be lacking in the knowledge of medicine. But yet, the doctors were literally goaded into participating. It was as if there was a purpose behind it. And if indeed there was, I pity those depraved minds for contriving a status quo that had the potential of belittling others.

Besides, one would also get the impression that the knowledge gained from discussing the battle strategies of World War II or how and why Napoleon lost the Battle of Waterloo would somehow enhance the quality of treatment provided at the hospitals and the MI

Rooms! It would have made more sense rather, if junior medical officers like us were made to attend clinical discussion sessions and classes instead, at the hospitals in the evenings, in order to enhance our medical and clinical knowledge and expertise for the service of the establishment.

In the spirit of fair play, I would have liked to have officers from the non-medical units attend such clinical classes with us at the hospitals, and then to have asked them whether or not they thought the knowledge gained thereby, could be used by them in the battlefield. To which, they would certainly have said, "Nonsense!" – a response the medical community was apparently not 'entitled' to when it came to doctors having to passionately discuss and debate military history and military strategies.

The one segment of the medical corps which actually had the power and the prerogative to be critical of such an imposition was the higher hierarchy of the corps. But, most unfortunately, they not only chose to remain silent, they seemed to endorse the practice. Though, at this point, I would not like to expound on the reasons for such a posture, I do believe the readers will be able to draw their own obvious conclusions in this regard by the time they reach the last page of this book.

Besides the Study Periods, the evenings were also often taken up by one of the 'nights'. It was usually a Dinner Night, a Guest Night or a Club Night, each with its purported significance and distinctive ceremonial rituals. Such was this institution's obsession with keeping everyone incessantly occupied and relentlessly active that people were always cutting the grass, weeding out the undergrowth or digging something somewhere. Interestingly, when they ran out of such objects, they descended upon their barracks and the trees – and painted them. "If you see something moving, salute it. If you see something standing still, paint it" was therefore a popular adage in the army, and not without good reason.

It is understandable that being the freshest and, more importantly, the junior-most in a field medical unit, I would continue to be delegated the most unenviable of responsibilities. In keeping with that modus operandi, I was the immediate and automatic choice for providing medical cover for a Brigade Boxing Competition.

It was a three-day competition in which boxers from various units under the Brigade were participating. The participants were mainly personnel of the Other Ranks, commonly referred to as ORs, which included anyone who was not a Commissioned Officer. In this case particularly, they were mostly young, recently-enlisted and freshly-trained soldiers. The competition was held in the evening in an outdoor boxing ring, and those in the audience had to be in their games dress. That dress, for the officers, comprised of white shorts, white T-shirts, white sneakers with white socks. The ORs, however, wore khaki pants and brown sneakers instead.

As the Medical Officer providing medical cover there, sitting ringside for three days along with the other officers, and exchanging pleasantries and making small talk with them could keep one engaged for only that long. And after that, things got rather boring. Though officers of other units who were as junior as I was – and therefore way below the radars of their senior officers – had the luxury of slinking out of there, I had to weather it out, being the medical officer on duty. It would have helped, of course, had there been some sort of an excitement going on inside the ring at least. But, unfortunately, the boxers there seemed to be throwing punches for the sake of throwing punches.

It was on the second day of the competition that one of the senior officers there, from a non-medical unit, suddenly started to raise questions about my attire. Perhaps he too was bored with the proceedings, both in and out of the ring, and was looking for some excitement on the side. The 'bone of contention' that he was chewing on was why I was in a games dress and not in my combat uniform. In all honesty, I think he did have a point. While everyone else was there in a recreational role, I was there on duty. But, did that necessarily mean that being on duty during games time in the afternoon, and after regular working hours, also meant being there in my combat uniform?

Were you to ask me that question, I would say "No" straight away. Let us examine why.

Firstly, I think it all depends on what time of the day the duty was being performed. During regular office hours we were as much in our uniforms at the hospitals and field medical units as anyone else in the establishment.

So, what about performing duties beyond regular office hours? Some may cite the example of sentries on duty being in uniform at those times. Fair enough. But so were doctors at the hospitals, while performing the duties of a DMO (Duty Medical Officer) after regular hospital hours.

The next question perhaps would be where that duty was being performed. In just the same way a doctor was not expected to be in combat uniform while performing a surgery, nor was I, in my opinion, expected to be in combat uniform while performing my duty during the afternoon game hours and providing medical cover for a boxing match. And more importantly, would my being in combat uniform make me a better doctor, and hence more proficient in providing treatment to a felled boxer, if needed? I do not think I even need to answer that question.

If anything, this was an example of how some in any establishment seek to fault others, perhaps even with the intention to belittle. And, in doing so, such individuals often seek refuge under the wings of certain archaic, profitless and impractical standards and practices to achieve their objectives. Dissociation from reality, and from a logical and efficient way of thinking and doing things, seemed to be the order of the day.

Other officers present at the meet, including those senior to the one chewing on the bone realized that, this time, this officer was perhaps not chewing on quite the right kind of bone, and so completely disregarded his groans and grumbles.

Most unfortunately, this was the kind of intimidating and belligerent mindset harbored by a few in this establishment towards the medical corps and those who represented it. It did not seem to matter to them that their bellicose behavior was being directed at a class of individuals who had, by way of merit, acquired one of the most sought-after qualifications. What perhaps figured here was the fact that deep down in the depths of their sub-conscious awareness was a lament of monumental proportions at not having been able to achieve what some others had. Who knows? Sadly, they also never realized that by doing what they did, they were not only revealing their own insular and discourteous mindset, they were also denigrating and belittling the image and worth of the establishment itself.

In the meantime, back to my personal life, I was left with hardly any time, or a personal life of my own. I realized only much later that there was probably a certain lofty purpose behind this imposed routine of relentless activities. Whatever it may have been, from my perspective, it was fifteen tiresome years of running incessantly like a mindless canine bent on retrieving "the stick" its masters kept throwing without ever letting up. It seemed like an imposed routine devised and designed exclusively to prevent any activities or thought processes outside of sanctioned beliefs and practices.

This was probably incited by an apprehension that one would otherwise go wandering about in search of whatever lay beyond the confines of the so-called 'established norms' – and in which case, there was always the risk that one might simply refuse to scamper after "the stick" every time that it floated through the air, be that for baseless or for justified reasons. And that was a prospect some in lofty places perhaps dreaded. Nevertheless, the powers-that-be did a commendable job at getting me to keep my attention sharply focused on the proverbial stick, as if it was my only avenue to heavenly salvation. Very soon, everything beyond the confines of my running track paled into meaningless insignificance, as I romped relentlessly and tirelessly between two fixed points like a mindless machine.

And so, here I was – young, energetic, excited and eager to dive headlong into a world of immense responsibilities. This was a stage of my life when I was confident of being able to take on the world by the scruff of its neck and accomplish any task, however daunting or intimidating. My superiors too, seemed to have shared the same opinion as I remember having noticed a glint and a sparkle in their eyes the day they welcomed me to 61 Field Ambulance. How I wish the lofty offices had realized at that point that it would have made more sense to have had a process in place instead, in which my energy and momentum were directed towards excellence in medical science. I say this because I realized soon thereafter that I was just another piece of raw material in a factory where the finished product came out with the stamp and the seal of a soldier, and not a doctor.

Considering the overwhelming burden being consistently shouldered by 61 Field Ambulance, I often wondered why this division or brigade couldn't have two field medical units instead of just one or, at the very least, some additional manpower at the existing field medical unit. But no, that was not to be, because everything was in keeping with an organogram conceived ages ago and chiseled in stone.

But, in reality, not everything seemed chiseled in stone. New units and new brigades were, at times, raised. But, unfortunately, that was done without any concomitant enhancement of the medical manpower required to provide services to those additional establishments. This, obviously, resulted in a deluge of new patients that clearly overwhelmed the medical establishment.

Since the authorities were most unwilling to tinker with the organogram of the medical organization under any circumstance, then the least they could have done was come up with one that dictated the number of sick allowed to turn up at the MI Rooms, or one that was capable of dealing with the runaway inflation of patients, or one capable of compensating for the manpower of a field medical unit otherwise stretched thin by activities often not quite medical in nature.

Not possible? Exactly! Which is where lay the crux of the problem.

This is what compels me to infer that, firstly, it could simply have been a matter of not only turning a blind eye to the overwhelming patient load of a field medical unit but, on top of that, exerting duress upon it to comply with activities beyond the scope of its primary role and responsibilities.

And secondly, it could have been that the institution was financially not capable of dilating the medical organization due to monetary constraints. Which, in my personal opinion, was not quite so, because I had witnessed non-medical units and brigades being raised for services much less essential, and for reasons even less relevant. To me, it seemed as if the medical functionary was being denied a piece of the pie. Because, had that not been the case, the field medical units would already have had equipment and facilities – starting from ambulances, to stretchers, to first-aid boxes, and MI Room facilities – commensurate with the rest of the establishment.

However, this was neither the core of the issue, nor was it the lone contributor to the situation.

In my opinion, a more relevant reason as to why the lofty offices didn't seem to bother with the situation was the outrageous reluctance of the medical authorities in expressing their concerns regarding the overburdened units under their command. It seemed as though they would rather have those units deliver the near-impossible than have the attention of the higher offices drawn to the fact that those units were actually struggling under the weight of numbers, suffering from a dearth of resources, or often being forced to do what was not their prime function.

It was as if the medical hierarchy did not want the wheels of their burdened and battered units to squeak – lest it awakened the 'fire-breathing dragons' that could, out of pure indignation, turn their meticulous plans for prominent positions and sought-after promotions to worthless cinder in an instant. All was well as long as the grease for the squeaky wheel was being provided for by the sweat of the officers and soldiers at every level of the medical institution. Understandably therefore, the medical authorities were more than willing to flay those under their command into ensuring that demands, however daunting, were duly met, and whims and wishes, however excessive, were adequately fulfilled.

The one useful lesson I learned early on in my career was that asking questions was never a good idea, which was why I hardly ever questioned the wisdom of the enlightened and the sagacious. An inquisitive mind obviously conveys the impression of a functional faculty of thought and which, I felt, was often not looked upon with any degree of appreciation. Rene Descartes must have, at some point or the other, been overheard declaring, “I think, therefore I am”, whereupon it was promptly decided that such proclamations be kept expressly out of any equation around here. A question – and therefore, a thinking mind – was likely to spoil not only the grand aura of time-honored traditions, but also the opportunities for undeserved ascendancy and inappropriate imperiousness. So, if anything was to be achieved around here, it was to be done with an exclamation mark, rather than with a question mark.

One of the pivotal principles of effective organizational management is discipline. It has, time and again, proved to be an effective weapon capable of enhancing the efficiency of any organization, particularly a military one. Discipline has served most military organizations well over the years, and the more disciplined an institution is, the more it is revered and feared.

However, my emphasis is also on the use of the word 'weapon' in discussing discipline. And, this is where I would like my readers to also understand that a weapon can be used either as an instrument of offense, or of defense. Understandably, when used for offence, it ought to be done with prudence and pragmatism because the slightest misuse can change the world, usually for the worse. And when used as an instrument of defense, it can also change the world but for the better. It all depends on how, and why, a certain weapon is being used, in the same way that we should also consider how, and why, discipline is to be enforced.

As already just mentioned, a rigid adherence to discipline happens to be the critical cornerstone of any institution, particularly a military one. This is to be expected, because without it such an institution simply cannot succeed in its mission and objective. However, we have also witnessed instances where the rigidity of discipline has been taken to damaging and detrimental extremes in certain establishments, both military and civilian, thus getting converted into an imprudent and malicious weapon of offense and regimentation, sometimes bordering on fanaticism. When that happens, the very fabric which holds the various elements of any institution together is likely to snap at some point as a result of the constant inflexible tensions and stresses.

Indeed, when a deviant practice of *discipline* and a distorted concept of *accountability* come wrapped up together like sticks of dynamite, as it so often does, then lighting its fuse – when it perhaps shouldn't be – remains the prerogative of the rash and the reckless.

I find it rather surprising too that some institutions of the 21st century sometimes cling dearly to certain puritanical attitudes and are fearful of the occasional Copernicus in its midst, examining the validity of some of its apparently antiquated philosophies and practices. It does not take a genius to realize that any pyramidal structure will not necessarily come crashing down if the mortar between its blocks are inspected and mended, if necessary, every once in a while.

Any system laid open to scrutiny logically stands a better chance at long-term survival through constant corrections and modifications. The pyramids at Giza, the relics at Machu Picchu and the ruins of Angkor Wat are prime examples, being in disrepair through lack of inspection and restoration. Constant readjustments help the blocks in any structure – be it pyramidal or not – to sit more snugly on a firmer foundation rather than cause it to wobble. Anything which is outdated, outmoded and antiquated does not carry much credibility.

I would like to conclude this matter by quoting Khalifa bin Zayed Al Nahyan, the President of UAE, and a noted philanthropist, who once said, *"The backbone of any improvement of governance, its development as well as its protection, from any form of wastage or excessiveness, is a mechanism to place laws under the microscope of revision and modernization"* – which is a concept that holds true for all establishments, at all times.

A Lamentable Divide

> *"Attitude is a little thing that makes a big difference." – Winston Churchill*

At my new unit I was overly awed by its Commanding Officer – both by the eminence of his elevated rank and status, and the distinctive prominence of his corporeal self. That, combined with my instinctive reverence for a senior officer, inculcated by weeks of indoctrination at the training center, made him look even more grandiose.

My Commanding Officer was a person of quiet and somber disposition – a little too somber perhaps, like many of similar or higher rank that I have had the good fortune – or misfortune – of having come across. I observed that he kept his conversations strictly reserved for only his Second-in-Command and hardly felt the need to communicate with anyone else in his unit, particularly those as junior as myself. This was certainly understandable, given the fact that this was an institution structured strictly along the lines of an ancient Egyptian pyramid, where those sitting at the very top had no business communicating with someone like me, sitting at the base. I concluded that it must be a fine point of military grace and aesthetic wisdom for a commanding officer to display a certain degree of reluctance, reservation and hesitation in interacting with a subordinate of my rank and length of service.

But from where I sat at the base of that pyramid, it was an agonizing observation that any amount of openness or frankness in the relationship between those at either end of the spectrum of seniority was not only lacking, but was also subtly discouraged, primarily by some perched safely at the top. It bothered me as to why a good number of senior officers, whom we held in high esteem and reverence because of their rank and appointment, should fail to reciprocate by way of cordiality and friendliness. Were they, by any chance, fearful that it would lead to a loss of precious self-respect and status? Was this prevailing practice and attitude a desperate attempt at concealing any sort of a professional shortcoming? Or was it an effort to cling on to prestige and prominence which might not have come about through entirely transparent means?

To be very honest, I do not have the answers to such questions. It is my personal inference, however, that some at the upper levels were simply not made of the fabric which would grace one with the capacity of certain lofty gestures. Moreover, they perhaps could never muster the courage to venture into a situation which could potentially put to test the frailty of the meticulously orchestrated pomp and splendor that their rank and appointment had bestowed upon them.

In this context I very vividly remember one sultry afternoon during a PET (Physical Efficiency Test) competition that I attended as the medical officer on duty. As I was walking down a path, an individual of average height suddenly confronted me. He was sporting a smart, gray military moustache and had a face that exuded exuberance, warmth and friendliness. I took his extended hand, and as he shook mine most enthusiastically, he introduced himself as Lieutenant Colonel Sabur, from a nearby medical unit.

I was genuinely taken aback to discover that a person of no lesser rank than a Lieutenant Colonel had the courtesy and the decency of initiating an introduction with a very junior Captain, and that too without the slightest hint of pretense or prejudice. For me, this was a little too overwhelming at first. Nevertheless, I soon gathered myself, and what followed were moments of pure magic. I was literally swept off into a world of boundless joy by the friendly effervescence of this articulate gentleman. There seemed not to be the slightest qualm in his mind, unlike most, that he was engrossed in enjoyable conversation with someone at least 20 years his junior in service. And above all, the conspicuous absence of all those drab, officious, authoritative and sanctioned military phrases, so often used with boundless passion by most seniors, truly felt like a cool refreshing shower in a sweltering afternoon, as we raced with great exhilaration from one interesting topic to another.

Though I never had the good fortune of coming across Lieutenant Colonel Sabur again, this encounter greatly assured me that there might, after all, be something to look forward to. It was much later that I learned that

that amicable Lieutenant Colonel never made it beyond that rank, and I think I know why.

Militarily Yours

> *"It is dangerous to be right in matters on which the established authorities are wrong." – Voltaire*

So, in spite of all that I had to endorse, entertain, endure and engage in, I endeavored to enjoy my existence within this enigmatic entity in which I found myself hopelessly entrapped.

This was largely due to the fact that I had finally come to terms with the reality that under the prevailing circumstances the opportunity for making any real progress – professional, academic, personal or otherwise – was still frustratingly far, and best not regretted about. I deemed it not only futile but also self-defeating to resist the resolute and consistent efforts of some, in transforming me into an efficient soldier, and not necessarily an effective doctor. By now, I had easily lost count of the number of times I have had to hear the ominous dictum, *"You are a soldier first, and then a doctor"*. This seemed to be the clearest and the most explicit statement that underpinned a certain functional philosophy which, in my personal opinion, was self-defeating insofar as creating an effective medical institutional base was concerned.

Furthermore, it was plainly obvious that I could not, by myself, defeat an entity that was, in certain ways, omnipotent, overwhelming and overbearing. I realized that it was way beyond my individual power to escape the all-pervading tentacles of certain antiquated philosophies and the all-consuming intensity of certain misplaced commitments. So, rather than ruining the exciting formative days of my career through contrition and remorse, I decided to turn things around for myself, and search for purpose and satisfaction in whatever I was commanded to do.

Almost every day for about 6 months at a stretch I accompanied, as the medical officer on duty, one unit or the other of the Logistic Area and the local Brigade, to a firing range some 40 kilometers away for their annual practice firing. It was the same grueling routine of waking up early every morning, rushing to my unit to board the famed Russian *UAZ* ambulance along with two medical assistants, and then falling in line with a convoy of vehicles headed to the firing range.

The only appealing aspect of this otherwise mundane routine was being able to acquaint myself with officers and soldiers from almost every unit of the Brigade and Logistic Area. Added to that, of course, was the exciting prospect of being able to fire a small arm on each occasion. Though, being the duty medical officer, this was not required of me, my colleagues from the arms and other services frequently invited me to participate in those firing sessions. This, for me, was the only sliver of excitement in an otherwise monotonous and dull ritual. Quite naturally therefore, over those few months, my marksmanship improved by leaps and bounds, often leading to moments when I would surprise even myself by out-performing my colleagues from the elite forces.

As already mentioned, there always seemed to be some sort of a consistent effort at making good soldiers out of medical personnel. And this was often adequately supplemented and endorsed by certain guardians of the medical institution itself. They frantically went about doing everything that pertained to 'good performance' in the eyes of those looking down from above. Needless to say, *good performance*, as interpreted by some usually meant *good military performance*, even if it was a medical unit.

I never could, and perhaps never will be able to comprehend a concept where a medical unit was required to excel militarily rather than medically. And it seemed that as long as a field medical unit gave preference to its military performance over its medical activities and abilities, some seemed pleased with the fact that things were going in the right direction. Hardly any effort was ever made to ensure that the level of medical support provided by a field medical unit was able to attain a standard adequate enough to fulfill the needs of those who solicited its services, both in terms of quality and ability.

In all the time that I had been looking after the various MI Rooms of the brigade, no senior officer of importance, either from 61 Field Ambulance or from the brigade itself, ever visited the MI Rooms to see for themselves whether or not any shortcomings existed, either in its setup, resources or service delivery. If ever they did, then obviously, I wasn't there – in which case it would be akin to chewing meat with toothless gums. Had there ever been a genuine good intent in this regard, the medical officers looking after the MI Rooms would have been consulted often, and their suggestions regarding any improvements in MI Room services given due credence. But sadly, that was not the case. And, regrettably, that was also a measure of the actual value and importance given to the medical efficiency of the field medical units. For some custodians of the medical corps perhaps, a collateral reward and benefit for catering to the practice of ignoring medical efficiency in order to meet the requirements of a militarily-inclined agenda was admiration and accolades of the higher offices, and its associated perks and privileges.

Furthermore, it did not seem to matter that the medical units were overworked and that their patient load was overwhelming. It did not seem relevant to the issue that patients could not be given due medical attention through lack of adequate manpower and resources. What mattered more was that a medical unit, in addition to its own duties, was toeing the line with its counterparts from the arms and the other services in participating in and conducting military activities. The medical units therefore, particularly the field units already overrun with a deluge of patients, had to regularly and sincerely participate in the drill competition, the firing competition, the physical efficiency competition, the games competition and every conceivable competition and activities. All that was in addition to carrying out their primary role of providing medical care in a setting of scarcity, inadequacy and, I daresay, inefficiency.

However, this does not necessarily mean that I do not subscribe to the notion of medical units participating in military activities. After all, military medical units are indeed an integral part of the military establishment and are therefore expected to take a part in its razzmatazz. But, in this case, there seemed to be a subtle – yet a defining – difference.

That difference was perhaps the preference and priority given to the allocation of energy and resources towards achieving a 'patronized objective', and the palpable duress exerted upon the medical functionary towards achieving that goal. That difference was perhaps how the custodians of the medical corps were rather compelled to tailor their medical agenda under pressure of mandated and enforced hoopla and jingoism. And in this matter, the medical functionary was swept away like a dead fish – which perhaps it already was – into undesired and awkward territories by an overpowering and overbearing tidal wave.

So we dutifully and cheerfully, and to the best of our abilities, performed the acts and the routines demanded of us. We swung dangerously from the trapeze, and balanced precariously on the tight-rope. We also jumped the hoops, played with fire, rode the elephants, dodged the tigers, and juggled whatever we were given. And we even became the joker at times, without even realizing it.

Marching to Orders

The apparent juicy freshness of someone like me, just back from my basic military training, made me the automatic choice for leading a contingent of military personnel representing the Army Medical Corps to a Drill Competition. This was a competition in which the ability of a team to march as flawlessly as possible to the beat of a military band was assessed. What made it difficult and interesting was that it had to be executed within a predetermined area, and the routine consisted of frequent complicated turns and stops, besides the synchrony of the march itself.

My role as the contingent leader was not to participate in the march, but to bark commands at my contingent – which would tell my marchers what to do, and when. I would be marked for the timing of my commands and the quality of their delivery, while the group would be marked on how well they had converted my commands into actions. If a command made a contingent step out of the marked confines of the marching area by as much as an inch, that team would be penalized. It was all about precision, timing, coordination and fluency.

Right from the start we knew we were the underdogs, because this competition had other participating units which habitually attached a superlative importance to marching. And why shouldn't they? After all, marching and drills seemed to be a large part of the reason behind their very existence. So, on the one hand, while a medical unit was rather constantly awash with overwhelming medical responsibilities, those units had all the time they ever needed to practice their drills and marching till they had it all nailed down to a tee. Evidently therefore, they had a clear advantage over us when it came to such matters.

But that did not seem to dampen our spirits or inhibit our enthusiasm in the least. Underdogs have always had an unfair advantage because they were hardly ever under any pressure to perform. And we knew that. Our competition was actually with ourselves, since we knew what our shortcomings were, and we therefore set about overcoming those. If that effort yielded an outcome which gave the best of the lot a good run for their money, that would be our victory. If perchance our efforts at bettering ourselves threatened to topple a few of the finest – that would be our conquest.

I was momentarily spared the responsibility of attending to the patients in the various MI Rooms as day in and day out we practiced on the unit's concrete basketball court. By the time the day of the competition finally arrived we had the routine down to the tee, and were confident enough to feel that we could perhaps up the ante. Or so we thought.

I will not fool myself by saying I wasn't nervous on the day of the competition, as I waited our turn with my contingent, each and every member of which had gone the extra mile the past month or so, trying their best to better themselves and not disappoint me.

When our turn finally came, I was surprised at how quickly and effortlessly I switched into a mode of focused automation. This could only be credited to the long hours of single-minded and dedicated practice on our unit's basketball court. The first few commands and their execution were well nigh flawless. This boded well, and seemed to instill some sort of a confidence in myself, as well as in the members of my contingent. I could clearly see a spring in their steps thereafter, which usually comes with the realization that the countless hours of practice was perhaps actually paying off. I noticed a kind of focus on the faces of my men and a glint in their eyes, which I had not seen before, and which could only be the evidence of a growing belief in themselves. As I barked out my commands, I caught a momentary glimpse of our Commanding Officer and the Second-in-Command sitting in the audience. The look of satisfaction and pride on their faces, as our routine progressed, told me that things were perhaps going very well from the perspective of the gathered audience.

Soon it was all over and I was left feeling totally spent and drained, more perhaps from 'adrenaline exhaustion' than anything else. My contingent was ecstatic, as the soldiers milled around me, congratulating me and each other. They knew in the depths of their hearts that not one of them had fallen out of step at any point, and that my commands had been spot-on.

But deep down, I was well aware of the presumed mindset of those who made the decisions, and seemed somewhat convinced that the elation of my contingent was perhaps going to be rather short-lived. Yet, I hoped. Because hope is what we always cling on to, even in the face of apparent adversity and hopelessness, and which transforms into the support we need, to take the next meaningful step. Therefore, despite the usual and well-known rigid and prejudiced mindset of some, I was hoping to be standing at least on the lowest rung of the victory stand, if not higher. But, at the end of the day, even that was something I strongly feel we were mercilessly denied – a disappointment which was also clearly visible on the faces of my Commanding Officer, the Second-in-Command and every member of my contingent. Nevertheless, and to this day, I remain grateful to every soldier of my contingent for having tried their utmost and for having given all they had, without any reservation.

Desperation on Display

A few months later I was on the runway of the Old Airport, as the team leader of a booth set up there, representing the Army Medical Corps. The occasion was a week-long military fair organized to mark the Armed Forces Day. The huge runway at the Old Airport was now used for such events, being largely abandoned after a newer airport had been built further to the north, in the outskirts of the city.

Almost every unit of the division was represented in this fair. And whereas others had more fancy and flashy wares to flaunt – such as field guns, armored personnel carriers, tanks, patrol boats, sea-crafts and the likes – the paraphernalia in our medical booth was rather severely restricted by the comparatively benevolent and humanitarian nature of our work, and the non-threatening equipment and instruments we used for that purpose. Of course, we could have brought along with us the fancy and complex equipment we often used during our surgeries, or we could have even had an X-ray or an ultrasound machine brought out for display. But sadly, those were too sensitive to be exposed to all the dust and the dirt. Unfortunately therefore, we were left with the drab and apparently unexciting exercise of measuring only the weight and blood pressure of visitors, which were understandably not quite as attractive or as awe-inspiring when compared to what the other booths had to offer.

My Commanding Officer then struck upon a brilliant plan, and which required my active involvement. He wanted me to procure, from Dhaka Medical College, specimens of human anatomical parts kept preserved in jars of formalin. These specimens were kept in the museum of the Department of Anatomy at the college, and had been useful study aids for us while we were students there. Knowing that I was from Dhaka Medical College, my Commanding Officer guessed – and quite rightly so – that the authorities there would be more agreeable to loaning those rare and valuable specimens to me than to anyone else.

From the day that the anatomy jars, displaying cut-out sections of almost every conceivable part of the human body, arrived at our booth at the fair, the visitor traffic increased substantially. The people who thronged our booth did not even seem to want to hear or care about my description and presentation of the human parts. All they wanted to do was to simply stare at the jars in awe and amazement, some with almost their jaws hanging. Perhaps human anatomy was as awe-inspiring after all, as were tanks and guns!

'Victory' on Victory Day

Fate brought me back to the runway of the Old Airport again the very next month, as I was sent off with a company of soldiers from 61 Field Ambulance to form a contingent of medical corps personnel who were to participate in the annual Victory Day Parade.

The annual Victory Day Parade was an event of national importance, always attracting national attention, and was undeniably a source of national excitement.

I was in my mid-teens when Bangladesh gained independence from Pakistan, and since then I remember having made it a point to watch this parade every year, at least on television, since it was always telecast live. This parade never failed to enchant, enthrall and excite me, as rows and columns of smartly turned-out soldiers marched in unison to the buoyant beat of a military band, as if a few hundred soldiers were one individual. It always seemed to instill in me a feeling of cheerfulness and optimism. To be very honest, there were times I had dreamed of being a part of that human column of precision and pride myself. And now, about ten years later, here I was – selected to lead a column of personnel from my unit to the very same parade, with the entire nation watching!

The practice and the preparation for the Victory Day parade was a month-long extravaganza. Practice sessions would begin early every morning and continue into the late afternoon. The entire runway would get busy and bustling with activity, as truckloads of soldiers and officers arrived for the practice. Each contingent was allocated a designated spot beside the runway in the order in which they would be marching during the practice sessions as well as during the final Parade itself. That spot would also be the place for the respective contingent to rest during breaks in the practice sessions. Like all other units, we also pitched our tent at our designated spot, in the shade of which we rested between the periods of practice. We also brought along with us a mess-waiter from our unit to serve us snacks and refreshing drinks while we rested in our tent during the breaks.

The contingent from the Army Medical Corps comprised of two companies, one of which was led by me, and the other by Captain Mizan from 11 Field Ambulance in Savar, and who was senior to me by a year or so. The entire contingent was led by Major Azad, a crisp, cut-and-dried archetype of a typical army officer, who knew his job well and carried it out with single-minded dedication and application.

It was with a tinge of bemused bewilderment that I observed, during the practice sessions, that the performance of our medical contingent as expressed by the Parade Commander was always below acceptable levels, however much we tried. Nevertheless, as far as I could see, we were performing well enough to give any other contingent a good run for their money – a fact amply and adequately supported by the accolades and applause our contingent received from the grandstand on Victory Day itself.

The author leading a Company of the AMC Contingent during the Victory Day Parade

Samina was at home, watching the parade on television. I was later informed by her and by those who had watched it telecast live, that the medical corps contingent did look very smart, confident and fluent as it marched past the grandstand. I was also seen on TV, leading my Company, and which I am proud to know, was watched by the entire nation, thus fulfilling one of my most cherished dreams. I had requested a relative of mine, who was a newscaster at the TV station which had telecast the parade live, to arrange for a video copy of the parade, so I could keep with me a cherished memento of one of the high-points of my career in the army. Unfortunately, that lady was never able to live up to her commitment to do so, and in all likelihood, after more than three decades, that video is lost forever. Nevertheless, that parade is still etched in my memory as if it had taken place only yesterday. And I am sure that from an audience's point of view it is also deeply ingrained in Samina's mind – and which, in itself, is good enough for me.

Insofar as the Parade Commander's disdainful view of the quality of our marching during the practice sessions is concerned, I have no way of ascertaining either the fairness or the bias behind it. Nevertheless, even if one deems his judgment to have been somewhat credible, then due consideration ought to be given to the fact that medical units exist not to march in rows and columns into enemy formations, but to provide life-saving treatment to the felled marchers. One of these days, I would very much like to arrange something like a "Medical Efficiency Competition" with an all-inclusive participation in order to verify how well the fighting forces fare in it. I am quite sure their 'medical performance' would be viewed with a much greater degree of forbearance and tolerance.

Conundrum in Comilla

In the midst of all my hectic activities at 61 Field Ambulance, there came time for our unit to go for its Annual Firing Exercise.

It was mandatory for every unit of the Brigade to have their personnel participate in a firing drill once a year to keep their skills with a rifle honed. That year it was decided that the contingent from 61 Field Ambulance would be going to the firing range at Comilla Cantonment for their Annual Firing Drill.

Comilla happens to be a rather modest township a little over a hundred kilometers south-east of Dhaka. Nonetheless, it is an important waypoint as one travels by road to the port city of Chittagong to the south of the country. Despite the fact that Comilla was nowhere near either Dhaka or Chittagong in area, population or glamour, Comilla Cantonment was nonetheless fairly strategic and rooted in quite a bit of tradition and history.

Major Mostafa, who later retired as a Brigadier-General, was designated as the commander of the contingent, and I, a fresh and energetic young Captain, was to be his second-in-command during this exercise. Though a medical graduate himself, Major Mostafa's appointment at 61 Field Ambulance was administrative in nature, and in this case, as a quartermaster. He was a warm and friendly individual who was always able to reach out with cordiality and amicability from his position of seniority. Small wonder, therefore, that I was hugely excited and energized to be going to Comilla with him. There were about thirty or forty soldiers in our contingent, and while they made the trip to Comilla Cantonment by train, along with the necessary arms and ammunition for the practice firing, Major Mostafa and I went there by road, riding the Toyota Land Cruiser of our unit. It was to be a four-day exercise, with two days spent in firing practice, and a day each for setting up and packing up our camp, and for travelling to and from Comilla.

Once at Comilla Cantonment, we set up camp in a thinly forested field designated for our contingent that was located fairly close to the firing range. As for myself, I was singularly excited at the opportunity of being able to spend the next few days eating and sleeping in a tent for the duration of the firing exercise. For someone like me, who have not had much of an opportunity of spending time in a tent, there was a certain degree of romanticism and adventure associated with the experience, and in which I literally reveled. And the fact that I was going to be able to spend those moments in the pleasant company of a personality like Major Mostafa, held the allure of it being all the more enjoyable.

We fell into our routine from the moment we pitched our tents, and things moved along with clockwork precision. We had two scheduled days of firing practice. I would have the contingent fall-in each morning, march up to Major Mostafa and report to him. After that, the senior NCO would take over, have the contingent march to the firing range and conduct the practice firing there. Major Mostafa and I would be there as well, supervising the overall proceedings.

However, just as everything in life has its good side and bad, so did this. As much as I was overwhelmed with euphoria in being able to live in a tent for a few days, I was not quite prepared to spend the inevitable and essential few morning-minutes in a tiny and cramped tent erected to one side of our compound, and which was monumentally different from what I was otherwise used to, at home.

Apparently, Major Mostafa seemed to be in a similar predicament. What it all boiled down to was a growing intestinal discomfort for the two of us as time went by. By the time we got into the second day of firing practice, the matter had gotten decidedly uncomfortable and was well nigh threatening to get out of hand. Major Mostafa, moreover, made no bones of how severely he was being tormented by this physiological nightmare.

On the second day of the firing practice, Major Mostafa and I were at the firing range when he perhaps could not take it anymore and categorically declared that something needed to be done urgently about our uncomfortable state of affairs – much to my own huge mental relief as well. I mentioned to him that Captain Ghani, a course-mate of mine from OBC-12, was posted at Comilla Cantonment, and that we could go to his residence to palliate our on-going distress.

So, while the firing practice was still going on, Major Mostafa passed on the responsibility of overseeing the firing to the senior-most Havildar there. We then jumped into our Land Cruiser parked at the firing range, and Major Mostafa instructed the driver to take us to Captain Ghani's residence as fast as he could. The tone in his voice adequately conveyed to the driver the necessity for speed, and the latter complied, combined with a fair bit of skill.

Captain Ghani's residence was one in a row of *Rupsa* accommodations. Readers may recall the *Rupsa* being mentioned earlier in this narrative as rows of barrack-like two-bedroom accommodations with sloping tin roofs, meant for junior officers of the armed forces, and constructed originally for officers being repatriated from Pakistan after the creation of Bangladesh. No sooner had our vehicle come to a stop in front of Captain Ghani's residence Major Mostafa was out in a flash, with me close at his heels. Simply standing at the door and waiting for someone to open it after we had rung the bell was, in itself, turning out to be a challenging exercise. Though I was in a bad shape myself, looking at Major Mostafa's face clearly conveyed the impression that he was perhaps a bit closer to the cliff than I was.

Since it was still office hours, Captain Ghani was not expected to be at home. And sure enough, his wife opened the door to let us in. In fact, she did not really have to let us in. Major Mostafa somehow mumbled a pathetic excuse of a greeting and just about pushed her aside on his way to the washroom. With the *Rupsa* being a typical residence for both Majors and Captains, we all knew well where the common washroom in such an accommodation was located – and into which Major Mostafa disappeared in a flash. That, if I may mention, had nothing to do with seniority. It had to do with the need of the moment.

Left to my own devices to fend off the intestinal turmoil raging within me while Major Mostafa attended to his own, I had no option but to take a seat in the living room with the express objective of at least being able to provide some sort of a resistance against the impending exodus. Mrs Ghani soon joined me, and while we made small talk, she must have noticed the agonized expression on my face and my constantly shifting positions. And having also witnessed Major Mostafa's dire straits moments earlier, Mrs. Ghani did not need to be a genius to figure out what was going on. Putting two and two together, she offered the services of the washroom attached to their bedroom, if I wished to use it.

If I wished to use it? You could bet your last dollar that I did!

We later cordially declined Mrs. Ghani's offer of tea since we needed to get back to the firing range as soon as possible. However, our expressions of gratitude as we took leave of her were most profuse, profound and plentiful.

Comilla is a place famous for a textile known as 'khadi' or 'khaddar'. Before leaving for the exercise, Samina had requested me to bring back a few lengths of that fabric, if it was possible. If truth be told, I was so caught up with various responsibilities over the two days of firing and so tired at the end of each day that I was hardly able to make any time to go into town during the first three days.

The morning of the fourth day was taken up packing our tents and our belongings, and cleaning up the entire area that we had occupied during our stay. Major Mostafa had decided on an afternoon departure for our contingent. In the same manner that we had arrived, he and I would depart in the unit vehicle, travelling by road, while the rest of the contingent by train. Unfortunately, I had been so occupied and involved the entire morning wrapping things up that we were precariously close to our time of departure when I informed Major Mostafa of Samina's request.

Major Mostafa was a stickler for punctuality and of uncompromising discipline. We were hardly about twenty five minutes from our departure time when I informed Major Mostafa of what was going on in my mind – and which was to go into town in our unit vehicle to purchase the 'khaddar' within the few minutes left. His immediate reaction was to look in my direction with a stare that was capable of burning holes in me. And then he looked at his watch with a body language that was intended to solely convey an expression of utter exasperation, disdain and disgust. This was naturally to be expected from someone afflicted with an obsessive-compulsive disorder for sticking to schedules.

In the social circle of military families, however, Samina and I were quite close to Major Mostafa and his family. He and his wife regarded us with great affection – a feeling that was not only mutual, but was combined with a lot of respect for them as well. Matters were different, however, when we were in uniform, when duty and responsibility stepped in – and hence his piercing stare a while ago. Anyone else in his place would perhaps have dismissed my request immediately. But, Major Mostafa simply said, *"I want to see you back here in twenty minutes."* I had this feeling that he was perhaps half-expecting me to abandon the entire idea upon realizing that twenty minutes was not going to be enough for this outlandish adventure. He could not have been more wrong. If Samina had made a request, I was going to go to just about any length to try to fulfill it.

Major Mostafa's reluctant assent and my subsequent leap into the parked Land Cruiser happened almost simultaneously. The driver was already behind the wheel, having perhaps anticipated the outcome of the conversation between me and Major Mostafa. Before I could even start saying anything to him, our vehicle was already picking up speed.

"Can you do it?" I asked him.

"I don't know, sir, but we can certainly try. We just might be able to pull it off. Let's see" the driver replied, with his eyes fixated on the road ahead as the needle on the dash continued to move steadily round the dial towards the other end of it. It was the tone in his voice that told me that he too probably had his misgivings

regarding the time we had in hand to be able to pull this thing off. But I had this feeling that was more than prepared to give it all he had.

One other reason I was inwardly feeling confident about it all was the fact that of all the drivers at 61 Field Ambulance, the one behind the wheel at this moment was the best and the most skilled. And this was an assessment being made by someone who had learned to drive pretty early on in life and had been driving for years together. Despite all the odds stacked against us, I was somehow quietly confident that if anyone could pull off this little stunt, this particular driver could. The one other thing that seemed to work hugely in our favor was the fact that he not only seemed to know his way around Comilla town pretty well, but also seemed to know where exactly to go for the 'khaddar'.

I will have to admit that rarely in my life had I witnessed, or been part of, a driving of such a level of skill and fearlessness. As I held on – or rather hung on – to whatever was within my reach, our vehicle raced down the roads of Comilla with merely inches to spare between it and the countless rickshaws, the other vehicles and the pedestrians. Finally, we came to a screeching halt on a road that seemed to be lined with stores selling 'khaddar'. I leaped out of the vehicle, literally flew into the closest store and, in a matter of minutes, was done with my purchase. The trip back was equally nerve-racking. But, what mattered at the end was that we were able to make it back with only seconds to spare, and did not have to contend with a venom-spitting Contingent Commander for being late.

Adventure in Africa

And then one day I received a phone call which, in retrospect, easily qualifies as one of the most momentous phone calls I had received in my career in the armed forces. It came from none other than the Director of Medical Services (DMS) at the Army Headquarters. To receive a call from someone so senior and holding such an elevated appointment was undoubtedly consequential. But what he told me over the phone was totally unexpected, and it left me thrilled.

The DMS informed me that I had been selected as part of a medical team which was to fly within three days to the Republic of Guinea in Africa, to provide medical assistance to the victims of an earthquake there.

The news of the earthquake had been received a few days earlier with a great deal of sympathy for the people affected, and naturally our hearts went out to them. But, the grievousness of the incident aside, I could hardly be blamed for almost letting out an earth-shattering roar of joy while I was still on the phone with the DMS. Fortunately, I had enough sense still left in me to realize I could not do such a thing with someone like him at the other end.

The DMS briefed me on the mission, including the preparation for it. And by the time I hung up, I was literally over the moon. The importance, implication and significance of the mission aside, this was to be the first time I was ever going to be out of the country. Perhaps the most heartbreaking disappointment at that point was that I was going to have to make this first ever trip abroad without the company of my wife.

The Directorate of Movement and Quartering (DM&Q) at the Army Headquarters dealt with matters related to army personnel going abroad. I was informed by the DMS that I would be attached to that directorate from the next day onwards and was instructed to report there the very next morning. That was where I met the other two officers who were also a part of what is known as a Mobile Surgical Team which had been put together to go to Guinea.

One of them, our team leader, was Lieutenant Colonel (later Brigadier-General) Majed Bukht, a neurosurgeon, while the other officer was Major Rezaul Alam (later Brigadier-General), an anesthetist. I was included in the team as a GDMO. The rest of the team comprised of a JCO (Junior Commissioned Officer), and eleven NCOs (Non-Commissioned Officers), all of whom were Operation Theater Assistants (or OTAs, as they were called). These individuals – that is, the JCO and the NCOs – were typically referred to as 'Other Ranks' (or ORs).

Having been attached to the Directorate of Movement and Quartering, we were consumed over the next three days by seemingly endless paperwork and procedures involved in getting a Service Passport issued, and obtaining the equivalent of our allotted amount for expenses in US Dollars. In the meantime, I also had to get my personal belongings in order, and if I may say, rather hastily.

Our journey was to take us from Dhaka to Amsterdam first, for almost a 3-day stopover there, before continuing on to Conakry, the capital of Guinea. We were to fly in a huge Boeing 707 belonging to Bangladesh Biman, the national airlines.

The first time ever that I had flown in an aircraft was in a now-obsolete Douglas Dakota DC-3 when I was perhaps ten or eleven years of age. That flight was from Dhaka to our home-town of Sylhet, and had lasted a little over an hour. The DC-3s, I remember, had a signature stance as they sat on the tarmac – with the front of the aircraft sitting much higher than the tail-end, looking much like a big bird of metal with its wings spread out and the head pointing up at the sky, preparing to take flight.

The surge of adrenaline that day, as I walked 'uphill' inside the aircraft, going up the aisle to my seat somewhere in front, was difficult to contain. The feeling of pure elation and excitement as I sank into my seat and put on my seat belt easily qualifies as a momentous childhood milestone. And minutes later, I was overcome by the rapturous sensation of being airborne. From that point onwards it was pure jubilation.

Since then, I had flown a few more times, and all in Fokker F-27s and ATPs which came into service much later, but which were not much larger than the DC-3s.

But, this time it was going to be different.

It wasn't about DC-3s or Fokkers anymore. It also wasn't about hopping from one city to another within

Bangladesh, as if it was a game if hop-scotch. This time, it was going to be a mammoth journey – a journey to which only the prefix *trans-* was going to be able to do any justice – *trans*-continental, *trans*-Atlantic! And obviously, an aircraft capable of undertaking such a journey also had to be nothing less than humongous. And, sure enough it was – the huge and majestic Boeing 707.

This was the same Boeing 707 I used to watch mesmerized, from the balcony of our house as a young boy, as they climbed out of the old Dhaka Airport at Tejgaon and made their way up into the blue sky. With our house being hardly five miles from the airport, it happened to be roughly in the flight-path of those aircrafts. So, as they flew by our house, they were still low enough for me to be able to clearly make out the features on it, including the emblem on the green tail with the letters "PIA" (Pakistan International Airlines), as well as the little windows along the sides.

And now, after all these years, I was finally inside one of those aircrafts. After the DC-3, the Fokker, and the ATP, it felt like I was inside a castle. I was amazed at how cavernous the inside of this aircraft looked, with seemingly endless rows of seats, as Colonel Majed Bukht, Major Reza and I took our places together somewhere at the back of the aircraft. I knew this was going to be a long haul flight and therefore likely to be grueling, and perhaps even boring. Nevertheless, the sheer thrill of the anticipated experience pushed that fact to the periphery of my concerns as the colossal castle-on-wings finally, and majestically, took to the air.

Sure enough, my initial excitement lasted for the first two to three hours only, and up to the consumption of the first of many sumptuous in-flight meals. The rest of the eighteen-hour flight soon turned into a rather tiresome and uninteresting affair, especially given the fact that in those days, in-flight entertainment comprised only of eating, reading or dozing off.

We landed briefly in Athens, Greece, in the wee hours of the morning for refueling, where we were allowed to leave the aircraft to stretch our legs on the tarmac, right beside our giant plane. Greece would not let us into their airport since we did not have a visa for that country.

It was late afternoon by the time we finally landed at Amsterdam Airport. By now I was drained, disheveled, and a bit drowsy as well. But the fact that we had finally landed somewhere, anywhere, so I may finally be able to egress this cramped flying metal tube – for that was how this castle-in-the-air seemed like, after about eighteen hours in it – and feel terra firma under my feet was reason enough for me to shake my somnolence and look eagerly out the window.

Amsterdam Airport was soon framed in it as our aircraft taxied along on the tarmac, and I was immediately disappointed. It looked like a grayish-black, drab, boring and uninspiring elongated box with the words "Schiphol" emblazoned on its façade. This was a far cry from the image I had in mind of a glamorous, classy, and stylish European airport. What made the spectacle even worse was the fact that this was the middle of winter, and the world around us, shrouded by a grey overcast sky, looked dreadful and uninviting.

Eventually we were within the airport. Rather surprisingly, and unlike the exterior, the interior looked elegant, opulent and gigantic. Soon we were all languishing on the comfortable chairs at immigration, trying to flush the tiredness out of us. The chairs here were certainly more spacious than the comparatively cramped seats we had been continuously sitting on for almost a full day. Lieutenant Colonel Majed Bukht, in the meantime, went through the apparently interminable formalities of obtaining visas for fifteen people for our two-and-a-half day stopover in Amsterdam. Finally, everything got done and we reached our hotel.

For me, however, our stopover in Amsterdam was an experience of a lifetime. Our brief stay there, as a matter of fact, seemed rather inadequate for the appropriate processing of the numerous unfamiliar and unaccustomed foreign inputs and experiences I was exposed to – starting with having to use Dollars and Schillings for purchases, instead of the Bangladeshi Taka, to witnessing the abundance of bicycles and trams on the roads, as well as the stately and ornate structures wherever I looked.

Everyone here seemed engrossed and involved in their own private little worlds, and not quite bothered with who the next person was, or what they were wearing or doing. This was in sharp contrast to the place I had come from, where everyone seemed to stare at everyone else for no apparent reason, and where your business was oftentimes everyone else's! People here also seemed to have a sense of purpose as they went about doing what they had to do. I was quietly amused at imagining how unseemly and inappropriate a sign like "No Loitering", so often seen back home, would seem in a city like this! I was also genuinely amazed to see that some of the pedestrians even jogged, ambled and trotted along on the sidewalks to get from one place to another. This too was an unfamiliar sight for me since, back home, people ran only during sporting events or in their frantic efforts at putting as much distance as possible between themselves and a life-threatening event!

Overall, I was totally blown away by the grandeur and the beauty of this stunning European capital. With almost three days to spare in Amsterdam, we immersed ourselves in exploring the city. Dam Square soon became our favorite stomping ground, and the shopping areas around it our choice haunt.

Dam Square seemed to be the hub and the heart of the city, from the point of both commerce and tourism. It was a wide open square adorned with little monuments and statues, where tourists walked, languished, rested and took pictures amidst flocks of pigeons. This square was lined at its fringes by both the ornate architectures of the past, and the crisp and smart structures of the present. Interspersed were numerous businesses – from shops to carts to kiosks – which catered mostly to the tourists who thronged Dam Square on a regular basis. On the other side of Dam Square was the famous canal, which seemed to flow right through the heart of the city, and was always bustling with boats carrying both tourists and commerce. The famous wax museum of Madame Tussaud's was also located in Dam Square, and which we visited at the very first opportunity, taking pictures with luminaries from the past, from Napoleon to Mata Hari.

At Dam Square in Amsterdam, with Lieutenant Colonel Majed Bukht

With Major Reza and the wax figure of Napoleon at Madame Tussauds Wax Museum in Amsterdam

The admission ticket the author had bought for his tour of Madame Tussauds Wax Museum in Amsterdam

As we entered and exited the numerous shops in and around Dam Square in our hunt for gifts for people back home, I was literally saturated by two Dutch words which seemed to appear almost everywhere - *voor* and *vnag* - and I had no idea at that time what they meant. I know now that *voor* is Dutch for *for*, and which, I noticed, appeared with the prices on merchandise that were on discounted sale. *VNAG*, on the other hand, was actually the acronym for *Vereniging Nederlands Antiquairs Genootschap* which meant "Society of Dutch Antiques Dealers". And sure enough, those letters appeared on stores which sold souvenirs, mementos and curios.

Just as certain inconsequential little things, at times, linger in our memories for life, so were these two Dutch words stuck in my head, as if with glue – and don't ask me why. But, every time I mentally utter those words now, I am immediately whisked into the past, to the Amsterdam of the early 80's, even if for a few fleeting seconds. The sights of the city, now blurry with time, take shape in my mind's eye, and the sounds of the city, though fading now, still ring in my ears.

What bothered me however, while we sprinted from one shop to another was the bone-chilling cold that seemed to literary cut through my pants and to invade the very marrow of my bones. The temperature in Amsterdam, now in deep winter, was perhaps hovering anywhere between three to five degrees Celsius. And this was, in no way, good news for me. Being born and brought up in a hot and humid tropical country, I certainly had no previous exposure to, nor the experience of dealing with such inconceivably low temperatures.

As I shivered and shook miserably and uncontrollably, I was oddly, and rather irritatingly, puzzled by the fact that the local populace did not seem the least bit bothered by the cold, which was otherwise almost killing me. I obviously presumed that being the residents of a city which got this cold during the months of winter, they must have gotten used to it. The situation of my traveling companions was no better, as I also noticed in them the uncontrollable urge to dash into the next toasty-warm shop as quickly as possible. However, as far as both keeping warm and shopping were concerned, this served my purpose well! It took me a number of years to realize why the residents of Amsterdam didn't seem to be bothered by the cold while I shivered and suffered in it. It was only after I moved to frigid Canada that it dawned on me that those walking along on the sidewalks of Amsterdam must have been wearing thermal pants or 'long johns', as they are commonly known, while at that point I didn't know such things even existed!

While we often loitered lazily in Dam Square when we had the time to spare or when tired from our shopping, I often spotted couples my age, and surprisingly from my part of the world, having a whale of a time just being with each other in the delightful and attractive surroundings of the city. That was when I promised to myself that I would one day come back here with Samina in my arms – and which I was thankfully able to, some fourteen years later.

Three days later, we were again at Amsterdam Airport for the second leg of our trip which would take us to Conakry, our final destination. Our team checked in quite early, and soon we were all at the duty-free area of the airport, meandering, loitering, window-shopping or simply languishing on the chairs, since there was little else to do, with so much time to spare.

This, I felt, was my opportunity to buy a good and decent camera for myself, since the one I was carrying was most basic, and old enough to warrant replacement. Major Reza was with me while I scanned the many cameras on display at a camera shop. Finally, I chose a Praktica camera for myself, which I thought would be right for my needs and was within my budget as well, and made the purchase. That was when Major Reza decided he too needed the exact same camera for himself. I was rather flattered at the thought that he had enough confidence in my choice and knowledge of cameras to feel that he could own one of the same. I realized only much later that that was Major Reza's way of saving time, energy and more importantly, the hassle and confusion of having to choose one from more than a dozen or two on display!

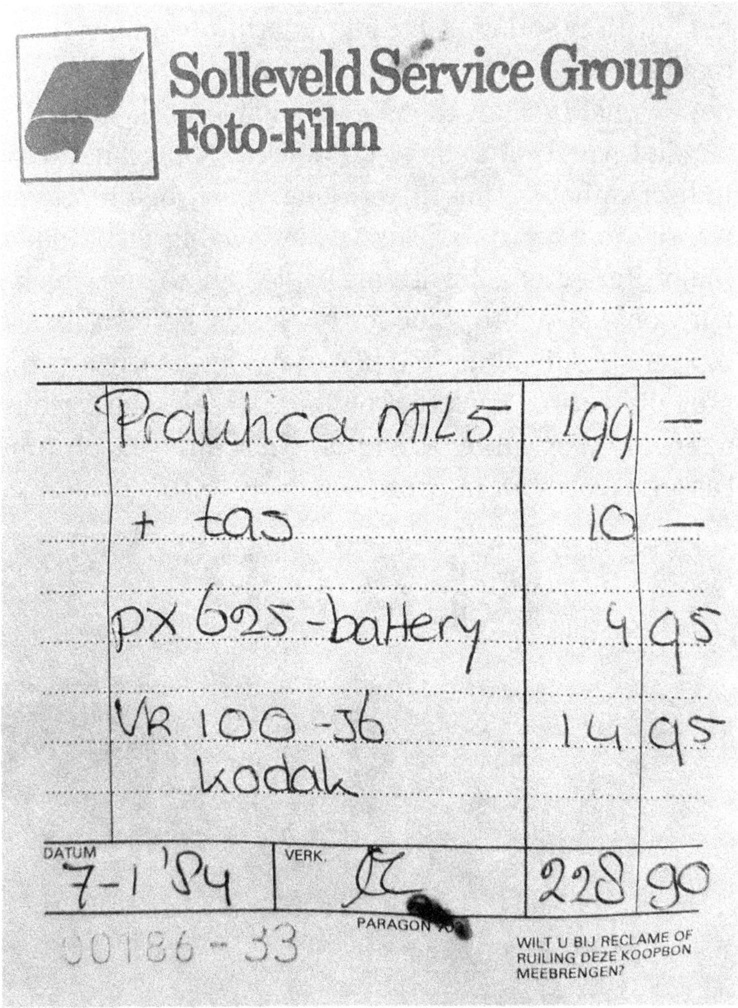
Solleveld Service Group
Foto-Film

Pralchca MTL5	199	—
+ tas	10	—
px 625-battery	4	95
VR 100-36 kodak	14	95

DATUM	VERK.		
7-1 '84		228	90

00186-33

PARAGON

WILT U BIJ RECLAME OF RUILING DEZE KOOPBON MEEBRENGEN?

Invoice of the Praktica camera the author bought from the duty-free shop at Amsterdam Airport

While we loitered and wandered around some more in the duty-free shopping area, it again occurred to me that it would be a rather novel idea to buy a cassette player too, for myself, while we were still there. I knew it would be a useful addition to our home, since we did not have any sort of electronic entertainment worth the mention. Moreover, I knew it would perhaps be of a better quality than the ones available back home. In fact, it turned out to be so durable that I used it, rather indiscriminately, for fifteen long years, before giving it away to a ward assistant when leaving for Canada. Major Reza was still with me while I chose one which I felt would be appropriate for my needs, and within the budget I had in mind. And that was when he, once again, pulled the same trick that had made life easier for him a few minutes earlier – and purchased the exact same cassette player for himself too!

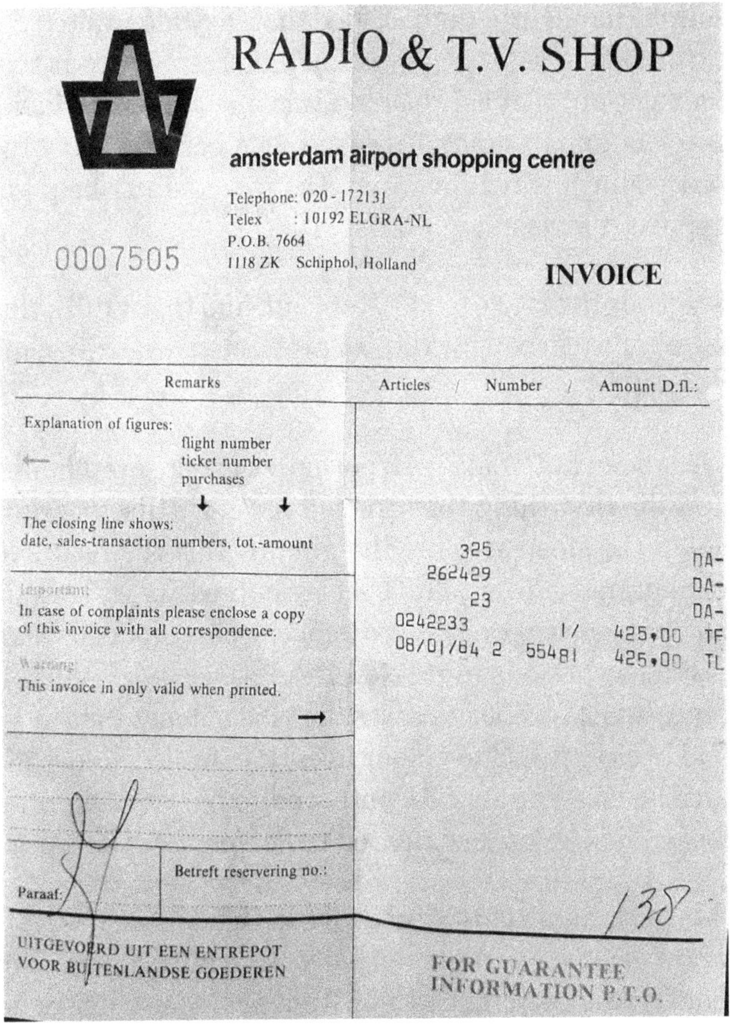

RADIO & T.V. SHOP

amsterdam airport shopping centre

Telephone: 020 - 172131
Telex : 10192 ELGRA-NL
P.O.B. 7664
1118 ZK Schiphol, Holland

0007505

INVOICE

Remarks	Articles / Number / Amount D.fl.:
Explanation of figures: flight number, ticket number, purchases. The closing line shows: date, sales-transaction numbers, tot.-amount	325 DA- / 262429 DA- / 23 DA- / 0242233 1/ 425,00 TF / 08/01/84 2 55481 425,00 TL
Important: In case of complaints please enclose a copy of this invoice with all correspondence. Warning: This invoice in only valid when printed.	
Paraaf: / Betreft reservering no.:	138
UITGEVOERD UIT EEN ENTREPOT VOOR BUITENLANDSE GOEDEREN	FOR GUARANTEE INFORMATION P.T.O.

Invoice of the cassette player the author bought from the duty-free shop at Amsterdam Airport

By now, however, a good number of the ORs, having nothing better to do while aimlessly meandering in the duty-free area gravitated to where we were and witnessed our purchase of the cassette player. And as if on cue, they suddenly seemed overcome by a collective 'eureka moment' – and decided that they too wanted the exact same cassette player for themselves! From that moment on, that salesperson was one busy individual. He was apparently so pleased and ecstatic with the proceedings which followed, that he couldn't help but express it in as many words.

Soon our flight to Conakry took off, and thankfully, this leg of our journey was not as protracted or as tiresome as the first.

We landed at Conakry Airport after about seven hours, and the first thing that greeted us as we disembarked down the steep steps of the aircraft was the heat and the humidity. To us, it felt rather oppressive, especially having been in the near-zero temperatures of Amsterdam just a few hours earlier. Nevertheless, we got used to it pretty quickly, since this was the kind of temperature we had been exposed to all our lives. We walked across the tarmac into Conakry Airport, and to be very honest, it looked like a shack compared to *Schiphol Amsterdam*.

We were met by an officer from the Guinean Army, who welcomed us most cordially. Soon after, Lieutenant Colonel Majed Bukht, Major Reza and I were driven to 'Novotel Hotel Conakry' in a rather big and spacious sedan, while the Other Rank personnel were made to board a minibus and taken to another, and presumably less glitzy, hotel.

During our drive, I tried to soak in the sights of the city as best as I could so I would have a fair impression of the socioeconomic condition of the country, as well as the type of city Conakry was. In all fairness, it seemed to be a rank lower than Dhaka, but only just. Dhaka, being a typical third-world capital, had its usual mix of good roads and bad roads and posh locales next to slums – and so did Conakry.

Novotel Conakry, also called the Grand Hotel de l'independance, apparently had a five-star rating – and it showed. But, considering the impression I got of Conakry during my rather long sojourn through the city, the imposing and elegant structure of our hotel in the midst of a third-world mix of poverty and scarcity was rather surprising. We knew right away that our stay here was going to be comfortable for whatever number of days we were to be in Conakry. In fact, we were expected to be flown out to the region of the earthquake within a couple of days or so, as indicated by the official who had received us at the airport. Till then, we were asked to stay at the hotel and make ourselves as comfortable as possible since, being guests of the Government of Guinea, the entire expense for our stay was being borne by them. In the meantime we were at liberty to explore the city in a chauffeur-driven car which had been placed at our disposal.

With Lieutenant Colonel Majed Bukht in front of Grand Hotel de l'independance (Novotel Conakry)

The next morning, Lieutenant Colonel Majed Bukht indicated that we needed to convert some of the US dollars we were carrying, to the local currency of Guinea which, at the time, was called a *Syli* (pronounced much like the word "silly").

When the three of us went up to the front desk of the hotel, we were told by the concierge that for each US dollar we wanted exchanged, we would be given twenty five Guinean Sylis. Lieutenant Colonel Majed Bukht's face immediately lit up, since he knew that one US dollar could buy only eighteen Bangladeshi Takas – and *twenty five* was certainly more than *eighteen*! For him, this was the equivalent of striking a gold mine because, with the socioeconomic condition of the two countries being apparently almost identical, he was getting more Sylis than Takas for the same amount of Dollars! Lieutenant Colonel Majed Bukht half-turned around to inquire, almost in a whisper, of what we thought. And, from the look in his eyes, I could tell he was literally imploring us to maintain a poker face, lest the concierge got a whiff of the heist he was about to pull and re-considered his offer.

I, however, tried to warn Lieutenant Colonel Majed Bukht that there was a distinct likelihood of a black market existing somewhere in this city, which we would do well to explore before committing ourselves to the offered exchange rate. But neither he nor Major Reza were willing to listen, and proceeded to exchange fifty US dollars each, for Sylis – coming away with beaming faces, and a spring in their steps. I took my chances, and preserved my dollars.

Later that morning, we got into our car with the express intention of getting some more dollars exchanged to Sylis, before going anywhere else. I was in the passenger seat next to the chauffeur, trying to explain to him that we needed to go to a place where we could exchange currencies. Unfortunately, this turned out to be a tedious and frustrating exercise because the official and widely spoken language in Guinea was French, which we didn't speak. And no amount of gesturing at the chauffeur, or any of my instructions in deliberately broken English seemed to work. It was like talking to a brick wall. The chauffeur stared back at me blankly, as I frantically waved my arms at him. As far as he was concerned, I must have looked like a puppet at a carnival which needed psychiatric treatment – and soon! After much gesticulation, I suddenly hit the jackpot when I included the magic word 'dollar' in my diction – to which the chauffeur seemed to suddenly come to life! His eyes lit up, and his face literally exploded with exuberance, as he exclaimed, *"Dolla!!! ... Oui, oui [Yes, yes]!!!"* and promptly put the car into gear.

We were driven straight to a marketplace which looked more like a conglomeration of shacks sprouting like a sea of mushrooms around a dilapidated two-storied brick structure. That central structure, I assumed, had been the original market around which the later jumble of shacks and lean-tos were added. My two companions handed me fifty dollars each for any exchange I might be able to accomplish, and while they waited in the car I struck forth in search of fortune into the maze of shops that were teeming with people.

I knew I looked different, and that was plainly obvious from the stares I soon began to receive once inside the marketplace. Guineans had probably never seen a Bangladeshi before, and at that moment we were probably the only Bangladeshis in the entire country. They must have guessed, and quite rightly so, that I was in the quest for local currency, because the setting was just right for a couple of reasons. Firstly, I was a foreigner whom they had not seen in this market yesterday, and so obviously, I was a newcomer. And secondly, a foreigner at a marketplace would have to have dollars in his pocket and, to be able to buy their wares, he would need Sylis.

I decided to keep walking rather aimlessly for a while, because with all the stares following me, I knew something was bound to transpire shortly. And, sure enough, the mountain eventually came to Muhammad because, very soon, I had a small following of young teenage boys in my wake chanting, *"Monsieur, dolla? ... Monsieur, dolla?"* Nevertheless, I kept walking, but at a slightly slower pace than before. I was intentionally allowing the crowd to grow, since I wanted some competition to exist between my prospective business partners. This, I knew, would give me the upper hand in any negotiation.

Eventually at one point I stopped, turned around, and threw the million-dollar question out at the little crowd, *"How many Sylis for a Dollar?"* I knew this was a question in English, but at that point it didn't matter because it had the two magical words which made all the difference – *Dollar* and *Syli*. And moreover, these teenage kids following me obviously knew by now what I was here for. The best offer instantly screamed out at me from somewhere within the crowd was two hundred and fifty!

Two hundred and fifty Sylis for a Dollar! I felt like I was dreaming!

My traveling companions were given a miserly twenty five Sylis for a Dollar back at the hotel! This was clearly ten times that amount! Ten times! I was mentally drooling by now.

Nevertheless, by all measure of logic and common sense, this would have to be this individual's worst offer, and I wanted some more for myself from his creamy commission. Obviously, some arm-twisting was in order. So, I pulled the lanky kid aside, and in as solemn a tone as possible I said, *"Three hundred"* while at the same time I let my gaze caress the group of my ex-followers who were still milling around. I did make sure that my potential business partner saw this too because, for him, it came with the disappointing prospect of his business going elsewhere if he was not willing to negotiate. And in almost the next instant I heard *"Two hundred and seventy five"* – the number I was hoping to hear. "This is one smart kid" I said to myself.

As I nodded my agreement, he bade me to follow him. I was taken through a maze of shops no bigger than tiny little cubicles and filled up to their hilt with merchandise, some quite novel and exotic. We eventually ended up at a shop on the second floor, which apparently belonged to a tailor from neighboring Senegal. I was told later that Conakry actually had a huge number of Senegalese businesses, and this was one of them.

The kid then asked me to hand him the Dollars I wanted exchanged, and indicated with hand gestures that I would have to wait at that shop while he was gone to have the exchange made. At that point I had no way of knowing whether he was actually going to bring back the Sylis, or disappear with my money. Nevertheless, I presumed that since this was a business which regularly put bread on his table, he would not like it tainted in any way – hopefully. And frankly, under the circumstances, I had no option but to abide by his instructions, and put all my faith on gut instinct. I handed him the hundred dollars from my traveling partners, and added another hundred of my own. And as I began to pray, he quickly slithered out of sight.

After about half an hour the lanky kid reappeared from somewhere within the human wall, and this time he was literally weighed down by two huge zippered bags he was carrying in either arm. That was when it dawned on me that at the exchange rate decided upon, two hundred dollars would add up to no less than fifty five thousand Sylis! It was no big surprise, therefore, that my friend was lugging all that weight, and more so since Syli had no denominations larger than a hundred. What made matters worse was that this lot, as I later discovered, had a predominant mix of tens, twenties and fifties only, which was entirely understandable, since this fellow was not exactly returning from the Bank of Guinea. The counting, though tedious, was eventually completed, and the Sylis were then transferred into two huge plastic bags for me to carry back.

As I walked triumphantly out of the marketplace, I had to genuinely resist the urge to repeatedly look over my shoulders, since I was expecting to get mugged any moment. The wide-eyed look of surprise on the faces of my traveling companions when they saw the huge bags I was carrying, combined with the toothy smile of uncontrolled glee, was a sight to behold, and to this day remains etched in my memory. However, Lieutenant Colonel Majed Bukht and Major Reza spent a large part of our trip back to the hotel verbally vilifying the concierge at Novotel Conakry to their heart's content in both English and in Bengali – and which they did with carefree abandon, since they knew the chauffeur had no knowledge of either language.

With Lieutenant Colonel Majed Bukht
at the marketplace in Conakry, where
the currency exchange was made

That the Syli was indeed an extremely weak currency soon became known to the ORs as well. They used the bus, which had been placed at their disposal, for shopping and for trips to places around Conakry. Lieutenant Colonel Majed Bukht had informed them of the marketplace where, he told them, they could get their Dollars converted, as well as do some shopping. Incidentally, that marketplace was where we too, did the bulk of our shopping. The partitions between the small shops there were rather flimsy and therefore, acoustically porous. So, anything being said in one shop, including the proceedings of any bargaining, easily carried quite clearly to the next. Lieutenant Colonel Majed Bukht, Major Reza and I were in one of those shops one day, making a few purchases, when the voices of a bargaining process could be heard coming from the shop somewhere behind it. We guessed right away that a group of our ORs were involved in the bargaining. It soon reached a point where the shopkeeper was perhaps adamant on the price he was asking, when one of the ORs, perhaps out of sheer exasperation, could be heard exclaiming, "Your Syli is like paper!" That, I must admit, was tantalizingly close to the truth.

A currency note of Guinea – called "Syli" – which the author brought back with him

In the meantime, it was arranged for us to call on the President of Guinea, Ahmed Sekou Toure, at his office. Our entire team, meaning the three officers along with the JCO and the ORs were there. The President and Lieutenant Colonel Majed Bukht exchanged a few pleasantries, and the former then thanked our entire team both for our willingness and our efforts to provide our services for the earthquake victims. This was followed by light snacks and a photo-session with the President.

The Mobile Surgical Team with Ahmed Sekou Toure, the President of Guinea (seen standing 5th from right), with Lieutenant Colonel Majed Bukht to his left and the author to his right. Major Reza is seen standing to the right of the author

A few days later, it was communicated to Lieutenant Colonel Majed Bukht that most of the casualties of the earthquake had actually been taken care of by medical teams that had arrived earlier, and that those requiring further medical attention had already been evacuated to nearby hospitals. Obviously, we had arrived in Guinea a bit later than we ought to have, which must have been the outcome of some kind of a bureaucratic sluggishness.

We were informed, however, that both the government and the people of Guinea were nonetheless forever in our debt for our gesture of friendship and for our intent and willingness to provide help during their time of need. And when we expressed our intention to immediately pack up and leave, since there was no point in furthering our stay, we were told that there was no rush and that arrangements for our departure would be processed in due time.

Lieutenant Colonel Majed Bukht, thereafter, kept goading the Guinean authorities on a fairly regular basis to arrange for our departure, which the latter kept delaying for no apparent reason. What we had not realized at that point was that that was the way the Government of Guinea wanted to say 'thank you' for our gesture of goodwill – by having us stay a few more days in Guinea and passing a relaxing time at their expense, without telling us so in as many words.

In the meantime however, we were given an aerial tour of the earthquake-ravaged area in a plane which seated no more than twelve people. We also landed at a remote airstrip and were given a tour around the countryside to witness the devastation from up close. It was horrifying to see the amount of damage and havoc Nature had wrought on the land and our hearts went out to those affected, and to the people of Guinea as a whole.

In front of the plane used for an aerial tour and a visit to the earthquake-ravaged area in Guinea

We stayed in Guinea for a total of almost three weeks, during which we were driven around in our chauffeur-driven car to wherever we wanted to go. We made it a point to also visit the rural areas in the outskirts of Conakry during that time. Despite the poverty that is usually so prevalent in such areas in any Third World country, we were struck by the warmth and the friendliness of those living there.

With a group of children in the rural outskirts of Conakry (The author is standing at the back with Lieutenant Colonel Majed Bukht to his left and their chauffeur to his right)

In front of "Monument du 22 Novembre 1970", in Conakry, with Lieutenant Colonel Majed Baukht and the chauffeur (in white dress)

We also did some local sightseeing as well as spend a fair amount of time at the famous market where I had made the money exchange. I have to admit however, that despite its decrepit and dilapidated looks, it did have wares worth buying.

However, because of the language barrier, our haggling for prices often turned into an exchange which was as incomprehensible to the other as of a donkey trying to understand the language of the whales. For someone who had absolutely no knowledge of French, "Soixante Syli" or "Quatre vingt cinq Syli" meant nothing. Eventually, the shopkeepers came up with an ingenious solution to the exasperating problem they were facing with the three "non-French-speaking foreigners" who frequented their marketplace. Every time we opened our mouths to start to bargain, out would come a calculator on which to punch numbers. The frequency at which the calculator thereafter changed hands usually reflected the intensity of the bargaining process. In such purchases too, Major Reza stuck to his proven practice of buying everything and anything I did – from chocolates to curios and from clothing to cans of coffee.

During those few weeks in Conakry, the cameras which Major Reza and I had recently purchased at Amsterdam Airport were also tested to their near-absolute limits, as we took pictures of anything and everything we saw. At the same time, we were also yearning to check out the cassette-players too, which we had bought from there. But unfortunately, we had no cassettes-tapes with us. And so one day, during one of our strolls along a roadside

Conakry market, I purchased a few tapes of supposedly popular Guinean songs. And need I mention that Major Reza bought an identical set for himself too? Though we realized we would understand nothing of the lyrics, we bought those tapes anyways, basically for the music, which was rather lively and up-beat.

Back in my hotel room, I was surprised at how quickly and easily the tune, the beat and even some of the incomprehensible lyrics seemed to get stuck inside my head. Very soon, and quite often, I found myself humming those tunes. And it seemed I was not the only one doing so. I often caught Major Reza too, rather absentmindedly humming the same.

Thirty two years later, most of the tunes which had made their way into my head at the Novotel Conakry have been erased by Time. However, two words, along with their accompanying lively drumbeats from one of those Guinean songs still echo feebly within my head, and which I treasure with great fondness and nostalgia. Every echo of it seems to unfurl an individual canvas of the people and the places in Conakry, my room at the Novotel hotel and, of course, the marketplace! Those two words are *"Sailey, sailey"* – and that's the bit of Conakry I still happily and gratefully carry within my heart, even after all these years.

Oftentimes, Major Reza and I would simply relax by the pool behind the hotel, with the Atlantic Ocean in full and majestic view. The Atlantic Ocean could also be seen from the window of my room on the third floor of the hotel, and I spent a fair amount of time simply staring at it, mesmerized by its beauty and expanse. There was a lighthouse not too far from the shore right behind our hotel, and during low tides a narrow ridge of land would appear out of the water, connecting the shore to the lighthouse. During that 'window of opportunity' the rocky ridge would be packed with people seeking adventure – walking over it to the lighthouse and back, simply for the thrill of it. I, in turn, got my share of thrill watching them go out, and then scurrying back soon after, just in time before the choppy waters of the ocean returned to swallow that ridge.

The lighthouse on the Atlantic shore as seen from the window of the author's room at Novotel Conakry

Dinners in the huge and ornate dining hall of the hotel was always sumptuous, with dishes from the regular to the exotic. Lieutenant Colonel Majed Bukht, Major Reza and I would always prefer to be seated at a table on one particular side of the dining hall – the side which was rounded out toward the swimming pool and the ocean at the back. For some reason, chocolate mousse soon became my dessert of choice. I ordered it on such a regular basis that there were occasions when Lieutenant Colonel Majed Bukht would volunteer to tell the waiter, ahead of me, of what I would like for dessert.

All this while Lieutenant Colonel Majed Bukht kept reminding the authorities to make arrangements for our departure, and would often come back with a dejected look on his face. Finally, after almost three weeks we were, I must say, 'allowed' to leave. As much as I was eager to get back to Dhaka, I was equally sad to leave Conakry – the one city I seemed to have fallen in love with – not in spite of its poverty and so-called African 'backwardness', but *because* of it. And also because of its warm, friendly and simplistic people, who were as beautiful outside, as they were in their hearts.

Our journey back to Dhaka took us through London, with a thirty six hour stopover there. Lieutenant Colonel Majed Bukht had made a prior arrangement with his friend Dr. Khaled, a physician practicing in London, to pick us up at the airport, and to which the gentleman most kindly agreed. He even went on to offer that we, the three officers, stay with him and his family at his residence during our stay in London, which we most gratefully accepted. Arrangements were made for the ORs to stay at a nearby hotel.

This was the first time ever that I was in London, and soon after dinner, when Dr. Khaled offered to take us out for a drive around the city, I was visibly excited. Sadly, the long trans-Atlantic flight and the trip as a whole must have taken its toll, for I drifted in and out of somnolence during our tour of London. I vaguely remember having seen the Pall Mall, the Buckingham Palace, London Bridge, Trafalgar Square, Piccadilly Circus and a few other places of interest – through most of which I must have slept, and perhaps even snored.

Finally, after almost four weeks, we stood on Bangladeshi soil. Though this was a most enjoyable trip, I'm sure most of us carried a lingering discontent and dissatisfaction that our expertise, for which we were trained, and our services, which we were prepared to render most willingly, were not required. Nevertheless, from the standpoint of a geopolitical gesture of goodwill, I was given to understand that our 'Adventure in Africa' had served its purpose pretty adequately.

> *It is with a heavy heart that I would like my readers to know that Lieutenant Colonel (later Brigadier General) Majed Bukht sadly passed away some years later. He was a thorough gentleman, a dedicated professional and an accomplished neurosurgeon.*

The Reality of Illusions

> *"How strange when an illusion dies. It's as though you've lost a child." - Judy Garland*

It was almost a year now that I had been a doctor in the armed forces. I cannot say I was doing exactly what my education had prepared me for, nor was I convinced that I was going down the fairy-tale path to realizing my professional dreams and aspirations.

Here was a classic example of a situation where one gets somewhat shortchanged while conducting business with an entity called Life, in which labor, endeavor and caliber, are bartered with fate, fortune and fulfillment. From the perspective of my transactions in this institutional situation, it was not the consideration of what I was prepared *with,* but what I was prepared *for.* Because however much we put into the slot-machine of dreams, hopes, aspirations and ambitions, there is no guarantee we will hit the jackpot. Nevertheless, we continue to play to the best of our abilities, trying to make the most of the chips we hold.

This is central to what I call an 'existential satisfaction', where one embraces an existence, whatever be its quality, seeking not only to derive satisfaction out of it, but striving to make it better. Understandably therefore, I pulled out all stops and tried to make the most of the parades, the drills, the firings, the dinner nights, the study periods and the overflowing MI Rooms. All this while however, I had my eyes set on the first opportunity of pursuing a career as a specialist in the armed forces because, as far as I was concerned, my game of poker needed to come to a satisfying and fulfilling conclusion.

The armed forces regularly conducted courses in various specialties. This was an eighteen-month Grading Course which was considered equivalent to a full-time residency. One became a 'Graded Specialist' in a respective specialty on successful completion of the course in that specialty. This gave that person the license to independently perform duties as a specialist in a particular medical field in any military hospital. Furthermore, a Graded Specialist, after having served as such for a year, could then proceed to become a 'Classified Specialist' if he or she wanted to. This entailed the successful completion of a post-graduate course at a medical institution at the national level, and having at least six publications to that person's credit in any reputed medical journal of the country. Being a Classified Specialist also made an officer, with adequate seniority, eligible to become the head of a department down the road. It also qualified an individual to be promoted beyond the rank of lieutenant colonel.

So, towards the end of the first year of our service, both Samina and I decided to apply to become specialists, because that was what we had always wanted to be, and because that was the hope with which we had joined the armed forces. Interestingly, this served as an eye-opener for us to the absurd and outrageous reality that in the armed forces one actually needed *military experience* to attain *medical milestones*. Our applications were turned down on the premise that we had not completed at least a year of service. We both fell short by twenty four hours! This meant that we would have to wait a minimum of another six months before putting in our applications again.

In my opinion, an impulsive assumption that medical graduates were incapable of proceeding for a post-graduate course and training unless they have had at least a year of military service under their belts, was not only a wanton disregard for the value of medical education, but perhaps also an attempt at an excessive indoctrination. Moreover, certain restrictions imposed upon medical graduates in their ability to prescribe and treat, unless they had become specialists, were a further proof of how much their knowledge and expertise were curbed, confined and censured.

With a Bachelor's degree in Medicine and Surgery, and with the kind of experience and clinical exposure gained from internships and residencies done under the guidance and supervision of professors at civilian medical institutions, doctors inducted into the medical corps ought to have been given a greater degree of freedom in patient management, even if under the mentorship of a specialist. Not only that, they should also have been allowed a greater flexibility in getting into post-graduate studies. Personally, I felt a huge disappointment when certain restrictions were imposed upon me in terms of my freedom and permission to treat. That was when I groped around helplessly, suspecting the true value of my medical education and degree, while at the same time, trying my best to preserve my professional self-confidence.

It would have made more sense had the initial one-year period, or at least a part of it, been spent in building an academic foundation of some sort. But sadly, that was not the case. For a medical graduate, the entire first year of service was set aside exclusively for parades, drills, firings, providing medical covers, and participating in study periods on military strategy and military history. Why, I have no idea.

Realistically however, in terms of medical academics and career advancement, an early start to post-graduate training is always to the advantage of the individual, as well as of the institution. The epic question therefore, is this: In case an officer wanted to become a specialist, what did the authorities want that officer to prove or to gain through military activities that would help him prepare for a medical post-graduate course?

In my opinion, the location of the diverging point where one chose – or was chosen – to either become a specialist or to remain a GDMO (General Duty Medical Officer) ought to have been made much earlier than was the practice. From a pragmatic perspective, that choice and decision should have been made within only a couple of months of completing the basic military training. That way, valuable time would not have been wasted by future specialists doing things which had no relevance to their future careers. The armed forces too, would have benefitted from such a practice, in that it could have enjoyed the services of a specialist much earlier than otherwise, more so since there was a dearth of specialists in the corps. As for any lingering concerns regarding military indoctrination, that could be assumed to have been adequately taken care of during the officer's basic military training or the OBC.

I am certainly not saying I am an expert in policy-making, nor am I suggesting that my viewpoint and suggestion is the "be all and end all" of the policy regarding processing of doctors freshly inducted into the medical corps. But I strongly feel that it comes closest to being pragmatic, beneficial and workable. It promises progress in the right direction, and the attainment of standards which would have served the corps well. It is my firm belief that this suggestion, along with some others which I shall make later, regarding the conduct and the curriculum of the Grading Course, has the promise and the potential of enhancing the respectability and reliability of the doctors of this establishment – at least countrywide, if not worldwide. However, if things have turned around now, after all these years, and of which I may not be aware, then that would certainly be a cause for celebration.

Rejection of our applications for the Grading Course was more of a concern for me at that point than for Samina who, being posted to CMH Dhaka was getting adequate clinical exposure. Understandably therefore, she seemed somewhat content, though not entirely pleased, with six more months of the same. From my standpoint, however, not being allowed to enroll into a post-graduate course because I fell short by twenty-four hours, and instead, having to continue with military activities for six more months was clearly unjustified, absurd and illogical.

With that in mind we wrote to the Director General of Medical Services (DGMS) expressing our interest in post-graduate studies, as well as our concern regarding the rules of eligibility for enrollment into the Grading Course. We requested a reconsideration of our application on the premise that we were eagerly and overly interested in starting our post-graduate education at the earliest opportunity without wasting valuable time; that six more months of delay for a short-fall of only twenty four hours seemed rather harsh; and that perhaps the DGMS had the exclusive authority of making an exception in this case – at least for the sake of the institution, if not for us. Though tempted, my sense of propriety prevented me from also adding, "… … *and how much is six more months of military activities going to help me towards a medical post-graduation?"*

Our applications were, as expected, turned down – and this, for me, was the beginning of a ***profound disillusion***.

Chapter 5
THE PROFOUND DISILLUSION
The making of a surgeon at CMH Dhaka

"We turn to God for help when our foundations are shaking, only to learn that it is God who is shaking them." – Charles C. West

Going forward in Life is largely a matter of constant adjustment, adaptation and compromise. The essential relationship between the amounts of work shouldered by an individual, versus his or her capacity of getting that work done is, by and large, symbiotic. That is because in such a relationship, an individual's ability to perform actually grows into and adapts to the workload shouldered, while the workload itself somehow seems to get adjusted to the individual's abilities. Eventually, both settle into a workable, and often a productive, relationship.

Understandably therefore, I soon became accustomed to the hectic and relentless activities at 61 Field Ambulance and was, before long, carrying out the multifarious responsibilities vested upon me quite comfortably and contentedly. The reality was that I had somehow been nudged into a situation where the previously urgent need for a post-graduate education had inexplicably slid down my list of priorities. On the contrary, and to be very honest, I was actually beginning to enjoy my time at the field medical unit. However, what eluded me at that point was the answer to whether all this was the result of my intrinsic sense of duty and dedication, or the manifestation of some extrinsic diabolical design.

It was just when things seemed to have started to move forward on a fairly even keel for me that I was faced with a sudden, unexpected and a rather unsettling turn of events. I was called into the office of my Commanding Officer one morning, to be told that I had been posted to the nearby Armed Forces Medical Institute as its Adjutant.

The Armed Forces Medical Institute (or AFMI) was where we had completed the second phase of our basic military training. The Adjutant at that time was Major Shahidul Haque Mallick, a quiet, mild-mannered and mostly-somber officer. I still remember how elevated his appointment had seemed when we were trainees there during the Phase-2 of our OBC not too long ago, and how distant that appointment had appeared to us at that time. And quite surprisingly, within hardly a year, I was being offered that same appointment!

Pleased as I was with this posting, it nevertheless left me somewhat bewildered, perhaps because it was both good and bad news for me. And I shall soon try to explain why. But, I believe to this day, as I had believed then, that the Commandant of AFMI, Brigadier-General Shahjahan Hafiz – the person who, after my extempore speech on the education system of Bangladesh had indicated that I could make up something despite not knowing anything about it – must have had a role to play in it. But that, of course, could merely be a figment of my imagination. But even so, it somehow made me feel good thinking that it was true!

Besides conducting the Second Phase of the AMC Officers Basic Course, the AFMI was also entrusted with conducting courses on various medical and surgical specialties, as well as being responsible for the publication of the Armed Forces Medical Journal. Needless to say, the duties of an Adjutant there were mainly administrative in nature.

The good news was that the appointment to the post of the Adjutant of the AFMI carried with it a substantial measure of honor and prestige. It was an appointment traditionally reserved for officers with a length of service much longer than mine, and with an experience much greater than what I had at that stage of my career. So obviously, such an appointment, in just over a year of joining the armed forces, was profoundly flattering.

As the Adjutant of AFMI (Armed
Forces Medical Institute)

But the bad news was this:

The course of my career was merely changing from being a GDMO doing one kind of duty at a field medical unit, to being a GDMO doing another kind of duty at a medical institute. This, in effect, was one and the same – since I was, and would still remain, a GDMO. This wasn't career advancement by any stretch of the imagination. This was something comparable to a chameleon changing its color only, and not necessarily turning into a different kind of a reptile.

Rather, a GDMO at a field medical unit at least had the opportunity of attending to patients, be that brief, hurried, and cursory, in its various MI Rooms. On the other hand, an adjutant at a medical institute had to remain confined to a desk and immersed in administrative paperwork, with no exposure, whatsoever, to anything medical or clinical in nature. And that, I knew, was certainly not the direction I needed or even wanted to take at that stage.

I was also somewhat bewildered and flustered by the fact that the higher hierarchy of the corps actually knew of my eagerness to pursue a career as a specialist, and not as a GDMO. I would have thought that that would have been the message conveyed to them after the little storm I had raised a few months ago by requesting the DGMS to condone the 24-hour shortfall in my service so I could enroll into the specialization course.

And yet, here I was, being goaded into a cattle pen, by certain 'cowboys in positions of power', who seemingly had plans of their own for me. Perhaps, someone sufficiently senior in the corps, senior enough to be able to call the shots, wanted to avail of my services as a GDMO before I, in all likelihood, disappeared into the crowd of specialists.

Whether I am right or wrong in making such an assumption, I do not know. But frankly, at that point, I also didn't want to know. I didn't want to know because my intense preoccupation with my current responsibilities at 61 Field Ambulance and my total immersion in non-academic activities had distracted me enough to be dazzled and dazed by the presumed prestige, pomp and splendor within the 'cattle pen' that I was being driven into. In effect, I had already been converted into an automaton for which matters beyond the immediate vicinity were out of focus and blurred, and of no particular concern. And that was to be expected because all this was happening at a time when I was caught up in sorting my priorities and preferences from the jumble of disorderly milieu that I faced. This was not only proving to be challenging for me, it threatened to throw me off my track as well.

In all honesty, a posting as the Adjutant of AFMI would have been a giant leap forward for those aspiring to make a career in the corps as a GDMO. As for me, this was a great leap sideways – into undesired territories. In golfing terms, it would seem as if I had scored a hole-in-one – but, unfortunately, the ball had plunked into the wrong hole!

All this meant that it was time for me to say farewell to 61 Field Ambulance – the first unit I had served in, following the completion of my basic military training, and the first unit which had given me the true taste of life in the armed forces.

Needless to say, I would be leaving behind memories both pleasant and painful. I would also be leaving behind colleagues who had always been friendly, caring and supportive, especially officers of the likes of Major Matin, the Second-in-Command, and Major Golam Mostafa, the Quartermaster. They had always been gracious enough to have consistently praised my achievements, and conscientious enough to have made allowances for my transient impediments. It saddened me too, to be leaving behind my other colleagues at 61 Field Ambulance who made the moments we spent together worth cherishing. I will always remember them all with great fondness.

By tradition, an officer posted out of a unit is presented with a unit 'crest'. This is an emblem with the unit's insignia or monogram on it, and with an inscription which carried a message of affection, comradeship and farewell from all colleagues. It was a memento which, in a very material way, declared how important a part of the unit an officer had been, and how much that officer would be missed following his departure.

A few days before the party to bid me farewell I was on my way back from the only washroom in the unit, located on the other side of the Commanding Officer's room when, in the midst of my stride, a critical phrase floated to my ears. It was our Second-in-Command, habitually a loud speaker, in conversation in the Commanding Officer's room, and saying something to the effect of, "... ... it doesn't matter that he has not been with us for a year, but I think he deserves a crest."

It did not require a genius to infer that my Commanding Officer was emphasizing on the fact that since I had served his unit for ten months only and not for a year, I did not qualify for, or deserve, a crest. Obviously, his inherent instinct to mindlessly and obstinately adhere to rigid and mundane military practices and protocols had gotten the better of him, and he was therefore willing to ignore the energy and the enthusiasm I had placed at his disposal whenever it was required of me. There was obviously no room in my Commanding Officer's dispassionate and uncaring heart for any gesture which would, in any way, convey a sentiment of appreciation or of gratitude.

But this was his unit and, if I am not mistaken, he certainly had the prerogative of making an exception when it came to presenting a crest to one of his officers, even if he had served only ten months instead of twelve. No one, I think – not even in the lofty offices – would ever have held him accountable for having exercised this option. In fact, I don't think anyone there even cared. But no, one had to be careful in such matters, lest the rank and the appointment were in jeopardy!

So, therefore, the long and arduous hours of practice for the Victory Day Parade and the enthusiastic participation in the various competitions which brought the unit honor and prestige, were obviously all meaningless now.

The endless journeys to provide medical cover for countless firing sessions and Physical Efficiency Tests, and the daily rush from one MI Room to another to treat and to provide medical advice to a mind-boggling number of patients just so the unit under his command had an unblemished image were all apparently irrelevant and immaterial now.

Not to mention the sleepless nights spent in apprehension of whether or not I was doing it all right – of which the Commanding Officer had no inkling. Everything was now being most casually disregarded because I fell short by two months to qualify for a crest, and also because someone was perhaps apprehensive of how the higher offices would interpret the conduct, if I was presented with one!

At the end, however, the Second-in-Command prevailed, and during the farewell party I was presented with a crest on behalf of all the officers of the unit. This was the first of a few crests I have received in my career, and to this day I cherish it and hold it close to my heart. I owe it all to the Second-in-Command and perhaps none to my Commanding Officer. Nevertheless, I hold no grudge against the latter, for he perhaps never possessed in his heart the element of appreciation, or the capacity for being magnanimous – not unlike many that I had come across during my career.

Dreams of Deception

> *"Seldom, very seldom, does complete truth belong to any human disclosure; seldom can it happen that something is not a little disguised or a little mistaken."*
> *– Jane Austen, "Emma"*

About six months into my tenure as the Adjutant of the Armed Forces Medical Institute, I was informed that I had been selected, along with about ten other colleagues of my level of seniority, for a specialization course in a neighboring country.

However, when we reported to the headquarters for the necessary formalities, a senior medical officer there informed us that that course was actually not for us; that it was, in fact, meant for those already working as Graded Specialists in the various military hospitals. We were told that there had been some sort of a misunderstanding, and therefore, we did not qualify. Only later was it revealed that all this was the result of a bureaucratic error. And, at that point, I was left wondering whether the lofty offices could actually have been so clumsy as to make an error of such a magnitude. Or was it something else, of which we were not being told?

Nevertheless, processes were swiftly set into motion that would neither expose any failing, nor leave room for any potential dissension. It was right then and there that we were given the opportunity of enrolling into the Grading Course in our subject of choice by being interviewed by a board of examiners. The fact that this was neither the time of the year for enrollment into the Grading Course, nor were we being required to take the customary written test preceding the interview seemed like a tacit admission on the part of the authorities of the immensity of their blunder

This interview panel comprised most of the top officials of the medical corps, both specialists and administrators. Prior to the interview, we were given a form to fill, on which we were also to indicate two specialties of our choice in order of preference. It was more by way of natural instinct that I checked the box beside the word "Surgery". It is not that I had any particular fascination for that subject, but compared to all the others on that list, surgery somehow seemed more adventurous and glamorous.

Insofar as adventure and glamour are concerned, the future that I have always had in mind was one which involved flying, or anything to do with rockets and space. Becoming a doctor never actually figured in my list of possible future professions. In fact, a good portion of my time during childhood had been spent sitting behind the wheel of my father's car, even before I had learned how to drive, imagining I was a pilot in the cockpit of an aircraft, preparing to take off. This included turning the knobs on the dashboard at random – perhaps much to my father's later consternation – and talking aloud as if I was in conversation with the air traffic controller. I made gliders out of balsa wood and rockets out of toothpaste tubes. More often than not, the gliders either nose-dived into the ground or the rockets exploded on lift-off. But, whether or not my contraptions took flight didn't quite matter. What mattered was that it gave me the thrill and the pleasure of doing what my heart desired. Why I ended up becoming a doctor instead, is quite another story. Suffice it to say that surgery, at that moment, came closest to giving me the thrill and the adventure I always sought.

My second preference was Radiology, for no reason other than the fact that I needed to check a second box. When asked during the interview as to how interested I was in Radiology as compared to Surgery, I said "Ten percent", without batting an eyelid. Thankfully, the panel of interviewers believed me!

That day most of us returned home with the satisfaction of having been selected for a Grading course. The fact that we were originally destined for a more widely recognized and a more prestigious course abroad was the least of our concerns. It was only much later that the proverbial cat leaped out of the bag, and we realized that the so-called 'bureaucratic blunder' was, in all likelihood, man-made.

To begin with, the country which had offered the course supposedly never required that specialists be sent. It was actually an entry-level post-graduate course for fresh medical graduates like us, wanting to pursue a career in a specified specialty. It came down the grapevine that those already working as Graded Specialists, and therefore higher up in the pecking order, considered it rather unfair and unacceptable that they were being ignored, and that junior officers like us were being considered for the course. The fact that they were already specialists, and that this was merely an entry-level course, did not seem to matter at that point. What mattered, perhaps, was the fact that this was a course *abroad*. And who, in their sane mind, would want to let such an opportunity slip through their fingers?

Allegedly, known and acquainted channels weaving their way up to the lofty offices were very quietly and effectively put into action – and quick changes to the conditions for qualification made. What amazed me was the swiftness with which all this was accomplished. It was as if the entire setup was jolted into action by some sort of a widespread frenzy which fired dedicated neurons up, down and across the so-called 'web of control and influence', to culminate into the singular act of sending 'preferred' individuals off to the course. If this was a war, and if this was the kind of response this chain of command was capable of mounting, it certainly made the brilliant generals of the Great Wars look rather pedestrian!

If there was even a shred of truth in what was being alleged then, quite obviously, we were at the receiving end of an exceedingly conceited and unfair conduct underlined by deception and cunning. So flawlessly had the web of disillusion been weaved around us, that the end result actually left us all feeling happy and rather grateful.

The Revealing Incision

> *"Correct me if I'm wrong, but hasn't the fine line between sanity and madness gotten finer?" – George Price*

So that was how I entered into the Grading Course in Surgery – and into a realm of deception, deprivation, dilemma and denial. Here was a world which, interestingly, resembled a soap opera more than anything else. Academics, it seemed, was merely a footnote in the script.

This course entailed a full-time placement at CMH Dhaka, the largest and the busiest military hospital in the country. Hospital duties, as a trainee in Surgery, included being in-charge of wards by rotation, assisting the senior surgeons during their surgeries, attending classes on theory and clinics, presenting cases at the weekly 'Clinical Meetings', and performing the duties of a DMO (Duty Medical Officer), the last of which I shall discuss at length.

During this period too, groups of trainees were attached to either one of the two most senior surgeons at CMH Dhaka by rotation. Like some of the things in the corps, all this looked very impressive from the outside, and would have been, had it not been for the failings of the faculty in some of its vital roles and responsibilities, where it came up shamefully short.

To begin with, the two of our very senior surgeons had differences which neither seemed willing to set aside, even at the risk of looking utterly childish and frankly comical about the whole matter. Malicious remarks suspecting the other's clinical abilities, and open shameless criticism of the other's surgical capabilities, frequently culminating into deafening and undignified verbal affronts, sometimes within the closed confines of the Operating Room, seemed to be a way of life for the two of them.

Overall however, one seemed more verbose and spiteful in his tirades than the other. Interestingly, the other's comparatively quieter and more somber disposition often also seemed to incite a runaway rage in the former, sometimes bordering on pure frenzy.

One of the bones they were fighting over was the coveted appointment of "Senior Surgeon", which was very soon to be decided upon. With post-graduate training and degrees from two different institutions, each felt he was better qualified for the appointment.

All hell broke loose however, when the one with a few days more of seniority was finally given the much-sought-after appointment, and the other felt his self-presumed 'higher' qualification had been willfully ignored. What followed thereafter were a constant and protracted open and shameless comparison of qualifications, and the attempted belittling of the other's degree, more so by the one who felt he had been unjustly deprived of and denied a prized crown.

With both of our top mentors consumed in mutual annihilation of qualifications and personalities, our education and training understandably took a back seat. Most of us would avoid interacting as much as possible with either of the senior mentors, particularly the one simmering with discontent. We felt it not worth the while being around someone bent on berating us for even the slightest mistake – or sometimes none at all – before, during, or after the surgeries. The fact that we were actually untrained in surgery, and still grappling with new concepts, practices and techniques, did not seem to matter in the least to either of them.

The faculty also didn't seem to care much about attaching a trainee to a particular mentor by turn, which should ideally have been the case, and which ought to have been clearly documented and practiced, as part of the curriculum. A trainee, therefore, arbitrarily went along with the mentor who was in-charge of the ward that the trainee was looking after. In fact, it should have been the other way round, where a trainee would have to be attached to a mentor first, and would therefore be looking after the wards of which that mentor was in-charge.

Left to such an ambiguous state of affairs, a trainee usually attached himself to the mentor he took an overall fancy to. In some cases this was dictated by whether or not one wanted to side with the contented composure of seniority or the infantile agitation of egocentricity. Nevertheless, whichever camp a trainee belonged to, that trainee usually ran the risk of immediately falling out of grace with one of the mentors if seen with the other, either during a medical round or at any other time.

For us, therefore, it was more like being in a course where we were training ourselves not in surgery, but in the art of staying out of trouble and steering clear of harm's way. Unfortunately, Fate had placed us in the same sandbox in which two giants were fighting, hell-bent on demolishing the other's esteem, fame and personality. So naturally, our instinct for self-preservation prevailed. Tragically nothing – including us, the trainees – seemed relevant to the two giants besides the assassination of the other's academic and professional standing. It was as if they existed for that one purpose only.

Besides, other junior instructors and surgeons too, never seemed to have the time or the inclination to instruct us in the theory, clinics or the practice of surgery. And why would they? This course did not appear to have a curriculum. And even if it did, the faculty never felt it necessary that we should see it, or be explained what it entailed. Understandably therefore, all our instructors, senior and junior alike, felt they had been excused of fulfilling the roles they were meant to play, or from assuming the responsibilities they were expected to shoulder. A question or two during the morning rounds, tossed out like charitable loafs of breads from a Red Cross truck in Ethiopia, was certainly not an example of proper post-graduate education. And as far as I can remember, the number of theoretical classes on the principles of surgery over the eighteen months of the course could perhaps easily be accommodated in the fingers of both my hands.

Another aspect of our training which further put us at an unfair disadvantage was the dearth of clinical exposure.

The number of patients admitted to CMH Dhaka was a trickle compared to any civilian teaching hospital. Obviously therefore, the number of surgeries performed was trivial too. It was like comparing a tiny rivulet with a mighty river. As a result, our exposure to the myriad of surgical conditions was severely curbed when compared to what our counter-parts at the civilian medical educational institutions were being exposed to. The latter greatly benefitted from the useful experience they gained from the sheer weight of numbers. Though I cannot speak for the other specialties, the lack of proper instruction combined with a dearth of clinical and surgical exposure was probably the reason surgeons trained in the armed forces, except for a pitiful few, were either not particularly accomplished, or considered not to be very proficient on a country-wide scale of comparison.

It is my opinion, therefore, that some part of our training, perhaps six out of the total of eighteen months, ought to have been obtained at a civilian medical institution. This was something so necessary and so glaringly obvious, that I fail to understand how those who conceived, conducted and supervised the Grading Course could ever have missed. Or maybe they simply didn't care. It has been more than thirty years now since then, and if this is something which has already been introduced into the Grading Course, then I will admit that it is a step in the right direction. Otherwise, the authorities would do well to seriously look into the matter. It's never too late.

Overall therefore, though the authorities did not seem to be concerned with what we, the trainees in surgery, took away from this course, I knew exactly what I had come away with. It was the disappointment and discontentment with how much I had not been permitted to accomplish, and the anguish of how little I had been taught.

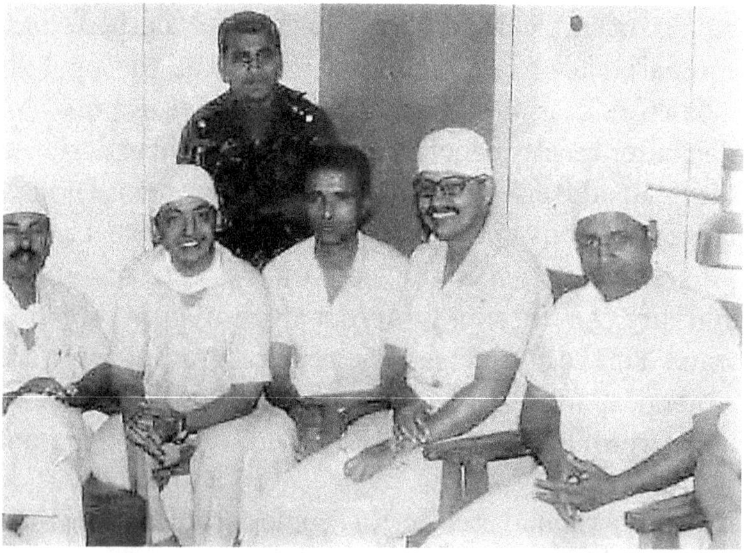

With fellow surgical trainees at CMH Dhaka
(The author is seated 2nd from left)

But, of all disappoints that I have had to deal with during my surgical training, one stands out prominently: Not because it was the most disappointing of all, but because it was representative of the general attitude of academic negligence and irresponsibility of the faculty. The truth of the matter is that any institutional shortcoming, big or small, in the propagation of proper education easily qualifies as a disappointment for those not receiving it. Individuals committed to its proper propagation, by virtue of their appointment need to understand, first of all, that knowledge is not their personal property and, secondly, that the sacred onus for its proper dissemination lies squarely on their shoulders.

I still quite vividly remember a time when I was assisting the ever-disgruntled 'verbose' surgeon during a chest surgery. Incidentally that was the first time ever that I was peering into the human chest, not to speak of handling all the contents within. For me, this alone qualified as an awe-inspiring experience of mind-boggling proportions. I was like a kid in a candy store, inquisitive of everything that was going on before my eyes, and tempted to stick my hand into every jar of candy!

The surgery, at one stage, threatened to get a bit out of hand when the surgeon, while working on the pulmonary vessels, inadvertently nicked it. For me, a mere trainee in surgery, this was a frightful sight, as blood kept welling up within the chest cavity more rapidly than the suction machine could deal with it. All this obviously demanded all of the surgeon's attention, and which also made him anxious, edgy and irritable. Personnel in the OR, particularly those who qualified to be rather needlessly and viciously berated by a habitually-acrimonious-surgeon-battling-a-messy-situation, held their breath. Eventually, and I must admit, through sheer skill and experience, the surgeon was able to contain the situation and everyone, thereafter, began to breathe easy. Finally, when everything was back on course, the atmosphere in the OR was calm and settled, and the surgery was in its final stages, I decided to ask the surgeon a question pertaining to the pulmonary vessels. To my utter surprise, the stern reply I got was, *"Don't ask irrelevant questions"*.

Maybe my timing was wrong. Maybe the surgeon was still in the process of getting drained of the adrenaline that had been pumped into his system, or maybe he was the sort of person who felt no obligation towards educating his students. At the very least, I would have expected him to have said, "I will explain this to you later" or maybe even "Look it up in the textbook".

But, *"Don't ask irrelevant questions"*? There was no way I was ever going to be able to come to terms with a response as mindless and as arrogant as that.

The point I am trying to make is this: If an academic query, made by a student of surgery during the course of a surgical procedure and pertaining to the surgery being performed was irrelevant, I am very tempted to ask my mentor as to what, in his opinion, a relevant question was. I don't remember having asked him an academic question ever again while assisting him during his surgeries, or at any other time. That, probably, was an arrangement very much acceptable to him.

A Stroll with the Giants

> *"Remember that when you think you are seeing giants, they may not be giants at all; perhaps it is you who is the dwarf." – C. Joybell C*

And then there was the Commanding Officer (CO) of the hospital who also figured prominently during our Grading Course.

He was the archetype of a top brass with the frills and trappings of aura and megalomania and in whom moreover, I could detect a hint of insolence towards junior officers from the medical corps, particularly us, the trainees. On the other hand, and surprisingly, I sensed a subtle undercurrent of friendliness in his disposition while dealing with non-medical officers regardless of their rank. And, I wouldn't be particularly surprised if one were to suggest that that was in an attempt at preservation of status and appointment. Nevertheless, this gentleman was rather meticulous by nature, and did seem to be able to run the hospital fairly well. Included in his arsenal of measures in running a tight ship was conducting a round of a ward once every week. And that was where we, the trainees, came in.

During the course of our training, we were in charge of different wards, between which we rotated every 2-3 months. Our responsibilities included looking after the overall management of the patients of the ward, including ensuring they got the proper medication, and on time. But most of all, we needed to know all there was to know about every patient in the ward, starting from their name, age, and where they came from, to the detailed history of their illnesses.

A ward round by this CO was almost as ceremonial as the Trooping of the Color. The ward in-charge, meaning the trainee, and all uniformed personnel were required to receive him in a state of spit-and-polish. The CO would have his assistant call up the ward as soon as he stepped out of his room for the round. That way, all concerned could be prepared to receive him with due honor. This meant the trainee officer and all uniformed medical assistants lining up outside the ward in order of seniority, and in keeping with a semblance of martial pomposity. The howls and screams of a military welcome, accompanied by the thunderous sounds of boots stomping on concrete just outside the hospital ward, pretty much completed the picture.

The CO would then go to each and every bed, while the trainee in-charge provided him with all the facts regarding the patient. Following this, he would inspect the patients' toilets and the ward storeroom, and reprimand the trainee if those weren't found to be as clean or as orderly as he would have liked. That was probably how he was able to keep this hospital in such a prim and proper functional state.

I was the in-charge of the JCO Ward when the CO once came in for his round. I proceeded to provide him with the medical history of the patients in a summarized format, the way I had been taught to, while in medical school. I was about half-way through the presentation of the second or maybe the third patient, when he suddenly stopped me cold in my tracks. Looking at me with his typical and famous penetrating stare shooting out of an impassive face, he said, *"I am not here to listen to such a sketchy account of your patients. You need to be more detailed and more elaborate. You need to tell me everything."* And so I did. Needless to say, I did grope and flounder at times, trying my best to pull out relevant and correct information from past memory. Overall, however, I believe I was able to put together a fairly decent performance because the CO wasn't too agitated when he finally left the ward that day.

For the next week's round, I made it a point to remember how the CO had wanted the cases presented. I spent a fair amount of time and effort in getting to know the cases to a much greater detail, so I could make an impression. This time I was ready for him. And when the CO's round began, I proceeded to provide him with a detailed account of the patients, the way he had wanted it. I plunged into the first case, and was only about a quarter-way through, when the CO threw his head back in a fashion so typical of him whenever he wanted to convey an expression of disgust, and said, *"Don't ramble on. I don't have time for that. Give me a short account."*

I stared dumbfound at him for a moment or two. The incredulous look on my face must have conveyed the impression that I had just been told that the first human to walk on the moon was Adolf Hitler! Didn't he remember what he had told me just a week ago? Or was all this being done on purpose? Was this a whimsical impulse of some sort, for playful entertainment, devised with the intent to harass? I guess I'll never know. But, whatever it was, in an instant I was demoted from having to steer the Titanic to rowing a dinghy, as I immediately switched modes from presenting a detailed account to providing only a summary. And that, I can assure you, was most unsettling and disconcerting. At the end of the day, however, I did manage to paddle furiously to the nearest shore before my dinghy sank!

The Cyclone from China

It was during the first six months of my Grading Course that an acrobatic team of the Peoples' Liberation Army (PLA) from the Peoples' Republic of China visited Bangladesh. They were to show-case their performances at different venues within Dhaka Cantonment. This was obviously a gesture aimed at bolstering the already-existing warm relationship between the armies of the two countries. With China being fairly well-known for its prowess in acrobatic performances, there was a certain degree of excited anticipation at the news of their arrival. The contingent of acrobatic performers was to have an almost equal mix of male and female performers, of which there were to be about forty in all.

Samina and I were called into the room of the Commanding Officer of CMH Dhaka one morning to be informed that we had been designated as the medical officers responsible for looking after the health of the acrobatic performers. Understandably, high-performance acrobatic acts, such as those performed by this team, were fraught with the danger of injuries, sometimes serious. Besides, other minor ailments could also occur from time to time, and which needed to be promptly looked into and treated. And since this contingent comprised of both male and female performers, it was important to have both a male and a female medical officer available for them. Samina was spared of her duties at CMH Dhaka, while I was taken off my Grading Course activities for about a week or so.

On the morning that the acrobatic team arrived, both Samina and I were at the airport, having travelled there in our ambulance. The Officiating Team, comprising of three Conducting Officers from the arms and other services, was responsible for ensuring that the programs of the acrobatic team went off without a glitch, and that their administrative, logistic and personal needs were properly looked after. Senior-most among them was a lieutenant colonel whose name I don't quite remember anymore, and two majors, Major Akbar and Major Humayun – those being their fictitious names.

Major Akbar was a most jovial individual with a constant smile on his face. With him, there was always this impression of constant fervor and activity, a good amount of which was not quite focused and which, therefore, often dissipated into thin air. Major Humayun, on the other hand, was quiet, somber and rather grounded.

It is at this point that I would like to get a pertinent fact cleared, and this relates to the status of medical officers in the context of an 'Officiating Team' of the armed forces.

"Officiating" has variously been defined in the dictionary as 'acting in an official capacity' or 'acting as an official in charge of something' or 'performing a duty' or 'holding the position, responsibility, or function of an official' etc.

With Samina and I having been given the responsibility of looking after the health needs of the acrobatic team and to advise and direct them in case of sickness, we were technically very much a part of the officiating team as well. Because, in the language of the dictionary, we were 'acting in the official capacity of medical officers' or 'acting as an official in charge of health' or 'performing the duties of a medical officer' or 'holding the position, responsibility and function of medical officers'. Whichever way one looks at it, it is beyond any reasonable doubt that we were technically – and logically – very much a part of the 'Officiating Team'.

However, the usual time-honored preference and practice was to ignore a fact such as this – that medical officers could also be a part of anything important, like being considered members of an 'Officiating Team'. And the incidents that follow will explain why, and how.

The initial greetings, introductions and exchange of pleasantries at the airport expressly excluded the presence there, of Samina and I, as the designated medical officers in charge of the acrobatic team. It was either by design or a failure to fulfill one's duty and responsibility that we were both relegated to the periphery of the flurry of activities by the other members of the officiating team. Thereafter, we all departed for the hotel where the team was to stay during their visit.

Our destination was the prestigious Hotel Purbani in the heart of Motijheel Commercial Area in downtown Dhaka. It was quite a crowd which gathered in the lobby as the formalities for checking in the guests were completed, and after which we all headed down towards the elevators. Included in the sea of moving people were the other members of the Officiating Team. Being as tall as he was, Major Akbar stood head and shoulders above everyone else – his height being further accentuated by the fact that he was in the midst of nothing less than a crowd of Chinese performers! I spotted him smack in the middle of the group, enthusiastic and animated as usual, as he moved toward the elevators with the crowd. Samina and I, in the meantime, brought up the rear.

Medical Officers always brought up the rear. While providing medical cover during Physical Efficiency Tests, the medical officer in the ambulance brought up the rear of those either running the two miles or walking the sixteen kilometers. In a convoy headed out to a firing range too, for example, the medical officer in his ambulance brought up the rear. But all that is understandable, because in such instances the medical officer was playing his designated role, which was to keep an eye on the physical well-being of everyone up ahead. Under the circumstances, being at the rear was obviously the best place to be.

But when the armed forces went about displaying its components and flaunting its prowess – as in ceremonial parades, for example – and the formations came in order of priority, the Army Medical Corps brought up the rear as well. Perhaps there was some sort of a 'martial wisdom' inherent in such a practice. Who knows? The Army Medical Corps was usually grouped with the Army Services Corps (ASC), the Ordnance Corps, the Education Corps, and the Corps of Electrical & Mechanical Engineering (EME) – none of which, with all due respect, were quite considered the elites of the forces.

So here too, Samina and I were bringing up the rear. It was as if after having spent so much time behind the rest of this army, the act of instinctively placing ourselves at the rear had become second nature. Moreover, had we, the doctors, been anywhere else, other than the rear of the group of people moving towards the elevators that day, we would probably have had to face a question like, *"Doctors, what are you doing here? Shouldn't you be at the back! What if someone behind you suddenly falls sick?"*

It was quite obvious that the members of the acrobatic team were being shown to their rooms upstairs. But at that point, we didn't know that there was also going to be a briefing session regarding the itinerary of the acrobatic team, and other logistic and administrative matters. Samina and I were approaching the elevator when I remember having seen the face of Major Akbar, from somewhere in the middle of the crowd of Chinese performers, turning around and yelling at us, *"Doctors, you stay outside and wait for me. I will be out soon."*

In hindsight, if this was a briefing for the team of acrobatic performers, then we, the medical officers, surely needed to be there, if not for anything else, but for the fact that we needed to be introduced as the designated medical officers so that members of the team at least knew who to go to, in the event of a medical need. And most of all, if this was a briefing then we, the medical officers, being an integral and essential part of the Officiating Team, also needed to be there.

But no, that was not how some of the great minds thought or acted. They perhaps always felt that doctors weren't as important, except when sickness arrived. And here too, we were being excluded from the briefing and literally being 'tossed out', perhaps because we were considered unimportant, and because no one was sick – at least, not yet.

Since we were expecting the rest of the officiating team to emerge at any moment, Samina and I went out to our ambulance and waited in it, instead of waiting for them in the hotel lobby. If this was about showing the members of the acrobatic team their rooms, we reasoned that it shouldn't take too long. But, we waited, and waited. An hour went by before we inferred that showing guests their rooms, irrespective of the number of guests, was not supposed to take that long.

And so I went back into the hotel and inquired of the concierge as to which floor the acrobatic performers had been accommodated. I took the elevator to that floor and after some exploring, pushed opened the door to what seemed like a conference room of some sort. It was largely empty, with Major Akbar sprawled on an ample sofa with a glass of juice in hand and chatting away with some the members of the acrobatic team. Logical inference told me that some sort of a briefing must have taken place in that hall-room, following which Major Akbar was lazing away, totally oblivious of our existence outside the hotel.

As I entered, Major Akbar sat bolt upright on the sofa, as if he had seen an apparition, and exclaimed, *"Doctor! You're still here! I thought you had left!"* He had apparently forgotten that he had asked us to wait outside, and that he would be coming out soon. This was ample proof of the fact that he was either seriously lacking in the faculty of mental retention, or that he didn't care, or maybe both. Whatever it was, I felt not only demeaned, but totally disgusted by this incident.

That afternoon, we drove from the hotel straight to the office of the Commanding Officer of CMH Dhaka and narrated what had happened. He was visibly perturbed, and more so when we mentioned it was going to be difficult for us to discharge our duties under the prevailing attitude of indifference and disrespect from the members of a team of which we were an integral part. The Commanding Officer sent us off saying he would look into the matter.

So, the next morning, when we went back to his office, the Commanding Officer informed us that he had had a talk with the lieutenant colonel in charge of the officiating team, who felt the incident was regrettable, and assured him that anything similar wouldn't happen again. Here was a rare instance of a senior medical corps officer having the courage and the assertiveness of standing up for what was right and proper, and demanding what was due.

That morning, when Samina and I returned to join everyone else, the leader of the Officiating Team informed us that he had had a conversation with the other members of the team about what had transpired the day before, and assured us that anything similar would not be repeated. He regretted the incident and apologized for it. His apologies were most courteously and graciously accepted.

The next week or so of our time with the team of acrobatic performers – as well as the other members of the Officiating Team – was pure bliss.

Besides the members of the Officiating Team being always very civil and cordial with us, the performances of the acrobatic team was a sight to behold wherever they performed. They seemed to know almost every act in the book, from the seemingly routine to the insanely difficult, and had those literally down to the tee. And they performed those acts with impeccable precision, immense confidence, and amazingly, with a constant smile on their faces.

We also soon discovered that almost each and every member of the acrobatic team were extremely friendly, frank, outgoing, and with a profound sense of humor. And it was amazing how they transformed themselves from this, in an instant, to being a totally focused persona of precision on the stage. Over time, a few friendships developed, more so between Samina and some of the female performers, who often also marveled at some of the traditional dresses Samina wore to their evening performances.

The author and Captain Samina with some members of the acrobatic team of the Peoples Liberation Army of China

Though the members of the acrobatic team were a bit wanting in proficiency in spoken English, we seemed comfortable, nonetheless, communicating in sign language, with a few basic English words thrown in here and there. The female members of the team often used a phrase *"Hai mei lee"*, specifically directed at Samina which, when translated meant, *"You are beautiful"* or thereabouts. Samina, for her part, was glad to have been taught that phrase because she then used it liberally and profusely for the female acrobatic performers too – and not without good reason!

Towards the end of their visit, the entire team of acrobatic performers, along with the members of the Officiating Team, was invited to a dinner hosted by the Chinese Embassy in Dhaka. I am yet to see tables at an official dinner spread out as elaborately, with dishes ranging from the most delectable to the most exotic. This also included the famed "thousand year egg" with the white of the chicken egg having turned into a tasty brown or green translucent gel-like covering. This, we were told, was a special dish made from eggs which had been processed in a particular way and kept buried underground for several months. In fact, every dish we tasted that evening had a touch of the extraordinary and a taste of the exceptional and remains, to this day, the most extraordinary official dinner I have ever had!

About ten days after their arrival, the team of acrobatic performers was at the airport again on their way back. Samina and I – and I am sure the rest of the members of the Officiating Team – bade them farewell with a heavy heart. And as we all waved them goodbye, we knew in the depths of our hearts that a few wonderful friendships had been forged over the last week or so, and that our Chinese friends were leaving behind their scintillating performances deeply etched in the memory of those who had seen them perform.

Samina and I returned home that day knowing that from the next day on, we would be back to doing what we have always been doing before our friends from China had arrived – Samina having to return to her work at CMH Dhaka, and I back to my Grading Course.

Duty Medical Officer: A Medley of Miseries

"Bad is never good until worse happens."
– Danish Proverb

From the day that we were at CMH Dhaka for our Grading Course we had to perform the duties of a DMO (Duty Medical Officer) from 2 p.m. of one day to 7:30 a.m. of the next. On holidays, however, it was much longer – a 12-hour duty starting at 7:30 in the morning of one day, all the way through to 7:30 a.m. of the next.

During the period of duty, a DMO had to be stationed in the MI (Medical Inspection) Room where he acted as an emergency medical officer of sorts. He had to an make initial assessment of all emergency cases reporting to the MI Room during that period, institute their initial treatment, arrange to have such patients admitted to the appropriate ward, and if necessary, organize to have the relevant specialist brought to the hospital to attend to those cases. The DMO also had to visit and treat admitted critical cases whenever called upon by the ward duty nurses or the medical assistants to do so and if need be, arrange to have the concerned specialist brought, for further care of that patient.

All this looked very prim, proper and impressive from the outside, and was inspiring up to a certain point. Chaos set in when a disproportionately overwhelming number of patients and other unnecessary and superfluous activities for the DMO were brought in to bear upon the overall scenario. That was when the whole system fell apart at its seams, and for which the quality of patient care, and therefore the patients, suffered.

To begin with, besides the basic duties of assessing, admitting and instituting treatment for emergency cases, the DMO also had to keep track of and co-ordinate the movement of all the vehicles in the hospital, especially those meant to bring specialists over whenever their services were required. Usually, ambulances were sent out for the purpose, but the number of those was severely limited. To make matters worse, not all were in good working order either. So, military Jeeps and 'staff cars' – that is, cars belonging to officers of the rank of Brigadier-General and above – and also parked in the hospital garage, had to be drafted in to cope with the mounting load. Unfortunately, even that did not seem to be adequate at times.

And as if all this was not quite enough, vehicles being sent out to fetch the specialists sometimes needed to be prioritized, more on the basis of the rank of the specialist being called in, rather than on the seriousness of the illness – unless of course, it was a life-threatening situation. Some senior specialists seemed rather reluctant to have to wait any longer than what their patience or seniority would allow. It was as if this hospital was a parade ground where the motions of rank and status were being played out rather meticulously and ruthlessly, regardless of the amount of human suffering. A patient with a more serious illness would sometimes have to wait because the specialist being brought in for him or her was junior to another specialist coming in for a less serious case.

It does not take a genius to infer that having only one emergency medical officer in a hospital with about 600 – 700 patients at any given time was not only being imprudent on the part of the authorities, but that it was being downright callous as well. I am not quite aware of the present-day situation, but the authorities back then perhaps felt that that was enough for a hospital this large to be looked after quite adequately and effectively. In my opinion, this was obviously a case of either a misplaced confidence on the abilities of the Duty Medical Officer, or an open disregard for the loss of lives through inadequacy of manpower or divided medical attention.

Whatever may have been the reason, it was quite obvious that the odd disasters and tragedies which sometimes resulted from a peculiar approach to hospital management and a bizarre concept of patient care did not seem to bother most people. And the reason for that was quite simple. Somewhere within the pages of certain trusted manuals lay a solution with the promise and the potential of ensuring that the establishment's reputation, despite the number of casualties sustained, would not be tarnished in any way. Interestingly and regrettably, the doctors somehow seemed to be the key to that 'magic solution' – and I shall soon explain how and why.

Treating the Healthy

> *"We are too busy mopping the floor to turn off the faucet." - Anonymous*

CMH Dhaka was the only military hospital in the capital region.

It therefore had to handle the sick pouring out of two army divisions, one Logistic Area, the headquarters of the Army, Navy and Air Force combined, and all ancillary civilian installations. Being the largest military hospital in the country, it naturally assumed the distinction of being a teaching and a referral hospital as well. This meant that the sick and the infirm from all the other military hospitals of the country which were without adequate facilities or expertise were constantly being sent over to this hospital.

The burden of receiving such referral cases fell on the lone DMO, since for some uncanny reason, most arrived after 2 pm, which was the start of the DMO's duty period on a weekday. And if the referred case required immediate medical attention, it obviously took precedence over most others. On the other hand, if it was a chronic – and hence a complicated – case, the DMO needed to spend a fair amount of time going through the accompanying massive and voluminous case notes to determine what to do with that patient. However, none of these really were tasks beyond the abilities of the DMO. And, regardless of when the cases arrived or what needed to be done with them, that was not the crux of the problem.

The problem lay elsewhere. The problem lay where the administration didn't seem to want to look. And that problem threatened to contradict all laws of patient care, the very concept of hospital administration, and the rules of administrative obligations.

And allow me to explain how.

To begin with, the services of the MI Room – and hence of the DMO – were primarily meant for emergency cases only. Obviously, chronic cases, meaning those with symptoms not as intense or as debilitating, and which had existed for more than twenty four hours, had no place in the MI Room after 2 pm. Obviously, those cases could very well have reported to either the MI Room or to the respective out-patient departments before 2 pm, when the hospital was running at full strength. Nevertheless, it was after 2 pm that the MI Room seemed to turn into a sort of out-patient clinic.

All hell broke loose every afternoon as innumerable *people* – and not necessarily *patients* – lined up outside the MI Room for a consultation with the DMO much before his arrival. Some days, it was total pandemonium of the kind usually witnessed at a wet market. Quite amazingly, the complaints of the majority were nowhere near to deserving any emergency attention at all. At the risk of sounding cynical I will have to admit that there were times, looking at the line of people waiting for consultation, I felt that I had rarely seen a larger gathering of healthier individuals.

This is not to say, however, that none had an ailment worth a consultation. But frankly, the number of such was pitifully few. In my personal experience, I can say with conviction that only one, or at the most two, in about ten had any complaint worth a trip to the MI Room. As for the rest, they were either soldiers looking for a couple of days of rest on the pretense of a physical indisposition or, surprisingly, waves of members of soldiers' families, seemingly making this trip as part of an evening recreational activity.

The volume of such family members lining up outside the MI Room would typically swell considerably between the hours of 4 and 6 pm. It was well-known – though not quite openly expressed – that they were here at this time and not during regular hospital hours because they either had certain social or domestic responsibilities to take care of during the day, or because they felt that that was their time for a breath of fresh air. And there seemed to be no better place than the CMH for that, with its surrounding gardens and grounds, easily qualifying as the focal point for evening social gatherings.

For such people, the cherry on top was the *free* medical consultation and *free* medications available at only an arm's length. All that they really needed to do was saunter in at the slightest urge for medical attention and for the most trivial of complaints. And all this, at a time and at a place designated for emergency cases only, and especially when the lone DMO was literally on a 'survival mode'! More importantly, these people came well-armed with the knowledge that their mere presence in the MI Room would not only ensure that they would be attended to, but that they would surely be able to leave with an assortment of medications to fill their medicine cabinets, which were perhaps already overflowing.

Even if the DMO were to suspect such cases to be physically fit and healthy, he nevertheless had to take a meaningful medical history and carry out all necessary physical examinations before coming to such a conclusion. Understandably, doctors are bound by the Oath of Hippocrates to provide undivided and unmitigated attention to any individual reporting to him or her with either a physical or a mental complaint. And seemingly, such individuals, the setup, and the system were taking full advantage of both a divine doctrine and a host of other professional moral obligations.

This, unfortunately, kept the DMO otherwise involved for a significant amount of time, thereby interfering considerably with better care of the genuine cases requiring more of his attention. The misfortune and tragedy of being the cogs and wheels of an institutional system blinded by an attitude of indifference to what was right and proper, and driven by a desire for popularity was that even when deemed fit, such individuals could not be declared fit. Because doing so would mean going against certain implicit laid-down rules which, though not quite written in stone, were most certainly being waved at our faces through various implied undertones.

I have to admit of my own guilt as well, for having prescribed medications to apparently fit and healthy individuals. But it was not as if I was sitting there and partaking to such a vile and distasteful practice very willingly or very gladly. We seemed to be under a strange and intangible duress to do so. Some sort of a weird and unseen – yet oddly palpable – pressure emanating from somewhere deep within the Corridors of Power seemed to have a stranglehold over our thought processes and on our decision-making abilities. This consequently led to the universal assumption that since an individual, whether sick or not, had undertaken the trip to the MI Room, complete and comprehensive medical attention ought to be extended, and all necessary medications provided. And, worst of all, some in the higher echelon rather explicitly indicated that such a practice had their whole-hearted approval. And, in my opinion, this probably stemmed from the endeavors of some in making themselves popular among the rank and file – and beyond.

Interestingly, the root cause which led to such a high volume of attendance in the MI Room lay in the fact that medical consultations, investigations, dispensation of medication, and all forms of treatment were absolutely free for anyone entitled to receive medical treatment in any military hospital. Obviously, such a concept and practice was both expensive and wasteful. It led to a lack of consideration for the resources placed at the disposal of those who exploited the system. The matter of entitlement to free medical treatment in military hospitals will be discussed at length in a later section of this book.

So therefore, besides attending to the real emergency cases, a DMO, as stated earlier, also had to spend – or rather waste – a good amount of time looking into the needs of those who had reported to the MI Room on the pretense of an illness. He also had to complete the admission formalities for the patients transferred from other military hospitals as well as those advised admission from the various Out-Patient Departments of the hospital during regular hospital hours. And this was not taking into account the admission formalities of those patients that the DMO himself had admitted into the hospital. Added to all this was also the obligation of being present in person and doing the needful whenever a critical case, anywhere in the hospital, took a turn for the worse. And as if all this was not enough, the DMO also had to prioritize calls for a specialist while maintaining a critical, and sometimes tricky, balance between the severity of the case and the seniority of the specialist concerned.

When we were trainees at CMH Dhaka, the DMOs were also responsible for cases in the Intensive Care Unit and the Post-operative Ward, for which we stretched our physical abilities beyond limits to ensure that no mishaps occurred. But that, I always felt, was total insanity in terms of appropriate medical attention and proper patient care. More importantly however, it was indicative of an attitude of arrogance and recklessness on the part of some policymakers. But that, of course, was the rightful prerogative of the mighty and the mindless with the privileged license to justify the bizarre, and indemnify the distorted, in order to suit their needs and feed their vagaries.

And while the travesty of the DMO duty continued, something else arrived at the door of the DMO in the form of an arrogant and over-bearing attitude born of seniority.

Needless to say, the "DMO applecart", if you will, was already lying on its side, much like a stage coach in the Wild West overrun by warring Native Americans. All that remained now, in order to obliterate the last vestiges of any rationality and sanity, was for the tribal chief to come along and trample all over the cart's remnants. And indeed, he came – in the form of an officer senior in rank to the DMO!

It was a flagrant and perhaps a widespread – though erroneous – assumption of some that seniority gave an individual the license to bend rules.

There were times, therefore, that an officer coming in as a patient would discover, perhaps to his immense satisfaction, that the DMO was junior to him by rank. This individual would then not hesitate to saunter into the DMO's rest room either in the middle of the DMO's meal, or during his few moments of rest, instead of waiting in the designated consultation room – which would have been the appropriate thing to do. Through this inconsiderate and thoughtless act of his, this senior officer was obviously indicating his desire to be attended to immediately. The fact that he was probably jumping the line, and putting himself ahead of some other cases with ailments more serious than his, was perhaps the least of his concerns.

In my opinion, such an insolent attitude and discourteous behavior would seem have stemmed from a total disregard for others, and a malicious disrespect for the DMO, and everything that the DMO represented. Moreover, such people were also perhaps very quick to conclude that this single snapshot of the DMO in his rest room was symbolic of his overall activity as the Duty Medical Officer. Little did they realize that if this army was waging any war, that war was being waged in its hospitals and MI Rooms, and nowhere else. All those who harbored any disdain for what the DMO did and represented, would probably have left with a vastly different opinion if only they had the patience, the stamina and the courage to spend some time with the DMO during his period of duty, and experience all that he went through.

The medical authorities, however, did try to make life somewhat easier for the DMO during his period of duty by trying to bring about certain improvements in the DMO's rest room.

When I started my duties as a DMO at CMH Dhaka, the MI Room was a rather dilapidated tin-roofed structure, and the amenities in the DMOs rest room were most basic. Soon after, however, the MI Room and the OPD complexes received a make-over with newer structures replacing the ramshackle tin-roofed building. Nevertheless, the amenities in the DMO's rest room continued to be rather rudimentary. In terms of what could be provided for the comfort of the DMO, the authorities never actually bothered to venture beyond sanctioned supplies and stringent regulations. Unfortunately therefore, the bed continued to be as basic, the mattress as unyielding, the bed-sheets as rough, and the chairs as pedestrian and uncomfortable as always.

Surprisingly, occasional suggestions made by the DMOs with regards to improvements in the most basic comforts during the period of their duty went unheeded by the hospital authorities. It seemed as if the needs of the DMO lay somewhere out of sight of the true medical agenda. This, despite the fact that the DMOs actually were the ones who, almost single-handedly, kept this humongous hospital functional after the regular hospital hours, while the rest of the world, including the administrators themselves, relaxed and reposed through the night. In my personal opinion, such a wanton disregard for the comforts – and discomforts – of a DMO clearly displayed the administration's viewpoint, if I may, that a DMO was perhaps comparable to some lowly breed of a low-maintenance 'beast of burden'.

That, at least, was the overall impression I got of the worth of a DMO in the eyes of the administration, back in the day when I was a trainee at CMH Dhaka. I will admit, however, that I am not aware of the working conditions of the DMOs these days, either at CMH Dhaka or at any other military hospital. If perchance it has improved, it will certainly stand out as a refreshing step in the right direction.

The only time, back then, when an upgrade of any significance was seen of the DMO's rest room was when a very senior officer from the high offices – and not belonging to the medical corps – had wandered into it one day, and was apparently appalled at what he saw. Even so, I found it rather perplexing as to how the foggiest television sets and the noisiest air conditioners of the hospital somehow always made their way into the DMO's rest room, and stayed there as their final resting place.

However, all said and done, the DMO did eventually survive the ordeal and the agony of his duty, the unabated war of nerves, the constant race against time, the raw weight of numbers, the desperate attempts at prolonging life, the irks and the quirks of those leaning on him by weight of rank and, at the end of it all, came out victorious – albeit totally drained, fatigued and exhausted – both physically and mentally.

Anywhere else in the world, far less than this would easily have qualified for a full day of rest and recuperation. But this was not how things were done here.

The DMO had to be back in the hospital within two hours of having bathed, rested, eaten and dressed, and get busy with his hospital duties. Amazingly, there seemed to be no connection, whatsoever, between a hectic, demanding and strenuous DMO duty and then having to return to one's routine hospital activities in just a couple of hours. Any lingering tiredness or fatigue resulting from a lack of proper rest was not to cloud the judgment of a clinician or of a surgeon, and cause him to err – ever. And if perchance it did, the lifeless pages of the judicial manuals were always there to decide what was right and what was wrong, and conveniently setting things right.

A rather amusing spin-off of this was played out regularly on the morning after having participated in the bi-annual Physical Efficiency Test (PET).

This was a test, made compulsory for all officers, and held every six months to prove they were always at the peak of physical efficiency. The test was conducted on two consecutive mornings, and it commenced long before sunrise on each occasion. On the first morning, the officers had to run two miles in full battle gear, following which they needed to climb over a six feet wall, jump across a six feet ditch, clamber across a horizontal rope about twenty feet long and hanging about ten feet above the ground, finally ending with swimming. On the second morning, the officers had to walk sixteen kilometers in full battle gear.

The point I am trying to make has nothing to do with the fact that after the PET I had to be back at the hospital within two hours and be ready to pursue my profession with every fiber and sinew of my body screaming with pain. The point I am actually trying to make has to do with the bewildering and rather amusing fact that my colleagues from the non-medical units –supposedly the tough and resilient ones – who were with me at the same PET that morning were to be seen limping into my consultation room for my recommendation to be given the day off for their bodily pains. If my own pains were screaming before, they were wailing now at my own sorrowful misfortune of being imprisoned both within the ethics of my profession and the dispassionate mindset of this institution and, therefore, not being able to walk away from either my surgeries or the deluge of patients waiting outside my room for consultation.

Guilty, until proven guilty

> *"There is a higher court than courts of justice, and that is the court of conscience."*
> *- Mahatma Gandhi*

The periodic inadequacy of the medical functionary in accomplishing a medically-desired outcome in patient care, including of that during the period of DMO duty, was often a cause of considerable concern and anguish, at least for me.

Obviously, all this was the result of a lack of resources and a dearth of manpower. Added too, were certain antiquated and ineffective practices, as well as the habitual single-minded capriciousness and obstinacy of some at the helm. Those of us who provided the services eventually reached a point where we were literally imploring the authorities to revisit the principles and practices that would felicitate an unhindered and unencumbered functioning of a hospital as big and as busy as CMH Dhaka. With regards to the DMO duty in particular, we pointed out that there was a genuine and urgent need to either redefine its functional concept and criteria, or to simply increase the number of medical officers available to perform the duties of a DMO.

Problems, difficulties, inadequacies and shortages were all regularly being mentioned in the DMO's Report, which had to be made at the end of a DMO duty period. But I hardly know of a single instance when a DMO had been called in to discuss matters mentioned in those reports, and to look for viable solutions. However, it is not that the DMOs were never ever summoned. They were. But that was only to discuss complaints of varying magnitudes made by those whose expectations of this hospital were unrealistically and disproportionately over-inflated.

However, I have often wondered why the Offices seemed so neglectful of the problems and difficulties faced by the personnel of this hospital, including those by the DMO. And after much introspection I was rather compelled to conclude that the tools to deal with the adverse medical outcomes of a somewhat flawed concept and a pretty inefficacious system were indeed available.

Though quite cleverly guised as a measure which appeared to be logical and appropriate to the casual on-looker, in reality, it was a procedure and a practice that was inherently prejudiced and unfair from the perspective of anyone with a shred of justice and fairness in their conscience.

What I am about to say in this regard is my personal opinion. There may be some inclined to disagree with my viewpoints – and they are at complete liberty of doing so. I would like to remind my readers that it was mentioned at the very outset of this narrative that it is entirely up to them – at least to some – to not consider my viewpoints as being universally believed or accepted. Skeptics have the license to consider this as nothing more than a one-sided diatribe of speculative conjectures.

On the same note, I would like to point out to my readers that the observations and opinions in this narrative are of an individual who has had to live through a system, while serving to the best of his abilities regardless of griefs and grievances. And, by the same token that I have always strived to uphold the worth of the establishment that I served, I draw my conclusions with a clear conscience and an unbiased mindset.

And that applies to all that have been narrated till now, and all that is to come after.

It was a rather universal assumption within the sphere of influence, concern and control that irrespective of the cause of a medical mishap, as long as the medical institution, including the treating doctor, was agreed upon to have erred, everyone would feel reassured and satisfied that the cause had been correctly identified and that the right decision had been taken.

Perhaps it was in the profound wisdom of some to assume that that would succeed in putting an end to hospital casualties. But sadly, it succeeded in only making matters worse. Because when the burden of blame, whether substantiated or not, repeatedly falls on a particular class or group, it compromises performance, instills repugnance and reluctance, and culminates into a considerable lack of self-confidence. The possibility that either a lack of manpower, resources, or situations beyond human abilities could have led to a grievous outcome was hardly ever taken into cognizance. This, to me, seemed like an easy and convenient way out of a situation which excused those responsible, from examining and correcting the actual reason which sometimes rendered a hospital so grossly and dangerously ineffective, and so miserably unproductive.

To consider a case in point, this hospital almost always had anywhere between 5-8 patients in the "Seriously Ill List" or "Dangerously Ill List" (commonly referred to as SIL or DIL), and could therefore easily have more than one emergency related to these patients arising at the same time. For the sake of argument, let us assume that one – only one, not two – out of all the SIL or DIL cases suddenly took a turn for the worse. With the DMO already immersed in a plethora of responsibilities in the MI Room, how could he be expected to be at two places at the same time?

However, some were brazen enough to think that that was somehow possible. This was primarily because any discomfort on the part of any patient, or worse still, any loss of life, could easily and conveniently be dealt with by a procedure which often exercised its inherent authoritative clout to discredit the medical institution or its personnel, basically with the intent to mitigate assigned responsibility and to deflect criticism.

It always seemed to me that the premise of the procedure of inquiry into matters dealing with medical mishaps was based on the blatant, biased and a tacit assumption that the doctor was at fault, be that a fact or not. And, unfortunately, when any procedure begins with a blind assertion of culpability of any professional entity, and then makes its way through a collective paranoia for seeking errors in their proficiency, efficiency and judgment, not many are expected to be left standing after the storm passes.

Hardly ever have I witnessed a doctor come out of such an exercise without a scratch, whether or not they were at fault. A 'forfeiture of seniority' or at least a 'reprimand', both affecting future promotions and postings, were often kept handy to be readily meted out. That way, everyone involved – everyone, except the unfortunate accused – could come away with the satisfaction that the right step had been taken and that justice had prevailed. But unfortunately, some people failed to examine other aspects that could also have been intimately associated with such an incident, and which could have been a significant contributor to the outcome. And in failing to do so, they also failed to see the impropriety and the injustice embedded in such a practice.

It is quite possible that certain preconceived misconceptions, premature inferences and biased assumptions on the part of some involved in the procedure actually stifled it from progressing to a point where the very need for such an exercise could be properly addressed. I say this because, if properly addressed, any failings or shortcomings, either of the treating doctors', of the medical authorities or of the establishment's itself, could easily have been detected, and corrective measures taken. But most unfortunately, some were seemingly unwilling to view matters from such a perspective. Rather, with the underpinnings of an allegedly prejudiced and a presumptuous mindset setting the tone to the proceedings, it sometimes nudged the process down slippery slopes to flawed and biased conclusions. And under the circumstances, it would be unfair to blame those who could be somewhat inclined to actually suspect and question the accuracy, adequacy, transparency and legitimacy of a process in which facts and figures were sometimes dispatched to irrelevance, and truth often banished to worthlessness.

It would certainly not have been necessary to have this discourse had there been a degree of objectivity and neutrality evident in the process and which, therefore, would have given it a stamp of credibility and reliability. But instead, in keeping with the preferences of some, the procedure mostly seemed to churn out carbon-copy verdicts, with no consideration to truth, justice and fairness.

The Evils of Entitlement

> *"Everything we get, outside of the free gifts of nature, must in some way be paid for." – Henry Hazlitt in: Economics in One Lesson*

Entitlement to treatment at a military hospital was more or less a sword with two edges.

One edge sculpted what was right and proper, insofar as the humanitarian need for treatment was concerned. The other edge, however, ruthlessly and dispassionately decimated whatever was right and proper, in terms of the concept and the mode of its delivery. Some in positions from where they could dictate terms used both the edges with authoritarian flair and carefree callousness to carve out a self-gratifying status quo. And that was because their placements gave them the privilege and the prerogative to do so.

And in case you're wondering how, let me to explain.

Personnel of all ranks in the armed forces, including their wives and children, were entitled to treatment at a military hospital irrespective of the nature of the illness or of its duration. Treatment was also provided to all civilians in military installations who were receiving pay from the armed forces budget, and to servants and maid servants of all officers.

This encompassed the treatment for everything from abscess to asthma, and from corn to cancer, mostly without any limits to the expenses involved. The element of contention here is not that all such treatments were made available, but that those were also provided *absolutely free of cost.* At this point, I have no intention of getting into the complex implications and far-reaching consequences that such an expenditure was supposed to have on the meager resources – financial or otherwise – of the establishment itself, because that is far beyond the scope and intent of this book. However, what really concerned me, and which I am obligated to discuss, was the impact it had on the resources and manpower management of the medical functionary.

Generally speaking, when anything is provided free of cost, two things are bound to happen.

Firstly, heads turn, and people seem interested. Soon there is a curious group, followed by a crowd, which finally culminates into a mob. It could be considered as something analogous to a sale event where products are given away free of cost, instead of being sold merely at a discounted price. Suffice it to say that such a situation is bound to cause a riot. And, that was exactly what happened in this hospital. Resources were stretched and manpower was overwhelmed by those wanting a slice of the incredible pie. But when a hospital has to provide treatment to more patients than it is capable of handling, the quality of patient care obviously falls below expected levels. Services, however excellent or exceptional, are reduced to pedestrian quality, and personnel, however skilled or qualified, are made to look most ordinary.

That unfortunately, was the case – at least with CMH Dhaka.

The second thing which happens when anything is offered free of cost is a natural inclination to view it as being of an inferior quality. And that was exactly the attitude of most who walked in through the doors of this hospital, and for which they could hardly be blamed. The sad truth was that the quality of service did fall below expected levels, singularly from the sheer weight of numbers. With the number of patients steadily exceeding the scope and ability of this hospital, that much of attention and care had to be shaved off of every other patient – even the most deserving – whether the personnel or the patients liked it or not. The only thing which kept this hospital on its feet, however, was the fact that countless little miracles were taking place within its four walls on a daily basis. And those miracles were certainly not heaven-sent. They were born out of the strength, stamina and sweat of those who worked in it.

Not surprisingly therefore, the numbers, charts and graphs depicting the performances of this hospital, which adorned the walls of some high offices, did look very impressive indeed. The frequent proud and satisfied expansive waves of the hand at the striking and imposing accomplishments hanging on the walls hardly ever took into account the toil and turmoil behind them. What mattered more, perhaps, was that "the ship" was afloat, and therefore everything was in good order. Despite the fact that some who steered this ship from high above in the bridge were well aware of the appalling situation deep within its hull, the end always seemed to justify the means. It was the privilege and the prerogative of the ship's *Captain and his coterie* to decide not to notice – and this, they exercised with carefree abandon. After all, if one chooses not to see or to hear, then unjustified, irrational and reckless whims can easily be imposed to appease wanton desires, irrepressible urges and selfish dreams.

At this point, I would like to clarify that the ship's 'Captain and his coterie' is a collective term denoting only certain individuals in any establishment, who have the power and the privilege of calling the shots by virtue of their relatively elevated ranks and appointments.

Such individuals seemingly forget the sacred principles of proper governance and ignore the true spirit of fair judgment. Rather, they always seem inclined to re-arranging components around them into a special apparatus meant only to serve certain personal agendas and fulfill certain egotistic urges. They devalue the worth of any establishment with their prejudicial mindset and parochial posture. They, in my opinion, are the few exceptions – the 'worms' within an otherwise perfect apple. Though such individuals are plentiful in this world, and are to be found in any organization or establishment, in the context of the establishment in question, their existence hurt it badly.

This is not to say, however, that there aren't any in this or in any other organization or establishment who display outstanding devotion, dignity and discipline at all times. They are the ones who, thankfully, hold an establishment together through their untiring efforts and genuine commitment to uphold all that the establishment stands for. They have my deepest respect, and deserve my sincerest praise.

In the context of the existing state of affairs, which was already teetering on the edge of agony and just about waiting to fall into a chasm of caustic comedy, it did not seem to be quite enough for the ship's *Captain and his coterie* to care that the medical institution was already bent over under the burden of the entitled patients. Gripped by yet another of their extravagant and mindless desires and an unrestrained urge, they decided to take the matter a step further – and went ahead, rather blindly, and lengthened the list of those entitled to treatment at a military hospital.

This new category was given a somewhat perplexing title of "Civilian Non-Entitled" – or CNE – patients. In a strict sense, and in the context of the acronym and its description, these patients were 'civilians', and 'not entitled' to treatment at a military hospital. Technically therefore, they had no place at a CMH. Nevertheless, I watched with exasperated resignation as, yet once again, attention was drawn away from what mattered more, to what some thought should matter.

To me, it all seemed like an attempt at bolstering public relations, enhancing personal eminence, and ensuring permanence of official status for a select and important few. Apparently, the back-breaking efforts of the medical personnel, who were made to toil below the waterline in order make such an arrangement work, were of no relevance or consequence in the grand scheme of things.

Personalities of national importance, ministers and their deputies, members of parliament, individuals of foreign missions, secretaries of most ranks, political heavyweights and the likes were now not only knocking at the hospital door, they were literally tearing it down. To be pampered at a fraction of the cost in one of the best hospitals in the country in terms of cleanliness, discipline and quality of patient care was like the utopia of medical attention for such people.

Personally speaking, I didn't care much whether or not this military hospital was being converted to a 'VIP hospital' of sorts. What mattered more to me, at that point, was that neither the manpower nor the material resources at this hospital were adequate enough to be able to cope adequately with the added load.

But, that was beside the point, of course, since such an arrangement paid dividends. The mighty and the powerful from both sides were now brushing shoulders with each other. So obviously, the ship was now sailing full steam towards promising horizons and land of extraordinary opportunities, while those deep within its hull were being forced to feed the fire with just about the last ounce of their remaining strength.

Soon thereafter, bolstered by what may have seemed like a considerably 'useful' strategy, it was decided that 'brilliance' be flaunted once again by making another port of call – this time, at the 'Temple of Belligerence'. The definition of CNE was again extended, and now it was made to include the parents and siblings of Officers and of their wives. Suffice it to say that this too was done without taking into cognizance the capabilities and the resources at the hospital's disposal, which was pathetic at best and woefully meager, to say the least.

To be fairly honest, this was to be expected. The medical authorities, who actually had it within their rights and their responsibilities to impose restrictions on the over-indulgence of some in the higher offices vis-à-vis the capabilities of the medical institution, amazingly sat through the entire process, quietly chewing their cud. Obviously therefore, left to their own whims and wantonness, those in the ship's bridge did what their urges instigated them to do.

A hospital which was already struggling to provide the most rudimentary care to its soldiers by being burdened with the first category of CNE patients was now being handed yet another class of CNE patients to deal with. Once that floodgate was thrown open, anyone and everyone who happened to be hanging from any point of a genealogical tree – and sometimes even beyond – began showing up at the gates. Commotion gave way to pandemonium, and chaos to total anarchy. If things were hectic before, it was a nightmare now. If a crowd could be described as a large, definable group, we were now dealing with a mob, riotous at that, which was as difficult to define as it was overwhelming to handle.

It was at that point, while I was a trainee in Surgery at CMH Dhaka, that my elder brother required a surgery on his gallbladder. I had both observed and assisted one of the senior-most surgeons during his surgeries, and therefore felt I could trust him with the surgery on my brother's gallbladder. I also wanted the surgery to be done at CMH Dhaka, with my brother being admitted as a CNE patient, since according to the most recent rules, siblings of army officers could be admitted as such. What I needed next was permission from the Commanding Officer who, after having signed the papers, would send those off to the higher offices for final approval.

I was in his office one morning with the papers for him to sign, when the very first question he asked me was, "Who is performing the surgery?" And when I told him who it was, the immediate curt reply was, "Sorry, no. You cannot have it done here." And, then without even consulting the admission status of the hospital, he added, "We don't have room for any more CNE patients. Take him elsewhere."

Standing there, beside the massive glass-top table of the Commanding Officer, I felt my shoulders drooping with disappointment. Right then, I must have been the personification of despair, dejection, and to a certain extent, discontent. Here I was, an officer who was training to be a Specialist in Surgery, and my brother was being refused admission at CMH Dhaka when, by all measure of the existing rules and regulations, he could very well have been. My brother was being refused admission because of the non-availability of CNE beds in the hospital, whereas I knew that other CNE patients had been admitted the day before, as well as the day after. I know this because I was curious, and had gone down to the Admissions Section a day or two later to confirm my suspicions. It is my firm belief to this day, as it was then, that my brother had been refused admission because a peculiar process of patronage, prejudice and preference had suddenly been set into motion through the revelation of who would be performing the surgery.

I will not make a secret of the fact that some conflicts and collusions within the corps often underpinned schism and discord beneath the surface of apparent civility, cordiality and orderly conduct. From that standpoint, I would perhaps have encountered a much more accommodating attitude had I chosen a different surgeon – a surgeon perhaps more 'acceptable' to the Commanding Officer. Nevertheless, the surgery was eventually carried out a couple of days later at a nearby civilian hospital, and it went well.

Another thing that made the whole matter of treatment at a military hospital an exhibition of deceit and deception was the 'fabrication of entitlement' by those who chose to exploit it at the expense of their own conscience and dignity.

And this is how it happened.

There have been instances when an individual, somewhat distantly related to an officer – or perhaps not even – have been admitted for treatment at a military hospital as a CNE patient. They were admitted as an officer's brother, sister, servant or maid-servant, because such patients carried with them a so-called 'certificate' saying so. Interestingly, such 'certificates' could be issued by the concerned officer himself, without it being subjected to any verification regarding the authenticity of the declaration being made in it. Having done my share of DMO duties, I have had a front-row view of such improprieties and indecencies, regardless of what some may be inclined to say at this point. Obviously, a system so full of loopholes – be those intentional or otherwise – was always destined to suffer both at the hands of individuals full of guile and greed, and an arrangement geared to waste.

Just so matters assumed a semblance of fairness and propriety, the CNE patients were charged a fee for services rendered, which was clearly nominal compared to what they would have had to pay at any civilian hospital or clinic. The beneficiaries of such remunerations were the coffers of the establishment, the hospital, its allied pathology institute, and specialists of the rank of lieutenant colonel and above. Understandably, where it concerned such specialists, it seemed to instill in them a more-than-eager willingness to entertain the CNE patients – perhaps a trifle more than for whom this hospital was actually built. Unfortunately therefore, junior specialists and trainees like us found ourselves having to struggle under the extra weight of responsibilities, since the beneficiaries of the 'CNE arrangement' – aka the senior specialists – often seemed to drift towards their CNE 'benefactors' like bees attracted to nectar.

So, here was this proverbial camel, standing unperturbed in the desert heat, as its masters loaded whatever they pleased on to its back. But however much was loaded, the trusting camel always assumed that its masters would have the good sense of at least not loading the infamous 'last straw'.

But, what most of us do not realize is that the concept of the 'last straw' has deliberately been erased from the so-called rules of procedure and conduct of certain organizations and establishments. This has perhaps been done on the premise that if the 'last straw' concept existed, and was perchance reached, it was more than likely to evolve into the next stage – rebellion and mutiny.

The Prerogatives of Power

> *"Nearly all men can stand adversity, but if you want to test a man's character, give him power." – Abraham Lincoln*

I would like to round this chapter off by momentarily straying to another matter I have always felt was regrettable and, in a way, reprehensible, and therefore feel that it deserves a place in this book in its own right and merit. It deserves a place because, at times, the individual progress of officers in certain organizations and establishments seem not to be measured in terms of how useful they are for the establishment, but by how useful they are, for some in positions of power.

We all know of how a handful few at the top in such organizations usually reserve the right to chart a subordinate's career, posting and promotion. Problems arise when a select few – enticed into playing god – exercise that right without being answerable either to the system or to their own conscience. Predictably therefore, it is not uncommon to come across instances where some careers have been influenced either by personal annoyances, collective displeasures, or as an expression of gratitude for certain favors received.

And I am sure that a good number of individuals belonging to such establishments and organizations would unhesitatingly agree with such an assertion, be that implicitly or explicitly, because in all probability the self-styled gods of egocentric indulgence had played with their fate and fortune at some stage of their careers. I feel it is my moral obligation, therefore, to denounce such a practice – be it in any organization – because it comes with the distinct possibility of a lackluster organizational growth and a compromised efficacy of its personnel. Surprisingly however, that was a risk some seemed more than willing to take, perhaps because doing so actually took the fangs out of the tiger, and

domesticated it for the services of those who stood to gain from the resulting status quo.
To the good number of such unfortunate individuals, regardless of which establishment they belong to, who have either had to tolerate the ignominy of such a practice, or have had to suffer its heart-wrenching consequences, I say this: To have withstood the storm with indomitable courage and tolerance, and with unflinching faith in yourselves, you have emerged a better, greater and mightier person than those who denied you what you so rightfully deserved.

In my case, by not being able to say or do whatever went against my taste and sense of propriety, I found myself steadily falling out of grace with some who held the reins. Hard work sometimes went unnoticed, sincerity often went unappreciated and good performances were at times ignored – evident more so during my surgical training. Naturally, therefore, I seemed to be under the assumption that I was perhaps not performing to expected levels, and so kept trying harder. But, I consistently noticed accolades, appreciation and recognition going elsewhere, where I least expected those to go. And after a while, it seemed as if I was living a life on one side of a transparent wall, across which I could see the world of my dreams, but which I was unable to breach. And that was presumably because I actually totally out of synch with the real world.

I was soon to learn that going forward entailed more than just sincere commitment, hard work and professional excellence. And the eventual realization that the yardstick of progress and success could also be measured by parameters other than sincerity, diligence and merit, eventually turned into a waking nightmare for me. Whatever I did, and tried to do, within the scope of propriety and proper practice didn't seem to work as they were expected to. And at every step of the way, therefore, I seemed to be swimming ***against the current***.

Chapter 6

AGAINST THE CURRENT`

A surgeon discovers

"The hardest thing of all is to find a black cat in a dark room, especially if there is no cat." – Confucius

Our training and residency at CMH Dhaka lasted 18 months, and at the end of which we had to write an exam, which had both a written and an oral segment.

At this point, I cannot say with conviction that we had been adequately prepared for it by our instructors, because we hardly ever received any attentive training in either the principles of surgery or the practice of it. All through the eighteen months of our course, our instructors seemed occupied with just about everything, except teaching us surgery. And that is besides the fact that our top two mentors were either continually consumed in demeaning and slandering each other, or taking out their frustrations on us, the trainees, by berating us at almost every opportunity, and for apparently no reason.

As for ourselves, we hungrily chewed on whatever meager and sporadic educational 'handouts' we received once in a while, endeavoring at the same time to steer diligently away from the fallout of 'kingly confrontations'. There were some amongst us, nonetheless, who did attempt to create a 'favorable' status quo for themselves under such circumstances by 'siding' with one faction or the other – and oftentimes they succeeded. I cannot speak for the others but, as for myself, I can say that I was left with educating myself for the upcoming Grading Final Examinations.

A few days before the examination, we decided to go to one of our mentors for a few pointers as to what to expect during it. Understandably, this was to be the first ever post-graduate examination of any kind that we were to appear in. The need for a 'direction', in order to help prepare for such an exam, was even greater in this instance since none in the faculty had ever felt the need to properly apprise us of it at any stage.

After spending a few minutes with us, our mentor sent us off by saying, *"You will pass the examination if, during it, I get the impression that you will not wake me up in the middle of the night."* Looking back, I now know I should have laughed on his face because, by all counts, and considering what he and all the other instructors had taught us, he was probably going to lose a lot of sleep in the days to come. But the fact that we passed the exam, and never ever woke him up in the middle of the night during our careers was a testament to our individual efforts at self-education.

My dissertation for the course was a retrospective study of the various types of knee injuries sustained by personnel of the army. It was titled *"Knee Injuries in Bangladesh Army: A Retrospective Study of 42 Cases"*. This was done in an effort at focusing on those activities that produced the most injuries and the types of knee injuries that were mostly sustained. It also identified the incidence of knee injuries sustained by personnel of the various branches of the army.

A study of this nature is basically done in an effort to alert the authorities of the causal factors of orthopedic morbidities so that proper preventive measures could be taken. For a soldier in training or in service to be 'out of commission', so to speak, for any length of time for a reason that could easily have been prevented is, in the long run, detrimental to the resources of the armed forces. It is expected, therefore, that the results of such studies would be taken into cognizance by the relevant authorities and proper measures taken so that the root objective of such studies is adequately served and the tireless efforts of those who undertake such studies is properly appreciated.

But sadly, that is not the case. The dissertations, after the Final Grading Examination of the candidates, find their way on to one of the shelves in the armed forces library as their final resting place, where they collect dust and ultimately rot. In the meantime, however, the candidates usually submit the paper for publication in the medical journal of the armed forces. Though it usually is a matter of great pride for the author that the article has been published in a reputable journal that is where it all ends, in most cases. Some of those articles, however, are sometimes referenced in similar publications of others, as I recently discovered that the work of my dissertation was, in one later publication. But, are the lessons learned from such studies ever looked into after, or utilized to the advantage of the institution? During my years in this establishment, at least, I have never seen that happen. Unfortunately, the most that happens in this – and in most other institutions – is an article making its rounds in the references from one publication to another.

Qualifying soon after, as a Graded Specialist in Surgery, was a significant milestone for me because I knew I was finally on the road to the professional utopia of my dreams – be it late than never. Interestingly, this also turned out to be a journey through a patented maze, around almost every corner of which were extraordinary experiences, surprising revelations, and unanticipated twists and turns.

Following my qualification in the Grading Final Examinations, I was posted to CMH Dhaka as a Graded Surgical Specialist. Posting to CMH Dhaka, which was the largest and the best-equipped military hospital in the country, always carried with it an implication that was special, and an aspiration that was widespread. I got posted to CMH Dhaka presumably because Samina was already working there and not because the authorities felt I was a gifted surgeon of some sort and therefore needed to be at an apex institution – a thought, if true, wasn't particularly flattering!

To be bluntly honest though, the authorities actually had no way of knowing what kind of a surgeon I would eventually turn out to be. And that was because I do not remember any of my instructors ever assessing my performance during my solo surgeries while I was undergoing my so-called training. Therefore, what was perhaps more important regarding this posting of mine is that the authorities probably did not want to lose the services of my wife, had I been posted elsewhere at that point in time.

But, this is not to say that there weren't any instances of serving doctors in the corps who, being husbands and wives, were not posted to different CMHs, sometimes separated by hundreds of kilometers. However, that was rare, and took place usually as a result of what could be termed, informally, as a 'punishment posting', made as a result of the irk and the ire of some placed high enough to be able to call the shots.

From my own perspective, being posted to CMH Dhaka was a unique situational circumstance.

It came with the opportunity to live through and participate in the activities of this hospital, not as a trainee in surgery anymore, but as part of the 'surgical authority', so to speak. Having suffered all this while as a result of certain shortcomings of the faculty and the medical institution, and having constantly bickered about it, I was now going to be a part of the entity which I had always been critical of. This was to be the testing ground for me to finally discover whether all the discontent that I harbored were justified, or whether it had been a misplaced judgment all along. It was like staring at the world down the opposite end of a kaleidoscope to see how different it looked.

It did not take me long to realize that from the other end, the patterns and colors swirled in a rather odd fashion.

As soon as I joined the Department of Surgery I felt a strange intangible force permeating every corridor of that department. It was an unseen power which seemed to dictate the way the department thought and acted. It was a palpable under-current which influenced every decision, right or wrong, which that department made – the vortices of which seemed as overpowering as they were deeply entrenched. This, I was to discover soon, was the prevailing state of affairs in essentially most of the other faculties at CMH Dhaka.

To begin with, in the Department of Surgery, there was this gargantuan might known as 'General Surgery', and those practicing it being known as 'general surgeons'. They laid claim to anything and everything within the human body that could be cut open with a scalpel. The abdomen seemed to be their favorite playground, from where they made frequent forays into the breasts, the thyroid, and the hernias. And like spoiled children wanting to play with more toys than they should, they also often meddled with other forbidden organs and anatomies, sometimes with disastrous results.

Finally however, the general surgeons settled within the abdomen, but at a time when modern medical science had already allotted the different organs within it to those who specialized in them. But that didn't seem to bother or even deter the general surgeons. As central as the abdomen was within the human body, the general surgeons too, having settled well and truly into that region, felt they too were the center of the so-called 'surgical universe'.

This was perhaps the outcome of a legacy left over from the early days of medical science, when the understanding of the human body was so primitive and the practice of surgery so rudimentary that anyone with a scalpel in hand who could display their expertise on any part of the human body, could be called a surgeon – or more fittingly, a 'general' surgeon – because their activities, according to the Oxford Dictionary, were "not limited to one particular subject or aspect".

Since then, however, surgical practice has actually progressed to greater depths of understanding and newer horizons of refinement and, in the process, has converged down to focusing on individual organs and parts of the human body. But, for some inexplicable reason, the general surgeons of the medical corps refused to accept that, and continued to languish in the back-waters of antiquity. They seemed to be stuck waist-deep in the quicksand of their own ignorance or obstinacy, or both, and not the least inclined to come out of this quagmire of antiquity. Rather, they went about making arrangements to give their situation, and their status as general surgeons, a stamp of pretentiousness and of authority, and quite successfully ended up having a stranglehold over the department.

Since the days of infancy of this establishment, the general surgeons have had such an effective vice-like grip on the functional philosophy of the medical corps that specialties like orthopedic, thoracic, pediatric, and cardiac surgeries, as well as ophthalmology, dentistry, obstetrics, gynecology, anesthesiology and radiology continued to be under the organizational and administrative control and authority of General Surgery and hence, of the general surgeons. That this essentially prevented a proper evolvement of those specialties did not seem to bother either the medical authorities or some in the lofty offices.

Rather, from the perspective of the latter, it was rather reassuring that the general surgeons had everything sealed within a simplistic water-tight containment called General Surgery, be that outmoded or outdated. And that was perhaps because either they could relate to such a model or because they weren't bothered enough that the medical corps wasn't keeping pace with recent innovative changes in the realm of medical science.

To me, it always seemed as if the medical corps was more like a step-child which never really figured in the grand scheme, design and purpose of the parent organization. It was more like an irritating weight hanging on to its shoulders, and which needed to be carried around rather needlessly, deserving only an occasional cursory and, at times, a spiteful glance – until sickness arrived.

Understandably therefore, some in certain offices couldn't care less that the expression and maturation of the various specialties under the Department of Surgery were being stifled by the egocentricity and obstinacy of the self-styled masters of the so-called 'surgical universe'. One would have expected, however, that the conglomeration of alleged visionaries and luminaries within the corps itself would have had the will and the wisdom to have risen to the occasion and to have set the tone for the future. But no, that was not to be. And sadly, the corps, led by stalwarts of the 'old school' continued in a fashion that was in keeping with their limited concept and capacity. And that, in my opinion, wasn't surprising at all, since D. H. Lawrence himself had once said "What the eye doesn't see and the mind doesn't know, doesn't exist".

Just so my readers are better able to visualize the set-up of the surgical department vis-à-vis the locus of the general surgeons within it, I will stray briefly from the topic at hand.

The senior-most surgeon at any CMH held the appointment of the Senior Surgeon of that CMH. However, in the case of CMH Dhaka, the position of the Senior Surgeon later underwent a change in nomenclature, and was re-named 'Chief Surgeon'. The Chief Surgeon was the head honcho. He was the senior-most of all the Senior Surgeons of the corps and was bestowed with supreme powers which could be exercised at will and imposed with finality, especially where it concerned the modus operandi of the surgical departments at the CMHs across the country. There was only one other surgeon in the medical corps who was senior to the Chief Surgeon, and he was the Consultant Surgeon. The Consultant Surgeon was not posted to any hospital. His place was at the Directorate General of Medical Services, the highest seat of administrative and technical decision-making of the medical corps. From there he liaised with both the Director General of Medical Services as well as the lofty offices on matters ranging from policies to practices to purchases.

What confounded me all the time was that only a general surgeon was always considered capable and qualified enough to be the Senior Surgeon of the Department of Surgery at any CMH anywhere in the country. What sort of an institutional principle and philosophy, I wondered, would allow a general surgeon to play a pivotal role in the decision-making process of the other specialties? How much did the general surgeons know of the other specialties which would make them competent enough to have a say in their matters? And unfortunately, I have, at times, had to deal with the unsolicited and needless impositions upon my specialty – be it technical or otherwise –by a Senior Surgeon, who happened to be a general surgeon, and about which I shall discuss shortly. I am not sure of how often that happened with the other sub-specialties, but that was perhaps one of the reasons why certain specialties were oftentimes left with either a lopsided distribution of manpower, a shortage of instruments and equipment, or those that were either not needed or did not work. However, if things are different today, of which I may not be aware, that would be reason enough for a celebration!

While the Chief Surgeon and his cohorts in positions of power and influence quite regularly played their part in ignoring the needs and the necessities of the other specialties, it also served as an incentive for people beyond the borders of medical science to feel that their rank and appointment somehow also gave them the right to step in and dictate terms. And that was where it got interesting.

While working as an Orthopedic Surgeon at CMH Chittagong later on in my career, I had to attend a meeting to discuss and amend the existing Table of Organization and Equipment (commonly known as the TO&E) of the various departments in that hospital. The TO&E details everything concerning a particular department, including its hierarchical set-up, its exact manpower, and every equipment, big or small, that a department and a specialty needs for its proper functioning.

I was representing the Department of Orthopedic Surgery, while representatives of other departments were present as well, with suggestions, recommendations and proposals of their own. Prior to the meeting, it was communicated to me that the meeting was going to be chaired by the divisional commander, and not by someone from the medical corps.

There have been moments in my life when I have groped helplessly for a credible explanation to a seemingly incredible situation – and this was certainly one of them.

What made this even more ludicrous and lamentable was that those with adequate medical knowledge and in capacities to be able to make perfectly rational and acceptable decisions regarding the TO&E felt completely at ease with a non-medical individual deciding for them how a hospital ought to be set up and administered. I wonder whether any medical personnel, however senior in rank or elevated in appointment, would ever have been given the power and the authority to decide how a fighting unit ought to be organized and managed. And did I hear you say, "Never"? Right! So, why should a non-medical individual have the right to sit at the head of a table at a hospital to decide how that hospital should be structured and administered?

It did not come as any big surprise, therefore, when very little time was wasted in transforming this meeting from one of sensible discussion to that of a scathing inquisition. Looking back now, I know I should not have expected any better from a situation where someone from the fighting forces was chairing a meeting on medical matters. It seemed as if he had perched himself at the head of the table with the sole intent of preventing the surgeons and physicians from 'over-indulging' in matters of manpower and equipment. That, most unfortunately, was our esteem and worth in the eyes of some in this establishment, and that was the kind of confidence they had on us! We soon found ourselves caught up in desperately trying to justify and defend our proposals with someone who had not the slightest idea of what medical science was all about, or what it took to run a hospital.

As the representative of the Department of Orthopedic Surgery I proposed at one point that considering the number of beds and the volume of patients we handled, we would have to have at least twelve medical assistants working in shifts to ensure proper care of the patients in the orthopedic ward. To this, the person at the head of the table shot back, "You don't need that many. Take eight."

I wonder how much of orthopedic surgery he had learned over the years, and how much he knew of the kind of work we did, to be able to make such a sweeping and instantaneous proclamation. How could he have ever guessed that eight medical assistants were enough to run my department? Would he have ever allowed me to dictate the number of soldiers he could have, in order to achieve a military objective? I don't think so. What then, gave him the right to tell me how to achieve *my* medical objective?

It never failed to amaze me as to how an elevation by way of rank and appointment invariably seemed to instill in some individual a sense of suddenly being endowed with new-found knowledge and unparalleled wisdom, besides being empowered with unlimited rights as well. It is beyond any comprehensible logic as to why people who were trained to march into the battlefield, fire salvos at the enemy and rumble around in a tank should take it upon themselves to meddle in matters of medicine and surgery. Perhaps the dizzying and intoxicating heights to which their rank and appointment took them clouded their faculty of judgment just enough to make them feel adequately competent to impose their whims on issues better left alone.

The Ascendency of Attrition

There seemed to be an everlasting and spiteful in-house conflict between the departments of Surgery and Medicine, which not only stood in the way of any real progress of the corps, but also eroded deeply into its core dignity and self-respect.

I will admit that I have no idea of how these two departments are juxtaposed today in terms of respect and reciprocity. But, back in those days – days when ego superseded enlightenment – the criticisms, condemnations, disapprovals, denunciations and tirades between the two in terms of the other's handling of cases often deteriorated to levels which nibbled away at the very foundations of academic decency and mutual credibility. It was as if members of either faculty were involved in a never-ending war of annihilation, and the psyche of both seemed to be literally consumed by that pre-occupation.

The chosen battlefield where this was openly and blatantly displayed were the weekly clinical meetings, where almost every case presented by one faculty was invariably deemed by the other to have been most incompetently handled or badly treated. Interestingly, this was a battle led from the front by the senior specialists of the respective departments, blazing the way for the junior specialists and the trainees to emulate.

As a trainee at these clinical meetings, I realized that this war of attrition contributed nothing substantial towards preparing us for our future profession. If anything, it harbored the potential of instilling in us an attitude of doubt and disrespect towards our colleagues, which none of us really wanted. Understandably therefore, most trainees including myself, as well as some junior specialists, were to be found catching up on lost sleep during those clinical meetings, or disinterested to the point of indulging in self-study, while the battle raged overhead. A truly desperate measure was to manually cause our pagers to beep, and to leave on the pretense of having to respond to an emergency.

Moreover, when it came down to the strife and rivalry between the Departments of Surgery and Medicine, there were instances in which any relevance to reality was consumed and lost in the fire of illogical presumptions and resultant unrealistic measures. It hardly mattered that the value and worth of true academics were needlessly being defiled in the process. What mattered, perhaps, was that departmental – and sometimes even personal – egotistic values were being fulfilled.

A glaring example was when the armed forces was offered a scholarship in “Sports Medicine” in a neighboring country. Such a course involved training in the management of sports and musculo-skeletal injuries. Obviously, it belonged to the realm of orthopedic surgery. Even if the general surgeons had wanted that scholarship – which I don’t doubt for a moment that they would – I would have probably given it even to them. But surprisingly, the Department of Medicine pounced upon it, presumably on the premise that the title of the scholarship had the word 'Medicine' in it – or so I was given to understand! I felt like Nunez in "The Country of the Blind" as I struggled to come to terms with the sheer absurdity, senselessness, and perhaps even shamelessness, of it all.

Thereafter, I made it a point to inquire of the medical specialists returning from that course as to whether they thought it was of any value to them. And I was told every time that the course was a total waste of time, energy and resources. The medical specialists actually had no idea why they had been sent in the first place. They were sent. So they went. And who would not like to enjoy a few months of R&R in a foreign country, making the pretense of learning something they had no idea about, and something they knew they would never require in their careers?

This was the kind of wastage which resulted from the arrogance, obstinacy and almost-childlike mentality of some at the helm of the corps.

Undesirable Frontiers

> *"There are two kinds of pride, both good and bad. 'Good pride' represents our dignity and self-respect. 'Bad pride' is the deadly sin of superiority that reeks of conceit and arrogance." – John C. Maxwell*

Disagreements and debates involving a post-graduate qualification that was to be considered acceptable to the medical corps was another stumbling block on which this corps frequently tripped, stumbled, and often fell flat on its face. And with much time wasted in getting back to its feet, it often proved to be a deterrent to any real academic progress.

A handful few of the senior specialists – senior enough to not only dictate terms but to also literally own the corps – were aggressively intolerant of any post-graduate qualification other than what was known as a "Fellowship". According to them, only a Fellowship obtained either abroad or from within the country was to be readily accepted as the highest medical qualification sufficient for specialists to be promoted to the rank of colonel or beyond, and to progress to the level of being the head of a department.

It is my understanding, and I believe quite rightly so, that the real reason for such a rigid and uncompromising mindset was this:

That the senior specialists –crucial cogs in the wheel of policy-making of the corps – being already in possession of a Fellowship themselves, were perhaps not willing to figure in any other scale of professional comparison. Were they, by any chance, fearful that that would perhaps lead to a loss of credibility of their own qualifications? Frankly, I do not know. But open emphasis was made of the fact that any post-graduate qualification other than a Fellowship, including even a Master's degree in any medical subject, was always to be considered a class inferior. Clearly, the adoption of such a strategy of intolerance was an attempt at being able to exert control and domination.

It is for that very reason that I am compelled, at this point, to draw a few comparisons between a Fellowship and a Master's degree, particularly where it concerns Surgery – because Surgery is my concern, and therein lie my bone of contention.

It is not my intention to be unfairly or unreasonably critical of any post-graduate qualification, nor am I adequately qualified to conclude that one is better or worse than the other. In fact, when it comes to post-graduate degrees and qualifications, there are more similarities between their curricula than there are differences. My intention here is merely to focus on a few of the differences between a Masters Degree and a Fellowship from a strictly neutral standpoint. My intention is to emphasize, especially for the Fellows in the medical corps who looked down upon the Masters Degree with disdain, that the latter was, in fact, as good a post-graduate qualification as the former, if not better. If truth be told, I have always had this feeling deep down, that those very senior specialists with a Fellowship actually knew this all along, but were perhaps driven by some sort of an egotistical mindset not to admit it. Even so, I will expound on some of the differences since I feel it is pertinent at this point.

While doing so, and as I have already mentioned, I will not venture outside the realm of Surgery simply because I would not like any injustice done to the other subjects, not knowing everything about their post-graduate pre-requisites, programs and curricula. Let me emphasize once again, that I am not out to prove that one degree or qualification is better or worse than the other because, at the end of the day, that is something I would like to leave to the judgment of the readers.

First of all, let me be very clear about one thing. Strictly speaking, a "Fellowship" is not a degree, as many would be prone to believe. It is, in fact, a program of intensive training in a chosen specialty. It is merely an affirmation of the fact that an individual has met the training requirements of a certain College, be it the Royal College of Physicians and Surgeons of England, or the Bangladesh College of Physicians and Surgeons (also known as the BCPS).

On the other hand, the Masters Degree is actually a degree, such as of any University anywhere in the world. It follows the natural academic progression from a Bachelors Degree, sometimes leading up to a PhD – should an individual wish to progress further academically, after having completed their Masters. And moreover, both the Bachelors and the Masters degrees are conferred upon by Dhaka University, the oldest and the most prestigious post-graduate academe of the country.

The course leading up to a Masters Degree is a three-year program, with two examinations that need to be written. Between the two examinations is a compulsory two-year period of in-house residency, training and classes. For specialties that have an institute and a hospital dedicated to that subject, the training and classes have to be compulsorily completed at that institute and hospital. For example, in case of Orthopedic Surgery, the residency or training has to be done at the National Institute of Traumatology and Orthopedic Rehabilitation (NITOR) (previously known as the RIHD, or the Rehabilitation Institute and Hospital for the Disabled), while for Cardiac Surgery, it is the NICVD (National Institute for Cardiovascular Diseases), and so on. Even if a Masters student has had two years, or perhaps even more, of prior training at any other recognized medical institution other than at the apex institution on that subject, that candidate would still need to complete this mandatory two years of specialized training at the respective apex institution, to be eligible to write the final exams.

During the training period, the education and practical teaching of a student is closely monitored and supervised by the professors at that institution. Having been a part of that system and method myself, I know that there is always this definite synergy between teaching and learning in this case, in which the mentor and the student move forward together through the entire education process, from its inception to the final examination – a process which can only be expected to yield a more productive outcome and a better specialist.

The Fellowship also consists of two examinations that need to be written. However, the two-year residency/training can be done either before writing any of the examinations or between the two. Moreover, in most cases, it does not really matter in which hospital the residency/training has been obtained as long as, prior to writing the final examination, a candidate can produce a certificate to that effect from the respective professor. This obviously means that the involvement of a dedicated institution for training purposes is not as essential in case of a Fellowship. And the reason for that is simple. Specialized training in a specified specialty in case of a Fellowship is obtained after the completion of the Fellowship. This also means that to be an Orthopedic Surgeon, for example, a Fellow in Surgery would need only to be *trained* in Orthopedic Surgery – and not be required to obtain any degree in that subject.

Another significant aspect of the Masters Program is the essential pre-requisite of the completion of a thesis on an original work. It has to be a "prospective study" in which study participants are selected or identified and then followed forward in time, with interventions, to observe outcomes. It is for this very reason that medical bio-statistics is a subject of critical importance in the Master's course because it not only provides the students with the means of arriving at a meaningful conclusion of their thesis, but it also instills in them the ability to conduct future reliable studies and make dependable and viable observations. The thesis is supervised by one of the professors of the institution, and during the final examination it has to be defended satisfactorily and successfully by the student in the face of queries and criticisms from a panel of examiners.

Interestingly, medical bio-statistics is never taught in the Fellowship program because its candidates are not needed to write a thesis. They do, however, have to complete a dissertation which, in most instances, is a "retrospective study" where conclusions are drawn from pre-existing data and is essentially, therefore, a study which looks backward in time. Moreover, the dissertation in the Fellowship Program is not required to be defended. It merely needs to be submitted.

The Republic of Repugnance

> *"And do you think that his contempt shall not be bruising to you. When he hath power to crush?" – William Shakespeare*

Despite all this, those with a Fellowship in the medical corps, particularly the senior specialists, always held the Master's degree in contempt. I wonder whether that was the outcome of either ignorance or arrogance – or perhaps even both. Or could it also have been some deep-down awareness that a Fellowship perhaps didn't quite measure up to a Masters degree? I do not know.

But, I do know this, that when a certain truth is plainly obvious and conclusively undeniable – yet unacceptable – to some, they succumb to the most primitive and disgraceful of all human responses: *Conspiracy.*

Conspiracy is something which grows like a cancerous crop on the fertile fields of contempt, to be harvested by those whose hunger is fed by their perennial anguish and lamentation of not having had the best in terms of possessions, be those material or academic. This probably gnawed so abrasively at the psyche of the surgeons with a Fellowship that they did everything within their powers to keep those with a Master's degree from assuming positions and appointments of significance.

One morning, during my Masters course, I had to go to CMH Dhaka on an errand. That was where I came across one of the senior specialists who had been triumphantly riding the rewarding wave of a Fellowship all his life. He was walking at the head of a pack of junior specialists and trainees during his morning round. As soon as he spotted me, he asked me something, literally at the top of his voice, for the benefit of everyone within earshot, and which, to this day, I clearly remember – word for every insulting word.

"So, how many more years do you have, to roam around?"

Roam around? I was completely taken aback by the raw insensitivity and maliciousness overflowing from the question. Nevertheless, it was only logical to have expected something like this from someone who had, time and again, proved that age and education alone do not always ensure civility and humility. Deeply entrenched in his assumption was perhaps the fact that the Masters program was nothing more than some time spent 'roaming around' which, I assumed, was a revelation of the obstinacy of his depraved mindset, and the fertility of his vile contempt. Even so, I would like to think that the viciousness in his tone and his condescending attitude probably had nothing to do with me personally. It could very well have been the outcome of his fierce hatred of the Masters degree itself, and that I was being insulted perhaps because I represented something he detested – or maybe even feared? Who knows? Even so, at that very moment, the one thing that that individual desperately needed were my sympathies for the pathetic state of his psyche, which I am not quite sure I was prepared to extend.

In the ensuing conspiracy therefore, most specialties, including Orthopedic Surgery, languished in the barren fields of utter negligence, and were lost in the dark alleys of petty prejudices. The only specialties which did not suffer were those which the two or three of the senior-most surgeons took a fancy to. Those were the ones which, therefore, flourished with the latest state-of-the-art and top-of-the-line equipment and instruments, as well as a hefty and sizeable manpower. It was as if all human afflictions were restricted to what those few surgeons or any surgeon bestowed upon with 'special blessings' practiced.

On the other hand, what the other specialties had, were hardly adequate, and outright antiquated. Repeated requests for newer and better equipment and instruments were usually most perfunctorily brushed aside. Once in a blue moon, however, a newer supply, though barely ever adequate, would arrive at the door of one or the other specialties, primarily with the intent of effectively putting an end to their constant bickering and to lull them into a brief silence.

So, while the repertoire of inventory of the few 'favored' specialties continued to be replenished unabated, it was always a treat for surgeons like us, from the so-called 'lesser' specialties, if you will, to wander into an operating room where perhaps a urological, thoracic or cardiac surgery was in progress, and to marvel at all the fanciful and sophisticated instruments and equipment being used there.

When it came to orthopedic surgery, in particular, there seemed to be a total disregard for its essential and technical needs and necessities. No amount of persuasion seemed sufficient enough to convince the power-base of the corps that in an institution such as the armed forces, where trauma and physical injuries were a way of life, orthopedic surgery, with the largest share of patients in the hospital, needed the most attention.

Though I would prefer not to suggest any basis for this obvious attitude of neglect for the orthopedic specialty, it seemed that deep down, there was perhaps a reason. Maybe it all boiled down to the fact that the orthopedic specialists were the ones with a Master's degree, while the senior specialists of the Department of Surgery – and who, therefore, made all the decisions regarding the modernization of the department – were all Fellows.

But what could possibly be wrong with an institution which willfully downplays and intentionally ignores an orthopedic scholarship offered by a prestigious institution abroad? The medical corps was known to otherwise always display a keen interest in obtaining scholarships for its specialists from foreign institutions, and frequently took an eager initiative in the matter. Active measures were often taken to ensure that such scholarships were secured and which, if successful, would be considered an accomplishment on the part of the establishment.

I was on a visit to Singapore once, during the time when Samina was there for her training in a pediatric sub-specialty. It was out of sheer interest in orthopedic surgery that I, in an unofficial capacity, met with the departmental head of orthopedics of a renowned medical institution there. I wanted to observe how their department functioned, hoping to take some helpful pointers, which could possibly be employed in our department as well, at CMH Dhaka.

At the end of a couple of days of meeting with the professor, he expressed his intention to offer me a scholarship in an orthopedic sub-specialty at the institution. All that would be required of me was to produce a letter from my institution in Bangladesh requesting the scholarship which, in my opinion, was entirely logical. To be offered a scholarship at such a prestigious institution, and that too by an orthopedic surgeon well-renowned in the South East Asian region, was a matter of great pride for me, and something beyond my wildest dreams.

However, as soon as the news of this offer was conveyed to the upper echelons of the medical hierarchy, I instantly came up against a solid brick wall. The response was disappointingly muted and visibly condescending. I was astounded by the fact that here was a scholarship for the taking, but the administration, for some inexplicable reason, did not seem to want it! Here was a scholarship which the administration would otherwise have fallen head over heels for, and now strangely, they seemed disinterested!

Out of nowhere appeared insurmountable bureaucratic obstacles and bizarre questions. Questions like, *"Why should* ***we*** *be the ones requesting the scholarship? Ask them to offer it to us".*

What the guardians of the medical corps couldn't quite possibly wrap their heads around was that this was a scholarship that was being offered at the total discretion of the departmental head of an institution. Perhaps in keeping with the rules of procedure of his institution or his department, he required that such a scholarship be requested. After all, by providing it, that institution or that department was undertaking to pay for the tuition and living expenses of an individual, and which could easily run into thousands of dollars. So yes, if requesting for such a scholarship was a pre-requisite, one complied, if one wanted it. Sir Lancelot was never going to come galloping into the Court of King Arthur carrying that scholarship, wrapped up as a gift.

Amazingly too, I was also asked, *"Why should we send you? We could send anyone we like"*. It was as if there were scores of other orthopedic surgeons to choose from. Or maybe I was getting it all wrong. Maybe the authorities were hinting that they would rather have preferred general, urologic, thoracic or cardiac surgeons instead, to be sent off to Singapore! The fact that it was a scholarship in an orthopedic sub-specialty and that it was being offered to me after I had had sufficient academic interactions with the head of that department seemed totally beside the point!

For an institution striving to attain excellence in the field of medical science and aspiring to make a name for itself on a national scale, a scholarship offered by a renowned medical institution ought to have been accepted outright and readily. To this day, I wonder as to the reason behind this kind of a response. Scholarships didn't come easy, and this one was literally being served on a silver platter. But, for some reason, the institution didn't seem to be able to get over their apparent inertia of bureaucratic dogmatism, imperviousness, insensitivity, or perhaps even bias, in this particular case. I have a feeling that had that scholarship been offered in any other surgical sub-specialty – perhaps urologic, thoracic or cardiac surgeries – it would probably have had a more conducive conclusion. Finally it all reached a point where I felt it not worth the while pursuing that scholarship any further. It was glaringly obvious that I would get nowhere with it – not, at least, with this administration, and with this kind of an attitude.

When the gist of the establishment's response was conveyed to the professor, he was visibly perturbed and, if I may add, literally livid with anger. I do not blame him, because what had just transpired revealed an impoverished mindset and a preference for petty nonsensical prejudices over real academic needs. And, to this day, I vividly remember the look of incredulity, anger and, to some extent, indignation in the eyes of that professor as he asked me, *"What if they send some tom, dick or harry? I'm not giving that scholarship to just anybody!"* And, thereafter, the offer of the scholarship was withdrawn.

I felt empty, and I felt denied. A good part of my academic aspirations had been pinned on that scholarship which, I had hoped, would serve to not only enrich my professional acumen, but also enable the specialty of orthopedics of this institution attain a respectable and recognized standard. But, some in this establishment perhaps didn't care to be bothered by such facts, perhaps because orthopedic surgery didn't quite measure up to the other surgical sub-specialties in terms of grandiosity, pomposity and novelty, despite having to handle the largest share of surgical cases at most military hospitals in the country.

Meanwhile, back at CMH Dhaka, the orthopedic surgeons, with inadequate, worn-out, and the most unsophisticated of instruments and equipment at their disposal, were constantly improvising their way out of one nail-biting surgical encounter to the next. Forceps didn't hold and scissors didn't cut. Osteotomes weren't sharp enough and clamps weren't strong enough. Saws were blunt, chisels were eroded, drills were dull and screws weren't ever the right size. But, what was sharp and incisive, and held everything in place, was the ability, the ingenuity and the tenacity of the deprived and the denied.

What it all amounted to was this: Specialties and specialists, unilaterally sidelined by the favored and "blessed" few, were routinely being sacrificed unceremoniously in ***the killing fields*** of neglect, contempt and conspiracy.

Chapter 7

THE KILLING FIELDS

A surgeon discovers more......

During my tenure at CMH Dhaka as a Graded Specialist in Surgery I began to work under the mentorship of Colonel (later Brigadier-General) Fazle Rahim – an orthopedic surgeon who had completed his Masters in Orthopedic Surgery about a year earlier.

Colonel Fazle Rahim was an officer with a rare sensible and rational head on his shoulders. Always soft-spoken and mild-mannered, he went about quietly doing whatever he had to do. I cannot say I have ever seen him stressed, or heard him raise his voice – unlike most others with enough seniority to think they could – not even under the most trying or frustrating of circumstances, be that in or out of the operating room. It was almost as if Colonel Fazle Rahim, by some strange quirk of fate, was in the wrong place.

It may be worth mentioning that despite trauma and injuries being the most prevalent form of ailment in the armed forces due to the very nature of its professional obligations, Colonel Fazle Rahim was only the second surgeon in its almost twenty-year history to have been sent for a post-graduate training and degree in orthopedics and trauma.

Upon his return therefore, Colonel Rahim realized that the army actually needed more orthopedic surgeons than it was willing to admit it did. And it was during my mentorship that he took note of my passionate interest in the subject, and suggested to the authorities that I be sent for training and a post-graduate degree in Orthopedics and Traumatology. And when a person of his level of seniority suggests someone as his candidate of choice, the authorities usually take that into cognizance. And, therefore, when time came for army doctors to be selected for post- graduate courses I was called in for an interview to try to determine whether or not I qualified for the Masters Program in Orthopedic Surgery. Fortunately, the interview panel thought I did.

Three years later, I returned as only the third orthopedic surgeon of the Bangladesh Armed Forces in its twenty one years of existence. As an annotation of interest, it is worth pointing out that considering the total number of active personnel in the Bangladesh Armed Forces at that time, the ratio of orthopedic surgeons to the number of potential orthopedic cases was roughly in the region of a staggering 1:60,000 by a most conservative estimate. And it gets even more mind-boggling when one also takes into account the family members of serving personnel with acute, chronic and congenital orthopedic problems. Even so, some in this institution probably felt that training doctors in orthopedic surgery was not a dire necessity. Had that not been the case, then there would have been a minimum of ten orthopedic surgeons in this institution by now. At least one orthopedic surgeon in each of its major hospitals was an absolute necessity. And that was because the varieties of trauma in an organization such as this spanned almost every chapter of the textbooks on traumatology, since every active personnel, anywhere, was liable to be injured at anytime. It is also an undeniable fact that in order to be at peak performance and efficiency, they have to train anywhere between six to eight hours a day – primarily with their hands and feet.

Understandably therefore, the orthopedic out-patient department, ward and operating room had the highest volume of patient traffic. If glaringly obvious facts and figures were anything to go by, one could only wonder in dismay and disbelief as to what it was that the authorities couldn't comprehend that they chose to consistently ignore the needs of the Department of Orthopedic Surgery.

Expedition Rangpur

Overall, specialists in the armed forces, regardless of specialty, were not particularly plentiful. So whenever a specialist went on leave at a hospital where there were none from the same specialty to look after his or her responsibilities, another had to be brought in from a

CMH which could spare one, to fill in the role. For the specialist filling in for the one on leave, this was called a Temporary Duty.

In spite of being an orthopedic surgeon, I was sent on Temporary Duty to CMH Rangpur once, to replace a general surgeon.

Perhaps a spare general surgeon could not be found at any other CMH in the entire country – which did not sound quite credible to me. On the other hand, it could also have been the perennial and protracted obstinacy of the surgical authorities in maintaining that anyone who could hold a scalpel could be a general surgeon, and that orthopedic surgeons were nothing more than some sort of superfluous, fancy and unnecessary appendage who had obtained their degrees simply by "roaming around". And so, in their boundless sagacity, the authorities decided to send me to replace a general surgeon.

Though I had not had the opportunity of doing any sort of surgery other than on bones, joints, muscles, tendons and ligaments for a number of years now, I was nevertheless confident that my past experience as a general surgeon, during the initial years of my training, would not abandon me. Moreover, I was reassured by the realization that experience was one thing which was never known to have abandoned anyone.

CMH Rangpur was a rather small military hospital with perhaps around a hundred beds. It was situated to the north of the country about 350 kilometers from Dhaka. I made the trip by air to Saidpur Airport, from where I was driven over to CMH Rangpur, about forty kilometers away, in an Army Jeep.

The Commanding Officer and the other officers at CMH Rangpur were very cordial, and ensured that my stay there was as comfortable as possible. I was accommodated in the Officers Mess, which was within walking distance from the CMH. I performed a few routine and minor surgeries and dealt with a handful of patients who came to the out-patient department for consultation.

With much time to spare, I was able to take an interest in the other aspects of the ward and departmental activities. It was during one such spare moment that I stumbled upon a few boxes full of pulleys in the store room of the surgical ward. These pulleys were meant to be fitted on to the foot-end of a hospital bed to allow for weight traction to be provided for cases with major fractures, particularly of the thigh bone. No one seemed to either know or be bothered by the fact that they were there. I suggested to the Commanding Officer that those be fitted on to some of the patients' beds, to which he quite readily agreed.

Despite this happy ending, however, there were a few things about those pulleys that kept bothering me. Why was the number of pulleys at least twice more than what would normally be needed for a hospital this size? Who ordered those pulleys? Why were they lying unutilized? Why didn't anyone seem to know that the pulleys were there, or how they were to be properly used? And even if they did, why didn't anyone seem to care?

Perhaps the answers to these lay in the *basics*: The basics of the hierarchical set-up of the medical institution in terms of who should have the privilege and the prerogative to make decisions; the basics of using common sense and proper judgment, coupled with a realistic understanding of a situation; the basics of the need to have the right person in the right place; and finally, the basics of possessing appropriate vision and adequate wisdom.

I personally felt that those *basics* needed to be revisited as far as this corps was concerned. And I found myself also wondering as to how many more pulleys were lying around in how many more store-rooms in the various CMHs across the country. And that's only pulleys.

Back to my life at Rangpur, a batman had been detailed to look after my needs during my stay at the Officers' Mess. Besides getting my uniform in order every morning, he also brought my lunch and dinner over to my room. Returning to my room every afternoon at the end of my duties at the hospital, and having nothing much to do after lunch, I would look forward to reading Robert Ludlum and slipping into a blissful siesta in the process. Waking up in the evenings and getting dressed, I would walk over to the CMH and spend time chatting with the DMO and the other officers and specialists who habitually converged to the DMO's rest room in the evenings either for a hospital round or to attend to a call at the hospital. I also got invited to a few dinners at the residences of some of my colleagues, and which were rather enjoyable – both for the company I was in, as well as for the culinary quality of the food served.

Overall, my two-week tour of duty at CMH Rangpur was rather uneventful from the point of view of my workload and surgical responsibilities. After the overwhelming load at CMH Dhaka, my time at CMH Rangpur seemed more like an R&R. It was a welcome break from monotony and helped me catch up on some much-needed rest.

On the day of my departure from Rangpur, I called up almost every officer at their residences to thank them for their hospitality and to say farewell. Not being otherwise particularly skilled or articulate in the department of social etiquettes, I rather surprised myself for having done what I did. I believe I was so impressed by the hospitality of my colleagues at Rangpur, that I felt I needed to express my gratitude. But, I would have been happy had it been just that, because there was this constant and subtle awareness of a foreboding at the back of my mind since then. I had just done something quite out of the ordinary in terms of my usual social habit and practice, and I kept asking myself, “Now, why did I do that?” I am not a believer in the paranormal, nor do I subscribe to the notion which suggests any credible link between what one does, and what could transpire as a result of that – in a mystical sense, that is. Naturally therefore, and not unlike other similar inconsequential little incidents in my life, this soon got tucked away into an inconspicuous corner of my head.

I was driven over to Saidpur Airport to board an ATP (Air Turbo Prop) aircraft of Bangladesh Biman – the national carrier – for our flight back to Dhaka. As we walked down the tarmac to the waiting aircraft, I was rather disheartened at how aging and uninspiring the aircraft looked. But, then again, there was hardly any aircraft in the fleet of Bangladesh Biman at that time that wasn't actually aging.

As I was walking down the aisle to my seat at the very back of the aircraft I, rather jokingly, mentioned to an officer from Saidpur Cantonment, seated in the front row, that statistically it was the back of an aircraft – where I was headed – which was the safest in case of a crash. We had a good laugh, but as I got into my seat and fastened my seatbelt, I said a silent and ardent prayer that we have a safe flight. Little did I know that God had been eavesdropping in on our little conversation, and had decided to infuse a bit of spice into a journey which otherwise had the potential of being historically boring.

The one-hour flight from Saidpur to Dhaka was largely uneventful, except for a cloud-cover over most of its flight path. There must also have been a good number of air-pockets, therefore resulting in considerable turbulence, but nothing that could be considered a cause for concern. When we finally arrived over Dhaka I could see the city through the scattered and momentary breaks in the clouds. Very soon, as the plane lost altitude while approaching Dhaka Airport, it broke the clouds, and now the outskirts of the capital came into full view.

I have always had a passion for flying since the time I was very young, and therefore, a seat by the window was unfailingly my preferred place of choice, with my face literally glued to the pexiglass, especially during take-offs and landings. Every time that the plane took off into the air, it was a thrill to watch the ground fall away, as huge buildings rapidly shrank to the size of little match boxes, and mighty rivers turned into sparkling silvery ribbons. Landings too, brought with it a rush of adrenaline as the plane floated down towards the earth. I would hold my breath and wait in anticipation of the 'thud' and the 'bump' as the plane finally touched the ground – always trying to assess how smoothly and softly the pilot had been able to execute the landing.

This time too, it was no different. I watched with child-like thrill as the ground got nearer while the pilot, I assume, lined up the aircraft with the landing strip at Dhaka Airport for the final approach. The seat beside mine was unoccupied. Familiar sights and landmarks of Dhaka came into view and got rapidly larger – certainly much larger now, than matchboxes – as they began to rush by under us as our plane continually descended. Very soon we were almost on top of the runway and rapidly losing altitude. The scattered trees and the bushes beside the runway were now speeding by like bullets.

We were hardly about twenty or thirty feet from the ground when, for no particular reason, I leaned over across the empty seat beside mine and looked down the aisle – and my heart skipped a beat. I knew for a fact that at that point the front of the aircraft ought to have been angled up, so the wheels under both the wings would touch down first – something known as 'flaring', in aviation language. But, to my amazement, concern, and perhaps a tinge of panic, this aircraft did not seem to be flaring! What more, it appeared to be descending at a rate which was alarmingly greater than what I would have expected!

And then it came.

A thunderous metallic bang and crunch, the likes of which I had never heard before, accompanied by a bone-jarring shudder, the likes of which I never knew even existed. But nothing less than this, of course, was to be expected when an aircraft, loaded to full capacity, hits concrete at an unprecedented speed and angle.

While the cabin filled with the shrieks and screams of my fellow passengers, the impact forced the aircraft to bounce back up into the air to a height of about 20-30 feet. At that point the aircraft was wobbling from side-to-side, and as the wings swayed up and down, the tips came precariously close to the ground. My heart was stuck in my throat as I contemplated the devastating outcome of one of the wingtips catching the ground, which would have caused the plane to cartwheel and to break into fragments, amidst a ball of fire. Fortunately, that did not happen. However, the plane did bounce a few more times, with the height of the bounce getting less and less, as if it were a stone skipping over water. If my face was glued to the window before, it was literally a part of it now, as I gripped the arm-rests of my seat with a force that could have squeezed something much more than simply juice out of a lemon!

Soon the bouncing stopped and the aircraft began to scrape nose-down along the runway. The entire nose-gear had completely broken away on initial impact, taking the left propeller out with it. Looking out and down my window, I could see fiery sparks coming from under our aircraft as we slid and grazed along the runway. And now the aircraft was beginning to angle to the left. This brought with it the renewed and catastrophic prospect of either the wing-tip catching the ground, in which case the aircraft would surely break up and perhaps be set ablaze, or of it sliding off the runway entirely. Fortunately, none of that happened, and we came to a stop, sitting across at an angle on the runway. The loud sighs of relief all around, and the verbose thanks to the Almighty pretty much summed up the prevailing mental state of all the passengers.

By all rules of aviation safety, and by all measures of logic, we ought to have been instructed by the flight attendant to exit the aircraft immediately, and go down inflatable emergency evacuation slides – assuming they had already been deployed. But surprisingly, we got no such instructions. Maybe the senses and reflexes of the flight attendant had been numbed by the event; or maybe the chapter on emergency evacuation procedures had been ignored during the flight attendant training course; or maybe the inflatable evacuation slides of this aircraft did not even work!

Whatever the reason, it resulted in us, the shaken passengers, sitting inside the ill-fated aircraft for around twenty to thirty minutes before a bus and the stairs arrived from the airport to get us out of the aircraft and get driven to the airport. All of this, of course, begged the question of what would have happened to us, had the plane actually caught fire, and prompt and immediate action was required to save lives.

I am not quite sure whether or not the level of alertness and efficiency of the emergency services and procedures at Dhaka Airport is any better these days. But, if the quality of its services in other areas of activity is any indication of how well it is going to perform in an emergency, I am not particularly hopeful.

When I reached home and narrated the entire incident to Samina, it genuinely sounded like I was telling her the story of a thriller movie I had just seen. The wide-eyed expression on her face as my narration went on clearly indicated not only how serious the incident was, but also how easily it could have gone horribly wrong. It was then that I wondered whether there might have been any connection between what had happened at Dhaka Airport and, contrary to my social practices, my phone calls to almost everyone back in Rangpur.

It is commonly believed that events in life, be those delightful or dreadful, take place in clusters. And I am further told that that is perhaps dictated by certain stars and planets trillions of miles or hundreds of light-years away. It seems like it is not enough that some of those stars and planets are being whipped around crazily by immense gravitational fields, being blasted by deadly radiation and giant asteroids on a daily basis, or are locked in a deadly tug-of-war with some black hole somewhere in the universe that they feel they also have the time and the inclination to interfere with our lives, and from such great distances. I am no one to judge the credibility of certain age-old beliefs or widely-believed phenomena. But apparently, I was in such a 'cluster' on the day that the aircraft I was flying in decided to fall flat on its chin on the runway.

Right after the initial 'hysterics' were over, Samina insisted that we offer what is known as a "Sadaquah", meaning a voluntary charity. In this context it would have to be an animal donated, in the name of the Almighty, to a person of lesser means, who could benefit from the donation. All in an effort to display our thankfulness to the Almighty for the favor He had showered upon us by having kept me safe through an air crash.

It all made sense till the point that Samina suggested that I, within the hour, ought to make arrangements to purchase a goat for the purpose. And, under the circumstances "making arrangements" meant going down to the goat market myself, located at Tongi Bridge, which was roughly 20 kilometers away. Very soon, I set off on my Kawasaki motorbike, with my batman riding behind me. Finally, having made the purchase of the goat at Tongi Bridge, the only logical method of carrying that animal back home seemed to be on the lap of my batman. The constant bleating that accompanied us for the 20 kilometer trip back was rather disconcerting, besides being annoying as well. And, of course, I never had the heart to inquire of my batman of whether or not the goat had also had any urge to relieve itself, while on his lap! And even if it did, my batman had apparently decided to relegate that memory to the past as quickly as possible.

The news of the crash was on the front page of the newspapers the next morning, with a picture of our plane sitting across on the runway, and its nose on the ground. The reason for the crash was never made public. Newspaper reports of it the next morning seemingly attributed it to a mechanical failure. However, with someone in my family working for the same airline and sufficiently highly-placed, the facts behind the mishap were made known to me. That, combined with my first-hand experience of having been in the crash myself, compels me to conclude that it was, beyond any doubt, a case of piloting error.

Biman engineers trying to repair the nose gear of the ATP plane that met an accident at Zia International Airport yesterday.
—Star photo by Mohsin

Picture showing Biman engineers trying to repair the broken nose wheel of the ATP aircraft that crashed with the author in it. This picture was taken from a daily newspaper published the day after the crash

Supposedly, at a certain point during the flight, the Captain had become somewhat physically indisposed, and had requested the First Officer to land the aircraft. When the plane finally broke through the clouds while coming in to land at Dhaka, the First Officer realized he was still too high, and would therefore miss the runway at the existing rate of descent.

I do not know whether or not the airport at Dhaka was equipped with an ILS (Instrument Landing System), which provides pilots with a glide angle for descent, despite adverse weather conditions. I also do not know whether or not this aircraft had instrumentation which supported ILS landings, or even if it did, whether or not it was actually working.

Whatever may have been the reason, rather than aborting the landing and going around, the First Officer decided to make this approach count, which meant he had to lose altitude rather quickly. That was when he was not left with enough time or the distance to either slow down to landing speed, make the angle of descent more gentle, or flare the aircraft: all of which, unfortunately, came together to cause the crash.

All said and done, I now seem to have a phrase capable of stopping every conversation dead on their tracks at any social gathering, and handing me the center stage.

And that phrase is: "I have been in a plane crash once".

Then, with all eyes on me, and standing in the limelight, I begin my story. But every time I relate those tense and harrowing moments on the runway at Dhaka Airport, I gratefully look up at Heaven above with an inner eye, and thank the Almighty for having given me a second lease on life.

As an annotation of interest I would like to add that the runway at Dhaka Airport had been constructed some twenty years ago under the joint collaboration of Taylor Woodrow, a British construction company, and Omar Sons Limited, a engineering company of the then East Pakistan. And as the Chief Engineer of Omar Sons Limited, my father was intimately involved in the planning, design and construction of the runway. It would have been heartbreaking and ironic indeed to have his son perish on that same runway some twenty years later!

Into the Valley of the Blind

> *"There are two ways to be fooled. One is to believe what isn't true; the other is to refuse to believe what is true." – Søren Kierkegaard*

Back at CMH Dhaka, I soon realized that a lot of what went on in there in terms of priority for treatment was sometimes measured not by the seriousness of the illness, but perhaps by the rank and appointment of the individual being treated.

A retired soldier, perhaps suffering from some complicated illness and languishing in a remote ward was probably of less medical significance than the infected nail of an eminent institutional personality. This is not to say that no one cared about the retired individual, but that the medical staff had to be much more vigilant regarding the bacillus that had made a home under the high-ranking nail – and which had to be evicted promptly, painlessly and with much greater care, concern and attention.

It was never a question of *what* the illness was, it seemed. It was always a matter of *who* was ill.

What I say may not sound right to some, and I don't blame them. Perhaps I look at things differently. Perhaps that was the way things were supposed to be done at a place like this. Who knows? I do not claim to have had any measure of understanding of what shaped certain ethics and morals of a system which was sometimes found to adhere to a feudalistic philosophy and to preferential treatment attitudes. If I did, I would not have walked away when my career was finally within striking distance of an ascendency. And that was because my ethics and morals somehow did not seem to be sitting on the same set of values, principles and beliefs of some individuals. At almost every step of the way, I found myself having to consistently and resolutely resist the endeavors of some, which threatened to transform me from a humane Mr. Hyde to a hideous Dr. Jeckyll – and in which, I daresay, they almost succeeded.

Aside from that, I was also never able to make any sense of the institutional indifference to the fact that the innumerable complex cogs and wheels of a medical functionary, with its various subtle and sensitive ramifications, simply couldn't be stamped with a concept of functionality that was set in stone and scripted to be doomed to being counterproductive. In the context of running a hospital efficiently, a certain degree of independence of the specialties from the administration, as well as interdependence between the two, is always essential to the fruitful outcome of each and every endeavor which either of them undertakes. If that is not adhered to, the administration and the specialties will soon find themselves stepping on each other's toes. What eventually results is a meaningless exercise where everyone stumbles, and the desired outcome is hardly ever achieved. And the greatest loser is always, and invariably, the unsuspecting patient.

Furthermore, those in lofty offices weren't always prepared to appreciate or accept the fact that the making of a specialist is a process where knowledge, talent, expertise, experience and maturity comes together in a unique culmination. It would have been an indication of true institutional wisdom had a specialist been given the kind of incentive, freedom and latitude which encouraged and promoted the advancement of innovative and progressive ideas.

On the contrary, there was this constant effort to keep the specialists at the end of a tight leash. If this was anybody's way of keeping things in 'good order and discipline', they were certainly not going about it the right way. Every pioneering endeavor and every innovative measure was invariably tagged with an undertone of 'accountability', and which was sometimes taken to awkward extremes. This, unfortunately, stood in the way of any real progress.

A glaring example of this will be narrated in a later chapter when an innovative surgical procedure instituted by me, and which was based on the verified outcome of my thesis, was mindlessly thrown out the window by a set of shortsighted and obstinate mental predispositions.

Accountability, by definition, is an obligation to accept responsibility, and furnish a justifiable explanation for any action.

However, if justification for every conceivable action and endeavor is sought irrespective of its intent or outcome without properly examining its various interrelated facets and modalities, and then taken to unimaginable extremes, then the free flow of ideas, the birth of innovations, and the manifestation of skills – especially surgical – are severely curbed, and the growth of any specialty ruthlessly stunted.

If History is the holy scribe from which we take lessons, we would do well to remember that every pioneering human endeavor ever made since the dawn of Mankind, has had its share of casualties and catastrophes. The sinking of the Titanic, the crash of the Hindenburg, the Tacoma Bridge collapse, and the Challenger and Columbia shuttle disasters are but a notable few. Yes, equipment, instruments, structures and more importantly, humans, had failed. But, that never set the stage for a culture of viewing later pioneering endeavors with suspicion. It never stopped Mankind from continuing to sail, to fly, to build and to explore. In fact, lessons learned have resulted in better ships, planes, bridges and spacecrafts of today.

But regrettably, in this instance, novel and innovative surgical measures and medical endeavors were nearly always viewed with suspicion and, sometimes even disdain. Hindrances and obstacles were often carefully laid across the path to any pioneering progress. Consequently, the practice and profession of surgery, devoid of any improvement or innovation, were soon reduced to being nothing more than a boring series of mindless and endless repetitive actions reminiscent of the tree-dwelling primates.

The Artisans of Deception

> *"Your religion is what you do when the sermon is over." – H. Jackson Brown*

Surprisingly however, one particular medical endeavor was not eyed with the usual disdain and distrust that was otherwise so commonplace. Certain masterminds in certain lofty offices one day, collectively, decided it was time to gate-crash into the scene of cardiac procedures and major cardiac surgeries.

In fact, a good number of civilian medical institutions were already well on their way to establishing such a department, and practicing the procedure with, if I may add, considerable success and fame. And so, one fine morning, it was decided that cardiac surgery also needed to be a premier specialty of the medical corps. In fact, it eventually turned out to be much more than just a premier specialty. It became a "favored" specialty, if you will, and not without good reason.

To that end, the medical institution, first of all, set about hunting for a specialist in cardiac surgery from wherever it could find one. And, contrary to usual practice, it did not seem to want to put into motion the process of sending an officer or two of the corps to obtain a post-graduate training in the subject. That was perhaps because the rat race was on and certain quarters weren't willing to be left behind. And since time was of the essence at that point, they felt that cutting a corner such as this was acceptable. But, tragically, that set the tone to cutting a few more corners along the way, with appalling results. But, that is my point of view, which may not have been shared by those on the running track eager to breast the tape at an ignominious finish line. Notably too, the lofty offices also did not seem to want to solicit the recommendations and training services of experts in the field, either from home or from abroad, perhaps because that would be tantamount to an admission of ignorance and of inability which, of course, was unacceptable.

The medical corps – with the blessings of some in lofty offices – finally got hold of an individual who, presumably, had some training in cardiac surgery from somewhere abroad. They donned on him a uniform and gave him the rank of a lieutenant colonel right away, surpassing many who had joined years earlier and who perhaps deserved that promotion much more than he did at that point. And then that individual was fast-tracked down the lane of military indoctrination and basic military training at near-lightning speed.

At the same time, back at CMH Dhaka, some senior specialists went about hurriedly putting together a conglomeration of commodities thought necessary to get a department of cardiac surgery up and running in record time. Resources, which most specialties could only dream of and had a lifetime longing for, were poured into the new department most eagerly, liberally and generously. Strangely, the kingpins of the corps, particularly those of surgery and medicine – otherwise the perennial antagonists – seemed to be in a strange sort of collusion, at least in this particular matter.

It is my assumption that one of the reasons, perhaps, for some in the upper echelons being suddenly gripped by this frenzy and paranoia of having a functional and independent department of cardiac surgery within the establishment was the realization, particularly amongst the aging few, of their own potential need for cardiac interventions in the not-too-distant future – and hence the unprecedented outpouring of efforts and resources. But the fact that certain means to that end were a flagrant disregard for sensible practice, done to expedite a self-serving and self-gratifying agenda, was grossly and conveniently overlooked – or maybe not even properly comprehended in the haste.

The faculty of cardiac surgery was soon up and running and, in my opinion, much sooner than a specialty of such a complex nature ought to have. The fact that it was done in uncalled-for haste, under the tutelage of a person with questionable credentials, and the patronage of some with disputable intent, gave the entire exercise a dubious dimension.

Moreover, it did not seem to matter to anyone that there was a spate of needless casualties in the process. After all, this was an 'experimental lab' where the cardiac surgeon and his team – all of whom were still on a rather steep learning curve – were given the right and the liberty of figuring out the right way from the wrong, be that at the expense of needless morbidity and mortality. Cases which perhaps never met the criteria for a cardiac procedure or cases inadequately prepared for surgery were mindlessly put under the knife, only to be able to get ahead in the rat-race. That, in my opinion, was akin to sending 'probes' out on to a minefield to be able to figure out a safe path, based on which of the 'probes' got blown to bits. Because as far as some were concerned, this was a promising specialty in the making and casualties were to be expected. If today's casualties were to be the stepping stones to tomorrow's successes – especially where it concerned the hearts of those with the badges and the brasses – then such sacrifices were certainly not in vain. And, it was for that very reason that the brand-new department of cardiac surgery, and the medical institution as a whole, were both spared the otherwise habitual vicious response of the high offices in the event of a hospital casualty. Because, if that was not the case, how was a department expected to sail to success and fly to fame?

This, in fact, was quite contrary to the frequent practice of the powers-that-be to mostly jump to a one-sided conclusion in the event of a hospital casualty, and respond to it in an otherwise vehement, acrimonious and almost-vindictive manner. It never seemed to matter that the treating surgeons or physicians had exerted a most remarkable effort in trying to save a patient. Neither did it seem relevant to the issue that, in most cases, the resources at their disposal were most meager and rudimentary. The hierarchy never seemed willing to understand that a hospital too was akin to a battleground where casualties were to be expected despite a most sincere effort. And, they also did not seem to be bothered by the fact that in this particular battleground, most of their soldiers were fighting a 20th century war with crossbows and spears which, moreover, were in limited supply.

And this is what the following pages deal with.

The Vultures of Vengeance

> *"It is better to deserve honors and not have them than to have them and not deserve them" – Mark Twain*

Most regrettably, a good number of people who routinely solicited the services of the military hospitals always seemed to harbor the firm conviction that that was where the ultimate solution to all medical problems lay. Deeply entrenched in their minds was not the belief that all their medical needs *would* be solved at a military hospital, but that they *should be*. It was as if this hospital was the simple extension of a unique model where the answers to all medical concerns and issues lay within the basic and primal act of howling an order, and then marching to it in perfect unison. Even in a ritual as simple as that, people frequently fell out of step. We have also seen how a most brilliantly thought-out military engagement conceived by the most accomplished of military minds can also be fraught with a fair amount of error and resultant casualties – and failures. We have a number of wars of every scale of intensity to bear testament to that fact. Why then, should the matter of casualties in a hospital be so unacceptable?

Logically speaking, those who provide treatment at the hospitals and those who engage in battles are the same humans, only with different types of expertise. Yet, the former are expected never to falter or to fail, while those failing in the battlefield are generally found to be given a substantial measure of leniency, where a host of highly technical military logic and explanations are at hand to explain their failures. Understandably, if every military blunder was labeled with 'accountability' leading to a 'disposal' in accordance with the military penal codes, then the likes of Napoleon, Field Marshal Bernard Montgomery and General Douglas MacArthur would never have had a second chance.

Given the overwhelming number of patients in this hospital, the perennial shortage of doctors and nursing staff, and the perpetual dearth of adequate resources, every bed in this hospital was a skirmish, every ward a crusade, every outpatient unit a theatre of conflict, every department a battlefield and the hospital itself a war zone. But, most regrettably, a hospital seemed to be the place where casualties were least acceptable to those who were likely to sustain it themselves during a war, despite a most meticulous battle plan and the most valiant of efforts. It was as if this hospital was their private and prestigious backyard battlefield, where 'medals' of certain undefined cravings and unfulfilled aspirations were to be won.

Time was never wasted, therefore, as the so-called 'vultures of vengeance', frequently armed with the weapon of 'accountability' and in search of 'spoils', swooped down upon the hospital at the slightest hint of a casualty. In this private little battlefield of theirs, they seemed to want to ensure that for every casualty that the hospital sustained, there would have to be one other – and that was to be the treating doctor.

Not once did it cross certain enlightened minds that a patient could have died because the illness had come too suddenly or too swiftly or perhaps because the patient had reported too late to the hospital. It also never seemed to occur to them that the illness could have been complicated beyond the resources at the doctors' disposal to be able to do anything about it. Or because, this time perhaps, the overwhelming might of Nature was simply too overpowering for Man to handle.

Understandably, if Man could do everything, there would be no need for a "God". But when we put ourselves in the proper perspective of this Universe and consider our overall capability of influencing the way it works, it would be reasonable to conclude, by way of deductive reasoning, that a certain Power does exist. Whether one chooses to call that power "God" or anything else is a matter of personal choice. I call Him God.

Interestingly however, some people seemed to have decided that there was actually no God, and that Man – more precisely, the doctors at a military hospital – were omnipotent, invincible and, hence, could never lose a patient to death.

Therefore, each and every hospital casualty mostly brought with it a swift and severe response, sometimes unfolding a chain of events of horrific and lamentable proportions, and which usually ended up with the hospital turning into a virtual graveyard for the treating doctor.

Casualties of Capricious Desires

"Corn can't expect justice from a court composed of chickens." – African Proverb

It also seemed to matter to some people as to *who* the hospital casualty was – rather than *what had caused* the casualty. For some weird reason, *who* always seemed to come before *how* or *why*.

It is most likely that this so-called *'Who'* factor was, in reality, the outcome of a collective sentiment of 'rank and status worship', which lamentably overshadowed the need for fairness, neutrality and, most of all, objectivity. It was always the elevated status and the institutional eminence of a hospital casualty which seemed to instigate the time-honored instinct for blindly seeking a scapegoat, rather than searching sincerely for the Truth. Sadly, when Truth is not sought and good judgment departs, objectivity and rationality get replaced by certain sinister emotions – emotions such as paranoia, suspicion or a 'persecution complex' – all of which tend to cloud the mind and destroy everything they touch.

It was a similar sinister emotion which had clouded the mind of Marcus Brutus who, thus being robbed of his faculties of judgment and reasoning, drove a knife into Julius Caesar. And when Mark Anthony, in his famous eulogy, lamented, "O judgment, thou art fled to brutish beasts, and men have lost their reason", it epitomized the insanity and the tragedy at that time. And, in much the same way that this departure from truth, good judgment and reasoning had led to blood being spilled at the Theater of Pompey more than two millennia ago, it seemed to me that the present-day departure from such denominators also had the potential of ruthlessly slaying dignity and talent in the dark and dangerous alleys of the world around me.

The one effective instrument frequently used these days in any establishment or in the society at large, in order to either bolster the chances of an inappropriate opportunity or to seek retribution for a perceived misconduct, is 'connection'. These are mutually beneficial links, relationships and alliances between individuals, regardless of position, status and appointment. In fact, connection seems to be the key to a lot of what gets achieved these days. Interestingly, even in a hospital situation, a sound connection sometimes seems to evoke a commotion and invoke a sentiment capable of shaking the very foundation of the institution, in case of an unfortunate death, regardless of whether or not it was an act of omission, commission or beyond the limits of human capability to resolve. But sadly, on the other hand, if the patient is without any connection, the circumstances of their demise are largely inconsequential.

Interestingly, it is also often seen that when an inquisition does take place in order to ascertain culpability in such cases, the proceedings mostly follow the path to determining 'who' rather than 'what' had caused the mishap. I am certainly not saying that humans are infallible, but it is also equally important to examine, at the same time, the mechanisms that make a system function. If a car won't run the way it is expected to or supposed to, it is advisable to lift the hood, once in a while, to inspect the engine. While it is fairly easy and convenient to blame 'someone' for an uncomfortable ride, it is equally important to verify that the components that make the car run are in good working order. But unfortunately, rectifying a system anomaly always seems much more complex than simply laying a straightforward blame on a person. And that is probably the reason we often witness human sufferings being meted out in order to appease certain flawed convictions and inappropriate conventions.

What comes next will, perhaps, illustrate the point.

A mid-ranking officer with apparently very sound connections brought in his seven-year-old sick son, who had to be admitted to the Pediatric Ward.

The parents were preparing to leave on a trip abroad the very next day. With the patient's condition not being too well, the physicians advised the parents to postpone their trip. However, with all the plans in place, they choose to ignore the physicians' advice, and left for the trip with the patient's elderly grandmother looking after matters. Most unfortunately, this turned out to be one of those rare instances where, in spite of all the medication, attention, expertise, and experience, the child succumbed to his illness. The parents cut their trip short, and returned home immediately.

Soon after the funeral rites were over, the dreaded juggernaut of allegations and finger-pointing began to roll. It started with the obvious and inevitable process of the aggrieved party contacting and motivating people in high places. A witch-hunt was soon set in motion to identify individuals to be blamed for the unfortunate and untimely passing away of the child. The fact that a patient had died meant that someone had to be held accountable. But, interestingly, the hunting party did not need to venture too far because the preys – meaning the treating physicians – were, most conveniently, only an arms-length away. A lynching was in order, and everyone seemed to know right from the start who would be hanging from the end of the rope.

For those at the helm of the medical institution, this was an acid test of the commitment to their principles, of the confidence in their performance, and of the belief in their knowledge – in all of which they failed in a most disgraceful manner. With the posse on the prowl, certain bastions of the medical institution began to collapse like a house of cards.

That was when none in authority could stand up and say that in spite of the best medical attention and efforts, an unfortunate death was something that could very well happen, and does sometimes happen. That was when none had the confidence to declare that everything that was humanly possible had been done for the child and that it made little sense looking for lapses and scapegoats. That was when none had the courage to assert that the treating doctors, who had spared absolutely nothing to save the child, be left alone.

Sadly, that was also when the true nature of some placed high in the medical hierarchy finally came to light. That was when all the confidence placed on them was eventually shattered. That was when I saw long-presumed strengths, principles, ideals, ethics and morals get buried in the graveyard of cowardice, greed, and a shameless attempt at preservation of rank and status.

Administrators and specialists alike, placed high in the medical hierarchy began to glance nervously over their shoulders. Most wanted to absolve themselves of the case, and would not like to have anything to do with it. While the administrators were pondering how to preserve their meticulously orchestrated image as able custodians of the corps, the senior specialists were wondering how to assume a posture that would reflect their so-called 'genuine concern' for the now-dead patient, and portray their superlative attention to the case – however fictional and fabricated that might have been.

It was generally known – and a fact widely accepted – that some senior specialists at the helm of the department of medicine considered it not only imperative but also rather fanciful to have the department of pediatrics under their medical and administrative authority, much like an egotistic trophy to be toted around for the world to see and to applaud. In this, they succeeded. However, both as a matter of convenience and as a consequence of ignorance, they did not seem to want to concern themselves with the handling of pediatric cases which, I think, actually boded well for the sick children.

But now they had to be concerned. They had to be concerned because the blood-hounds were out looking for a meal, and those senior specialists did not want to be on their plates. This was an exceptional circumstance, and therefore it called for extraordinary measures. It all boiled down to the age-old preservation of rank and status, which had to be achieved at all cost. It did not seem to matter what the price was for it, or who paid the price, because such people were capable of walking into a pawnshop any day and more than willing to trade their honor and dignity for rank, status and appointment.

In one of the most shameful and disgraceful acts ever witnessed, some senior specialists of the department of medicine proceeded to give the impression that they were genuinely concerned about, and were actively involved with the case – which, of course, was more of a fiction than a fact. In a move perhaps unprecedented in any civilized society, let alone a hospital, the case file of the unfortunate patient was tampered with. This obviously was a desperate attempt at having the lofty offices believe they had played their part. And all this, because they knew only too well that, in this particular case, without the overt evidence of any active involvement, their cherished rank, appointment and status were bound to be in the line of fire.

Pages of treatment instructions purportedly written out later were covertly inserted into the case file of the patient, preceding those of the pediatricians' to make it look like those senior specialists had played their expected supervisory role and taken the treatment initiative. But being actually ignorant of pediatric principles and practices, they copied the already existing treatments of the pediatricians almost to their last letter. Even more appalling and disgraceful was the fact that on the pages they later inserted, they left instructions that the pediatricians were to follow their treatment advice! If ever was dignity and self-respect sacrificed at the altar of deception and downright shamelessness, then this had to be it. If ever had selfishness and cowardice been used as a shield for the devious and the deceitful, then this had to be the most outstanding example.

With the pediatricians' treatment now appearing on the following pages, those specialists finally had their tracks covered. They didn't seem to be concerned at all by the fact that they had just tossed their pediatricians heartlessly into the center of a school of sharks circling for blood. What mattered more to them was that they were safe for the moment, and so were their much-vaunted and oft-flaunted ranks and appointments. The medical administrators too, though fully aware of the outcome of such a heinous act, condoned it, perhaps on the premise that on the road to glory and greatness, junior specialists were expendable commodities who could be trampled upon at will.

The plot to pull off a most remarkable heist of deceit and deception then began to take shape within the four walls of the medical powerhouse.

The treating pediatricians were coerced, so to speak – though 'commanded' would perhaps have been a better word – to sign certain documents which apparently shut the door permanently to any plea of not being guilty of the charges being framed. Understandably, this was a military organization where one followed the chain of command, and refusing to comply with a senior's 'request' – aka 'order' – would obviously amount to insubordination. Besides, the signatories were assured that all such paperwork was merely a formality which was necessary, and that the matter was actually nothing more than an open-and-shut case. And they were also further assured that everything possible would be done to ensure that no one was unjustly or unfairly implicated or incriminated.

But sadly, that was not the case. The medical authorities, in reality, had no intention of following through on their promise. Their only objective was to demonstrate, for the benefit of those barking for blood, that the pediatricians – who actually had done everything within their knowledge, skill and resources to save the unfortunate child – had been penalized. And that was because a special brand of people scattered throughout the demography of the establishment were probably guided by an institutional philosophy which promoted an aversion to, and a misplaced mistrust on all that the medical establishment represented. And in this particular case, it seemed as if the only recourse for them was a closure that would satiate not only their own so-called 'hunger' but also that of those screaming for blood from the grandstands of the Roman coliseum.

It did not seem to matter in this case that responsibility was not shared equally by all which, in fact, it should have been by all measure of fairness.

If negligence and deceit were ever to figure in the overall scheme of things, then the senior specialists were certainly guilty of it. If deception was ever a denominator of misdeeds, then the administrators of the medical institution were its most ardent proponents. If carelessness and imprudence were ever to be a contributor to catastrophe, then the parents, who had so irresponsibly gone off on a trip abroad with their child in the hospital, had played their part. They needed to be there to see how much the pediatricians did, to try to save their child. They needed to know that sometimes the overwhelming might of Nature and the nature of certain devious diseases render humans helpless. And they also needed to know that there was a God who comes with a plan of His own, which is beyond any human comprehension or ability to alter.

Overall therefore, while the senior specialists conveniently turned their backs to all that was transpiring, and the administrators went about the business of preserving their prized positions and possessions, the parents did their best to ensure that those who had tried their utmost to save their child not go unpunished.

Statements pertaining to the events, situation and the circumstances leading up to the unfortunate death of the patient were obtained from the treating pediatricians during the course of an inquiry. At a certain stage in the proceedings it became plainly and painfully obvious to those being questioned, that the recording of their statements were, in fact, nothing more than a charade; that minds were already made up as to who were to be held responsible for all that had transpired; that the outcome of the inquiry was a foregone conclusion and that the authorities were going through the motions merely to give everything the semblance of a so-called 'orderly conduct'.

Predictably, it did not seem to matter that Truth was not revealed during either the recording of the statements, or the proceedings of the case. Truth, in this case, was nowhere be found, as the wolves of vengeance prowled the streets and terrorized Truth into fleeing out of sight. In the face of palpable pressures from certain influential quarters – pressure perhaps born of malice and a reprisal-focused frenzied state of mind – truth gave way to falsehood, trickery and treachery. The final verdict was a testament to one of the vilest chapters of human immorality and indignity ever written, where truth, fairness and justice were mindlessly, and perhaps deliberately, shown the door to oblivion.

That was when the pediatricians, like scores of other officers of the medical institution, including myself, realized that we had always been – and would continue to be – pawns in a game of chess that was being played with a motive beyond logic, a pretext just as frivolous, and intent full of guile, deceit and deception. Predictably, the pawns were regularly sacrificed with an expected degree of indifference because, in reality, it was their demise which paved the way for the kings, the queens, the bishops and the knights to move forward unhindered. The pawns, on their part, realized that they were mere casualties of war: a war which was as senseless as it was shocking, and as absurd as it was shameful. It was a war being fought for a grossly unwholesome and a totally unjustified cause on the battlefields of pure personal gains and egotistic satisfaction. This was a war fought by people blinded by a faith, an ambition and a commitment that was as repulsive and reprehensible, as it was disgusting and dishonorable.

And the winning strategy in such a war was pretty simple and straightforward: Place the pawns ***in the line of fire*** so the kingpins and the linchpins could survive to go on and write their own glorious histories. They needed to survive because they needed to come back the next day and sacrifice more unsuspecting pawns in a most despicable and decadent sport.

Chapter 8

IN THE LINE OF FIRE

The 'peaks' and 'valleys' of Chittagong

"There are sufferings that have lost their memory and do not remember why they are suffering." – Antonio Porchia

It was about ten years now that both Samina and I had been in Dhaka Cantonment.

And this is how.

Following our initial stint at CMH Savar, Samina was posted to CMH Dhaka in *Dhaka Cantonment*, while I had gone off to Rajshahi for my basic military training – where Samina joined me after about ten weeks. After we both returned from the training, I was posted to 61 Field Ambulance, while Samina to CMH Dhaka – both in *Dhaka Cantonment*.

Subsequently, I was posted as the adjutant at the Armed Forces Medical Institute (AFMI), which again, was in

Dhaka Cantonment. This was followed by my selection for the Grading Course in Surgery, during which I was attached to the AFMI, with a placement in CMH Dhaka for the training – in *Dhaka Cantonment*.

Following my qualification in the Grading Final Examinations, I was posted to CMH Dhaka – in *Dhaka Cantonment* – as a Surgical Specialist. In the meantime, Samina was selected for the Fellowship Course in Pediatrics, during which she was attached to the AFMI in *Dhaka Cantonment*. While Samina was in her Fellowship course, I was selected for my Masters course in Orthopedic Surgery, and for which I was again attached to the AFMI – in *Dhaka Cantonment*. It seemed as if Dhaka Cantonment was not quite willing to let go of us!

Following completion of our post-graduate courses, both Samina and I were posted to CMH Dhaka, she as a Pediatrician and I as an Orthopedic Surgeon. And yes, we were still in *Dhaka Cantonment*!

So, therefore, it was almost ten years now that we were in Dhaka Cantonment.

Obviously, selections to our respective post-graduate courses and, to some extent, our postings were to blame for that. Though, at this point, I would not like to venture into explaining the reasons for our selections and our postings, I would nonetheless like to mention that we were insanely, yet contentedly involved in our studies and our work to even notice how those ten years had flown by.

Postings to any military hospital or to a particular cantonment, in general, last an average of up to four to five years at the most. Evidently, we had long outlasted our tenure by being at a place this long – a fact which, we noticed, was gradually starting to seep into even the most casual of conversations and passing remarks being made by people around us. Such a sentiment, we knew, was soon bound to percolate up to the highest level of decision-making. And indeed it did.

We were on a trip to Singapore once, when we received news of our posting to another military hospital. Call it coincidence, if you will. But I have always believed that coincidence walks on two legs: one the 'mystic', and the other the 'malicious'.

The former is what coincidence is all about and, in keeping with its age-old novelty, sits firmly on the mysterious and the magical. It is purely unintentional, and happens by chance. However, it is the other leg of coincidence which perhaps represents what is sometimes intended, or even manipulated – a situation which a good number of people in any organization or establishment can perhaps relate to. In our case too, I would give myself to believe that for our posting order to have been published when we were out of the country, the so-called 'malicious' leg of coincidence perhaps had a big role to play.

It was a rather flimsy curtain which veiled the fact that measures, which were not always the most ethical or moral, were often employed by some, mainly through connections, to be posted to or to remain in coveted positions or enviable locations for tenures longer than normal. And, in our case too, it was perhaps an assumption by some – dubious though it was –that we were probably resorting to such a practice ourselves to stay where we were, for as long as we had been. Or, on the other hand, it could also have been the result of others resorting to such a practice themselves to effect a successful coup d'état and have us persona non grata at Dhaka Cantonment. Who knows?

It is not as if we were not expecting to be posted out of Dhaka Cantonment. In fact, deep in our hearts, both Samina and I were hoping it would come, and come soon. We were both actually quite overworked at CMH Dhaka by now, and felt it was finally time for a much-needed break. But, standing by a public pay-phone in a distant land I could only smile and shake my head in disbelief at the exquisite timing of our posting, because it had a classic Shakespearean deceptive plot written all over it.

We were posted to CMH Chittagong, the second largest military hospital located to the south of the country, with me as its only orthopedic surgeon, and Samina as the lone pediatrician.

Chittagong, the larger of the two port cities of Bangladesh, is situated on the banks of the Karnaphuli River, which flows into the Bay of Bengal. The beauty of Chittagong is in her location, as she sits primly by the sea to her west, while the lush forested hills of the Chittagong Hill Tracts flank her other three sides as if she were a princess out of a fairy tale, being guarded by three knights in shining armor. The fringes of the city actually undulate on to the smaller hills of the enchanting and captivating Hill Tracts, which in turn get higher and higher, and finally merge with the high hills and mountains extending into India and Myanmar. This gives Chittagong a beauty not shared by any other city in the country. Besides, a little over a hundred kilometers to the south of Chittagong is Cox's Bazaar, which boasts the longest sandy sea beach in the world. The Chittagong Hill Tracts and the sea beach at Cox's Bazaar, therefore, are the most frequented places in Bangladesh in terms of tourism.

So obviously, both Samina and I were visibly excited to have been posted to CMH Chittagong – a fact which seemed to puzzle some people, whose main purpose in life, it appeared, was to try to remain in Dhaka Cantonment for as long as they could.

The only painful part of departing for Chittagong was leaving my ailing mother behind, who had suffered a stroke a few years earlier, and which had left her with a paralyzed right side and without speech. In spite of our busy schedule at CMH Dhaka, Samina and I would always make it a point to visit her at least every other day to be by her side and to look after some of her needs. We also rented video cassettes of Indian movie classics from a video store, called "Rose Valley", near our house in Dhaka Cantonment, for my mother to watch, and which turned into her major and most favorite pastime.

For Samina and me, all this was not merely a routine – it had become our lifestyle, and which we both enjoyed doing. Besides, my mother also had the unwavering support of my siblings, as well as a personal care assistant, to look after her everyday essential needs. Nevertheless, with us being doctors, my mother had come to consider our mere presence by her side a huge moral and physical support for herself.

I vividly remember that moment when Samina and I bid my mother farewell before leaving for Chittagong. She hugged us both dearly, and as we were about to step out the front door I looked back and saw her seated at the edge of her bed, savoring every last bit of her sight of the two of us. That look in her eyes, and her countenance, will forever remain etched in my memory. She couldn't speak, but those eyes were saying a million words and expressing a billion sentiments. I saw sadness in them, as I also saw blessings and affection at the same time.

We had loaded our car with as much of our belongings as we could. Chittagong was a good 6-8 hours away under decent traffic conditions, despite being at a distance of only about 250 kilometers. This was taking into account the not-so-ideal road conditions and the fact that there was a river to be crossed on a ferry. My car, moreover, was not in the best of conditions, which was a cause for concern. Because without the services of organizations like the CAA or the AAA, one was pretty much left to one's own in case of a breakdown in the middle of nowhere.

We owned an aging 1970 Datsun Sunny which we had purchased from my brother at a rather reasonable price, but which wasn't exactly in the best of conditions. I had known for a while now that the radiator of the car had a leak, which the mechanics in Dhaka were not quite able put a finger on. Therefore, we made sure we were carrying enough water with us in a huge plastic jerry-can, in case the radiator decided to boil over and discharge all its contents.

As luck would have it, about halfway into the trip, that was exactly what happened. Fortunately, however, after a decent cooling-off period and about half a jerry can of water later, we were on our way again. For the rest of the trip, my eyes were riveted on the temperature needle on the dash, while I literally willed it not to rise. Whether the leak had decided to get plugged off through some divine intervention or whether my will was strong enough to cause the needle not to rise, I do not know. But eventually we reached Chittagong without any further unnecessary or unpredictable delays.

Our reception at CMH Chittagong was in sharp contrast to the one Samina and I had received at CMH Savar about ten years earlier, including the formalities we were required to go through in order to secure a proper accommodation. Perhaps our present ranks as Majors with ten years of service behind us, and the few extra alphabets of post-graduate medical degrees now attached to our names, made a difference.

It made a difference to the extent that we were immediately accommodated in a reasonably large and comfortable room in the main Officers' Mess in Chittagong Cantonment, since a proper family accommodation wasn't available right away. The difference was also the fact that the Second-in-Command at CMH Chittagong made time to come down more often than once to both look into our needs and to have a cup of tea with us. This, obviously, was in sharp contrast to being left alone in a rather decrepit room for days together in Savar, with only our new-found batman to keep us company and to look into our needs.

After only about a week or so at the Officers mess we were moved to an 'interim accommodation', since a proper accommodation wasn't yet available. This accommodation, though interim, was surprisingly quite modern and well-planned, and seemed recently-built. If truth be told, both Samina and I felt that that would have been more than adequate for the two of us for the period of our tenure at CMH Chittagong. But actually, a bigger and better apartment was waiting for us!

In the meantime, I did notice a particular eagerness in the efforts of the Station Staff Officer (SSO) of Chittagong Cantonment – the person responsible for the allotment of officers' accommodations – to try to get us one as close to his as possible. We eventually ended up moving into the ground floor of a most conveniently located apartment complex. Compared to it, the interim accommodation we were living in all these days now seemed almost like a shack. This apartment was that good! Not surprisingly too, the SSOs apartment was right across from ours. It is my feeling that the SSO was probably looking for that extra bit of psychological security in having two doctors living right next door, more so since he had two daughters who were both in the pediatric age group.

It was when we were moving from one accommodation to another, and a little over a month after we had left Dhaka, that we got news of my mother's sudden passing away. The news struck me with the ferocity of a vicious tropical rainstorm – which shed tears with a million raindrops and howled a most melancholy song with its wind. As the world around me shattered into countless little bits and pieces, I was left feeling strangely empty and unfairly robbed. Suddenly I was without the support I knew I always had since the time I had acquired comprehension and memory. I felt lonely, and the world seemed like a frightful place. It didn't seem to matter that I was a grown-up individual in my late thirties. The one person from whom I had always derived support, solace and wisdom wasn't there anymore, and would never again return!

However, the agonizing and unbearable grief of the departure of one important woman in my life was timely and adequately alleviated by the only other important woman in my life – through her support, solace and wisdom. And though I felt lonely, I derived comfort from the fact that she was there to hold the hand of this so-called 'frightened child' in helping him swim out of the sea of sorrow, and rise from the depths of anguish. Samina made me realize that despite my irreplaceable loss, I needed to get on with my life, or remain perennially bogged down in a pool of misery and grief. Time being the best healer, I eventually recovered enough to be able to get back to my daily routine and to my responsibilities at CMH Chittagong, albeit gradually.

CMH Chittagong was essentially in a zone where the military was conducting a conventional warfare against a secessionist movement and their armed insurgencies in the hilly regions to the south, called the Chittagong Hill Tracts. This was a region where the local tribal population was demanding autonomy and the right to self-determination. Therefore, the focus of all activities of the army at that time was on the Hill Tracts where they were, both militarily and through peaceful means, campaigning to counter the guerilla-type activities of the Shanti Bahini (Peace Force), as the secessionists called themselves.

CMH Chittagong was the military base-hospital closest to the region of conflict, and therefore the number of casualties arriving at that hospital on almost a daily basis was close to monumental. At this point, it is well worth remembering that CMH Chittagong had only one orthopedic surgeon, namely I, to deal with this overwhelming deluge. And this was not taking into account the fact that soldiers sustaining orthopedic injuries in non-combat situations and those with chronic orthopedic disabilities, as well as their families with both acute and chronic orthopedic problems, were all reporting to the orthopedic department as well. It is not surprising therefore, that the orthopedic ward was constantly overflowing with patients, the out-patient clinic was bursting at its seams and the orthopedic operating room busier than a metro station. I will have to admit nevertheless that during that period I was fortunate enough to have had the support of a staff which was as skilled as it was dedicated.

This hospital, much like CMH Dhaka unfortunately, was not spared the overbearing presence of the general surgeons. There were always three or four of them available at CMH Chittagong, including the Senior Surgeon. And in keeping with tradition, most came with their perennially annoying 'mightier-than-thou' attitude.

Being in the proximity of a war zone and given the fact that the army was an institution defined by relentless and intense physical activity, the number and turnover of orthopedic cases was always about three to four times than what the general surgeons had to deal with. Coupled with this was the fact that the coveted appointment of "Senior Surgeon", both by a default arrangement and a draconian law, always went to a general surgeon. Interestingly too, this also gave the rest of the general surgeons, cuddled and huddled under the cozy wings of the mother hen, enviable preferences and privileges.

It also needs to be mentioned that all officers – specialists and GDMOs alike – of the rank of lieutenant colonel and below in this hospital had to perform the duties of a DMO (Duty Medical Officer). Moreover, as in any hospital, a specialist also had to be "on call" to deal with difficult and complicated cases which arrived after 2pm, that is, after regular hospital hours. And, therefore, the duty roster was set in a way that a specialist was not both on-call and a DMO the same day. But, my case was different. Because being the on-call orthopedic surgeon every day, there were days when I was both at the same time!

That notwithstanding, being the lone on-call orthopedic surgeon, I was to be found running constantly back and forth between home and hospital for every trauma, regardless of severity. In sharp contrast, however, with two to three general surgeons available at any given time, they were on-call every second or third day.

Even that was something I was willing to live with, until the Senior Surgeon hatched a brilliant plot. He wanted me to join in with the general surgeons to be on-call for their cases as well! At first, I simply couldn't believe what he was suggesting. The fact that I was on-call every day for the orthopedic cases did not seem to be enough for the general surgeons. What they wanted was another surgeon falling in line with them, so their life would become even easier.

What the Senior Surgeon surely must have realized, but did not really care about, was the fact that I would be functioning as a combined on-call orthopedic and general surgeon every third or fourth day. The fact that every non-orthopedic case would eventually have to be referred by me to a general surgeon after instituting the initial management did not seem to matter either. What mattered was the fact that with another surgeon in their roster – be it an orthopedic surgeon – who could set up the initial care of a case, the general surgeons now had the luxury of getting into the management scene at their own leisure.

What I found most abominable was the Senior Surgeon's detached disregard for my inconceivable situation, and the unsympathetic finality with which he delivered his pronouncement of the extra burdensome responsibility vested upon me. Somehow, it reminded me of a ruthless medieval king from the Dark Ages dismissing a serf to the guillotine only because it gave him an immense, and perhaps a sadistic, pleasure.

In the meantime, a new phase of construction was undertaken at CMH Chittagong where a four-storied structure was built to accommodate the orthopedic ward, the general surgery ward, and wards of two other departments, one on each floor. This distribution was supposedly decided upon at the time the plan was made and sanctioned at the high offices in Dhaka. The wards which were to be relocated to the new building – including the orthopedic ward – had, till then, been inside tin-roofed accommodations, which looked much like the soldiers' barracks, getting unbearably cold during the winters and obnoxiously hot during the summer seasons.

It took several months for the construction to be completed. And once completed all the beds and the equipment of the orthopedic ward were transferred to one of the floors of the new building.

Remarkably, and contrary to the original distribution, the Senior Surgeon then had this sudden random urge to occupy two floors for general surgery, instead of just one. And quite predictably, he decided that he was going to get it out of orthopedic surgery, despite the fact that the number of patients in the orthopedic ward was always at least two to three times that in the general surgical ward. For want of a more appropriate simile, it seemed as if a whiny and cantankerous kid was pointing to, and wanting, another kid's toy, despite holding the exact same toy in his other hand!

Interestingly too, the Commanding Officer and the Second-in-Command of CMH Chittagong seemed suddenly gripped with the frenzy of having the orthopedic ward re-located back to where it originally was, without my consultation, while general surgery was allowed to spread its wings over two entire floors in the newly-constructed building. The need to get this done seemed so urgent that the Second-in-Command himself was seen supervising the entire re-location process.

When I approached the Commanding Officer to inquire into the reason for this sudden turn-around in the decision of the authorities, I was informed that whatever was taking place was in keeping with the 'desire' of the local lofty office! If that was indeed true, then it does not require a genius to conclude that the whiny and cantankerous little kid had somehow been able to persuade his so-called 'guardian nanny' to help him secure what was not his. It did not seem to matter to the Senior Surgeon that all this was not only contrary to the codes of professional propriety, but also contrary to the existing logistics of this hospital as well. What perhaps mattered more to him was that he desired another toy – regardless of whether or not he actually needed it – which he could then tote around like a trophy. Little did the cantankerous 'kid' realize, or even care about, was that all this whimsicalness of his would actually lead to the sufferings of the orthopedic patients.

If what I had been told by my Commanding Officer regarding the wishes of the local high office was indeed true, then this was another outstanding example of how those that had no business in the allocation of resources within a hospital, unnecessarily interfered in the process. Such uncalled-for meddling and intrusions were often made on the basis of bias and favoritism, and not on facts and figures.

Furthermore, this was also an example of how decisions taken within the medical functionary, and made on the basis of bona fide medical requirements could, in an instant, be perfunctorily overturned by those who were experts in military science and not medical science. But, then again, that was naturally to be expected when experts in medical science often took refuge under the powerful wings of their non-medical masters while seeking unjustified, self-gratifying and self-serving solutions. And that was exactly what had happened in this case.

But, then again, it could also be that the local lofty office perhaps had nothing to do with this case. Instead, it could very well have been a case of the Commanding Officer being coerced by the Senior Surgeon to give him the extra floor which, the former being the junior officer, was not quite in a position to refuse. And the Commanding Officer was perhaps 'exploiting' the name of the local headquarters merely as a 'protective shield' to preempt my protests and outcries! If that was really the case, then I will have to admit that it was indeed a brilliant move, since the Commanding Officer knew only too well that in order to voice my concerns and grievances to the local lofty office, I would have to go through him!

And therefore, in keeping with what the Senior Surgeon and perhaps his cohorts in high places desired, but not in keeping with the genuine medical needs of the hospital, the orthopedic ward was back to the tin-shed accommodation, and remained there till the day I left CMH Chittagong.

And that was how that chapter finally ended.

So, to get back to the on-call duties which I was discussing prior to this, the Senior Surgeon had, as already mentioned, laid out the meticulous scheme of getting me to carry out the duties of an on-call general surgeon every third or fourth day, in spite of being the on-call orthopedic surgeon every day.

And things would get rather interesting when, on some days, emergency orthopedic cases arrived when I was the DMO. Here at least, some good sense prevailed, as I was relieved by another medical officer to go into the OR to perform my surgeries. However, the duration, intensity or complexity of the surgery did not seem to matter as I had to be back at my post as the DMO, and carry on in that role till 7:30 am the next morning unless, of course, my surgeries continued well beyond that. On the whole therefore, I was performing, besides my basic duties as an orthopedic surgeon, those of a round-the-clock on-call orthopedic surgeon, an on-call general surgeon and the Duty Medical Officer.

But that was only one half of the story. The other half, regrettably, was equally dismal. If the first half of the story made life difficult, the rest completely obliterated whatever was left of it.

The stage for that was set in the orthopedic out-patient department, which functioned three days a week. I was literally overwhelmed by the number of patients reporting there each out-patient day – which was usually in the region of a staggering 80-100. Good days were those when only 50-60 patients lined up for my consultation. Interestingly however, a significant and shameless proportion of those patients, soldiers and officers alike, were there with complaints they would never have imagined bothering with, had this not been a free consultation.

Given that every individual reporting to me reserved the right to be treated as a patient, each and every one of them needed to be given a tolerant hearing, examined properly and prescribed the necessary medications. Given that I was working at peak efficiency and was at my outrageous best, I still required a bare minimum of five minutes for each individual. An average of ninety patients at my out-patient department therefore meant being there continuously for seven and half hours simply examining and prescribing. And this was besides the fact that I needed a break for lunch, and that certain minor orthopedic procedures (such as joint aspirations, intra-articular injections, and application of special plaster casts) also had to be performed by me during the out-patient session.

The author in his hospital office at CMH Chittagong

Interestingly, with only six hours of official hospital work time, one would begin to wonder how I ever managed to squeeze an elephant into a shopping bag. If necessity was truly the mother of invention, I am very much tempted to put my name up there, perhaps a bit below, if not beside those of Thomas Alva Edison, Benjamin Franklin and the likes. My earnest and sincere efforts in patient care had to be shaped by innovations and improvisations, in which certain repetitive and time-consuming actions were replaced by simpler and quicker ones, and some redundant corners cut without compromising on the quality of treatment.

An example of one of the desperate measures adopted, and for which I often pride myself, was having a rubber stamp made, of quite an ungainly size, which included all conceivable orthopedic treatment advice. This was stamped on to the blank official prescription paper that every patient carried, and all that I needed to do was simply check the appropriate boxes. This saved me the time and the effort of having to write almost the same thing over and over again, about ninety times. In this case, a desperate situation had called for a desperate measure since the authorities were obstinate in their unwillingness to change anything on the printed prescription paper that had existed almost from the time that Moses had crossed the Red Sea. It was either that, or me having to carry on to the point of utter senseless exhaustion, and perhaps even unintended negligence of monumental proportions.

The Cremation of a Creation

"A droplet can't perceive the extent of the ocean" – Aarush Kashyap"

My thesis during the Masters course was an operative procedure which helped to stabilize an unstable knee joint.

Ligaments around the knee were partially detached and then tightened, without entering into the joint, unlike some other stabilizing procedures in which the joint is invaded for the purpose. The procedure which I had adopted had the attractive advantage of leaving room for a subsequent more aggressive procedure should the need arise, in which case the joint could be entered, if needed. Moreover, it was assumed that with the joint not having been entered into, the chances of future degenerative changes would be minimized. Also, with the joint space not having been tampered with, this procedure was also expected to result in a shorter and easier phase of rehabilitation, returning the patient to an active lifestyle much sooner than otherwise. This last feature was an attractive attribute, particularly for the armed forces, where it was always important for soldiers to return to active duty as soon as possible.

The surgical procedure I had adopted was a clever modification of one which was introduced almost thirty years ago by two orthopedic surgeons by the names of Slocum and Larson, after whom the original surgery was named. The simplicity of my modified version for a condition as disabling as an unstable knee was considered novel and attractive. The outcome of it too, was an unqualified success. It was a success validated by bio-statistical calculations made in my thesis – a thesis which had been vetted and scrutinized by a panel of renowned orthopedic surgeons, and which I had to defend in their presence during the Finals of my Masters Examination.

Upon my return to the armed forces following completion of my Masters course I began performing, among other surgeries, reconstructions for unstable knees along the lines of my thesis. Patients with previously unstable knees made remarkable recoveries following an intensive phase of post-operative rehabilitation, as is required for any orthopedic procedure. Most of the individuals operated upon were back to active military duty usually within a year.

There are times that a single bad apple can give a batch of apples a bad name. However, this is not supposed to mean that the rest of the apples in the crate are unworthy of consumption either. Similarly, there was this one patient, amongst the many with a successful outcome, who could not overcome the wasting of the thigh muscles – an accompaniment of any knee surgery – in spite of a most intensive regimen of rehabilitation. Eventually this individual had to be declared physically unfit for active military duty and was therefore recommend to be sent on early retirement. Accordingly, his papers were sent to the divisional commander for his perusal and sanction.

This was the same person who, just a few months ago, was sitting at the head of a table with a visibly condescending attitude, deciding for the doctors how a hospital ought to be run. It did not come as any big surprise, therefore, when a very terse instruction came back to me saying that I should abandon such 'experimental' surgeries. What surprised me more than the fact that my procedure was being offhandedly dismissed was the use of the term 'experimental' in this context.

The surgery that the divisional commander, perhaps with advice from the director of medical services at the divisional headquarters, was calling 'experimental' was conceived by two of the most world-renowned orthopedic surgeons, and which I had modified and improved upon. This was a surgery that was my thesis, and during the course of which I had taken it to perfection. This was a surgery which had the whole-hearted support of my supervisor, who himself was a renowned orthopedic surgeon and was considered an authority on the knee joint. This was a surgery that had yielded such a good result that a panel of experts had deemed it totally acceptable during the defense of my thesis. This was a surgery that had been regularly returning soldiers to active military duty for the past four years.

Those enlightened luminaries, who had not the remotest idea about a knee joint, were certainly not doing this institution any justice or favor by rejecting outright a surgical procedure which not only had an extensive research behind it, but had also stood the test of time. It was simply not proper for a person who had mastered the art of military combat, to summarily dismiss a surgical procedure which he, in all probability, knew absolutely nothing about – and all for just one single patient!

But, perhaps the problem actually lay elsewhere. Perhaps it lay with those medically-knowledgeable people posted at the local headquarter who were meant to function as a bridge between the medical functionary and the non-medical elements of the Division, so one could understand the other's 'language'. There is this outside chance that the local area commander might have consulted with the director of medical services at the local headquarters before deciding to reject my surgical procedure. Even if I were to hypothetically assume that the two had 'discussed' that single failure out of a multitude of successes, the fact remains that that was done without consulting with the surgeon who had devised the procedure in the first place. In the case of the local director of medical services, it was probably the fear of falling out of favor with the mighty and powerful that took precedence over what was the right and proper thing to do.

All said and done, it is beyond any comprehension or conceivable logic as to how two people – one a non-medical individual and the other a non-specialist – could unilaterally effect the discontinuation of a surgery without even once consulting with the surgeon who had been performing it. With all due respect to what a director of medical services does, I wonder how much he, being a general duty medical officer, knew about my thesis, or the complexity and novelty of that particular surgical procedure. How much, I ask, did he know about the *Pes anserinus transposition for chronic antero-medial rotatory instability of the knee joint* and the bio-statistically 'significant' outcome of that thesis to be able to sign a directive ordering its discontinuation without consulting with me even once. That was what frustrated me then, and that is what infuriates me still today.

I keep wondering whether any of the epic decision-makers had any knowledge of the principles that underlines medical research analysis. The outcomes of all previous similar surgeries done by me should have been taken into account, and my thesis consulted again. Bio-statistical tests for validity ought to have been applied to the whole series of patients in the armed forces on whom I had performed the exact same surgery. The opinion of other orthopedic surgeons, including my thesis supervisor, should also have been sought in this matter. Much more should have been done, not least of all, consult me, before mindlessly rejecting with the dismissive scratch of a pen a procedure which the leading orthopedic surgeons of the country had deemed unique and very much acceptable.

What had transpired was akin to driving a knife mindlessly through the heart of a successful surgical innovation, perhaps not because the medical authorities thought that that was the right thing to do, but because the medical authorities knew that a high-ranking non-medical individual thought so. Appeasement in order to ensure continuity of rank and status raised its ugly head once again, as I stood aside and silently apologized to the countless patients of mine who could have benefited immensely from this technique. It marked the sad demise of an innovative procedure created specifically to serve an institution, which the institution, in its boundless sagacity and perpetual predilection for instant and hasty judgments, abandoned.

My loss was the fact that I had been robbed of a procedure which was my very own, and which I held close to my heart. The loss for this establishment, on the other hand, was that they never gave themselves the opportunity of benefitting from a novel and successful surgical procedure. They had, in reality, robbed themselves of it. And the real tragedy is that they didn't even realize that!

Endangered Ethics

Not all Senior Surgeons I served with had the fortitude or the common sense to realize that being a general surgeon with some amount of seniority did not necessarily and automatically endow them with powers, knowledge and abilities to perform what they were not formally trained to do. That there could be situations where decisions ought to be left to those who knew their job was, unfortunately, not quite appreciated by some. That was when they made a complete mess of not only the surgical situation, but of the patient as well.

My case in point involves a young boy, perhaps around fourteen to fifteen years of age, badly injured by a shell blast in close proximity. This particular patient and his friends were playing in a field one day, when they stumbled upon an unexploded shell, which was not quite uncommon in a region of armed conflict. Not knowing what to make of it or how to deal with the unexploded shell, the boys rightly sought the advice of a member of the paramilitary forces living in that area, and on leave at that time. The latter, for reasons best known to him, struck the shell with an axe with all his might. Unfortunately, the axe landed on the detonator! Shrapnel from the exploding shell tore through the belly of the soldier, and through both the lower limbs of the boy in question, since he was the next closest. The others, being much further behind, were fortunately not injured.

Both the young boy and the paramilitary personnel were evacuated to CMH Chittagong by a helicopter. I was about to get into my car at the end of the regular hospital hours one day, when my medical assistant came running to announce that patients were being evacuated from the hill tracts. The casualties were swiftly brought into the resuscitation and pre-op station, and as I began my assessment of the cases, the Senior Surgeon, accompanied by another general surgeon, walked in.

The soldier's belly was studded with shrapnel holes. Experience with similar cases in the past told us that he was likely to have multiple punctures in his intestines, and perhaps a few to some vital organs. However, his vital signs were stable, and as was discovered during the surgery, his vital organs had been spared. All it took, in his case, were a few straightforward repairs of the damage to his intestine.

The condition of the young boy however, was quite different. The muscles below both his knees were well-nigh shredded, and the bones, all exposed, were reduced to multiple small fragments. While I was assessing his situation, and making a mental plan of a management for him, the Senior Surgeon came up to me, took one long look at the boy, and said, "Amputate both his legs."

Inculcated in me as an orthopedic surgeon was an ethic, a philosophy and a principle built around the concept of reconstruction, re-growth and rehabilitation, eventually leading to locomotion. Years of education, training and experience had taught me to view and nurture muscles, bones, joints, ligaments and tendons the way a soulful gardener would regard the plants and trees in his garden – hopeful of a healthy growth, and happy at the prospects of a fruitful and fulfilling future.

And right there in front of me, at that very moment, I could see tissues which were not only begging to live, but which had an immense potential to grow back. Lying there too, was a very young boy in whose eyes I could see someone pleading with his God and with me, desperately wanting to be able to walk on his own two feet through the years ahead of him. My sense of obligation as an orthopedic surgeon simply refused to relegate this unfortunate boy to being merely another 'number' lost in the sea of hospital statistics. I was unwilling to condemn him to being a helpless amputee on a wheelchair for the rest of his life, more so since a surgical plan was already starting to take shape within my head, and I could see a light, however feeble, glimmering at the end of the tunnel.

And the second time that the phrase, "Amputate both his legs" floated to my ears, I looked up and said, "This boy will walk."

This marked the beginning of a battle which lasted the better part of a year. Fixators fell into place, bones were apposed to bones, and tedious sessions of muscle and skin grafting and transpositions followed. The young boy, to my amazement, went through the ordeal with the cheerfulness and resolve of one who was determined to go through life without having to lean on others. I was even more amazed at how his disposition seemed to bring out the best in me – something which kept me sharply focused, deeply motivated and eager to accomplish. It was as if this young patient, in his resolve not to need any support in the future, turned into a support for the person who could help him achieve that objective.

Almost exactly a year to the day that this young boy was brought in with both his legs almost shredded to bits, he walked out of the orthopedic ward on both legs, albeit with the temporary support of a pair of crutches. The sparkle that I saw in his eyes that day, the verve that I saw in his step and the spirit that I saw in his soul will forever remain with me a source of inspiration, a guardian of devotion and a trusted companion to any destination. I will also remain forever grateful to Providence for having given me the fortitude and the common sense of neither having listened to a general surgeon that day, nor having followed his principles of surgical practice.

One other reason for which I shall forever remember this young boy was the events and circumstances surrounding his discharge.

I was in my room doing some departmental paperwork on the morning he was to be discharged, when I seemed to hear the crowing of a rooster coming from somewhere in the ward. Perplexed, I called my medical assistant to inquire into the matter. He informed me that the boy's father, who lived in the hills, had brought with him a rooster for me, as a gift to express his gratitude for what I had done for his son. I was completely dumbfounded, because this was way beyond my wildest expectation. Simply saying 'thank you' was one thing, but bringing a rooster as a gift for a doctor had to be the ultimate in terms of social gesture and expression of gratefulness. Moreover, accepting any form of a gift for services rendered while in a uniform was way out of line of military service etiquette and custom. So obviously, I asked my ward medical assistant to tell the boy's father that he should take the rooster back because it was not within my abilities to accept it. Moreover, given his financial situation, I added that he probably needed the rooster more than I did.

About a quarter of an hour later my medical assistant re-entered my room with a rather apologetic expression on his face, as though he was convinced that what he was about to say would perhaps upset and infuriate me. To my inquiring look he informed me that as part of the on-going military operations to combat secessionist activities, he had served in the hill region for quite some time, and was therefore sufficiently aware of the social customs, etiquettes, beliefs and practices of the indigenous hill population. I was told that it would literally amount to a humiliating offense not to accept the gift being offered to me. My ward assistant went on to mention that such roosters were possessions these people held dear, and into which they invested most of their time and money in order to nurture and to nourish. It easily qualified as being one of the major possessions for such families – something similar to perhaps owning a flat-screen TV, a motorbike, or even a car. Obviously therefore, the sentiment attached to their willingness to part with it was profound, and the gesture truly magnanimous.

I looked at my medical assistant for a while, debating what to do. Finally, not wanting to hurt the individual's cultural sentiments, and as an exhibition of my reciprocity for his kindness and generosity, I relented. I drove home that day, with the huge rooster in the trunk of my car, for want of a better place to carry it in. And people around me on my way home must have been of the impression that I had outfitted my car with a new kind of a horn which sounded much like the crowing of a rooster, and that I was using it rather indiscriminately! Soon after, that rooster spent a rather extended session on our stove, just to get to the softness suitable for consumption!

The Economics of Poverty

> *""Not all doors open in the same direction and with the same effort" – Jasleen Kaur Gumber"*

Before moving on, however, this seems as good a place as any to relate another incident.

The common thread between this and the one just narrated is the performance of surgery on a young boy, neither of whom was technically entitled to treatment in an armed forces hospital. But while the previous was performed under circumstances of an emergency and in an area where the army was involved in an armed campaign against secessionists and therefore technically obligated to treat that patient, the latter was purely an elective procedure. More importantly, this latter case also had a touch of amusement as well as an air of sadness about it. And that is the reason I feel it deserves a place in this book. It happened a few years earlier when I was posted to CMH Dhaka as an orthopedic surgeon, just before being posted to CMH Chittagong.

It is a frequent occurrence at many intersections in Dhaka for a car, while waiting at a red light, to be swarmed by beggars of all ages. As to the reason they are begging, they indicate old age and physical disabilities, amongst a constellation of others, with some being literally out-of-this-world.

It was just after sundown one day that Samina and I were returning home. We were waiting at a red light, when a young boy of maybe about twelve years of age came up to our car, asking for alms. Since he looked pretty able-bodied to me, I rolled down the car window and said, *"You seem quite fit and young. Why don't you do something to help out your family instead of begging on the streets?"*

That was when he raised his right arm to show me why he was begging. He had, what is known in orthopedic language, a cubitus varus deformity. This happens when there has been a fracture in the lower end of the bone of the upper arm, that is, of the bone just above the elbow, which subsequently heals improperly due either to bad treatment or no treatment at all. So, when a person with such a deformity stands with both the arms hanging by the side, the elbow of the affected arm will be bowed outward.

I will have to admit that I was rather amazed and a bit amused as well that someone would be exploiting a deformity as simple, and as easily treatable, as a cubitus varus. Besides the corrective surgery being rather easy and straightforward, it was one that I had performed quite a number of times myself. And that was what prompted me to ask, rather spontaneously, *"Would you like to have it treated?"* And to which he instantly replied, *"Yes"*.

Since the lights at the intersection had already turned green by now, and the cars ahead of us were gradually starting to move, I hurriedly told him, *"Alright, I will be here tomorrow at this time. Bring your mother with you, and we can discuss this."* To which the young boy hurriedly answered, *"She is right there...there"* pointing to the side of the road. With us now having to start to move, I shot back at him, *"Okay, I am pulling over beyond the intersection. Bring your mother over."*

Soon the young boy and his mother were standing by our car. I first explained to the mother what I did for a living, and then informed her that I could correct her son's elbow deformity, if they wanted me to. She immediately replied that they were poor and could not afford the surgery. And when I explained to her that I could do it for free, the expression of utter relief on her face was worth a million dollars. It was decided then and there that the young boy was to meet me at CMH Dhaka at my out-patient department, and that I would be performing his surgery at that hospital.

Readers may recall, from a discussion in an earlier part of this narrative, the matter of entitlement to treatment at the hospitals of the armed forces. That was where I had also mentioned that in this regard all that an officer needed to do was to simply indicate on a hand-written note, called an Entitlement Certificate, the relationship of the entitled patient with the officer. This also applied to servants and maid-servants where they were needed to be mentioned as such, on that certificate. This latter instance was, unfortunately, such a gaping loophole that advantage was often taken of it by some, where non-entitled individuals, including far-flung relatives too, were sometimes admitted as a servant or a maid-servant to receive treatment at a military hospital. Procedures may have changed now, but that was how it was being done three to four decades ago.

When it came to doing a surgery at CMH Dhaka on this young beggar, I will openly admit that that was the only time during my entire career in the armed forces that I had decided to go through that loophole and admit someone into a military hospital as my servant who was not actually my servant. Understandably, all I was trying to do in this case was to be of some assistance to a family that was so poor that both the mother and the son were out begging at a city intersection. And moreover, in spite of being apprehensive about her son's physical deformity, the mother seemed rather resigned to Fate knowing there was nothing she was ever going to be able to do about it due to the expenses involved in having it treated. Clearly, there were thousands of such needy and poverty-stricken people on the roads and intersections of this city that could do with such a helping hand reaching out to them. Unfortunately, that did not happen often because this is not a perfect world.

At this point, I leave it to my readers to judge whether or not what I did was right and justified. Personally, I feel immensely pleased with myself that I had reached out to a family in need. My satisfaction lay in the fact that I was able to do my part in making the life of at least one such family a bit easier, and to have perhaps given them some hope for the future. Needless to say, I had circumvented the system to place resources at the disposal of those not entitled to it. But, truly speaking, those were the same resources that I had seen being placed either at the disposal of some who never really needed it, or used often for reasons not entirely justified. If anything, and as far as I was concerned, this was charity. And that was something I felt would make God happy. That, at the end of the day, was what mattered to me.

Long story short, the young boy was soon admitted to the hospital, and the surgery on his arm subsequently performed. It went well and his recovery was rather commendable. Several days later when time came for his discharge, we arranged to have his mother come to the hospital to escort him back home.

On the morning of his discharge, I had the patient brought into my room to take a last look at his operated arm and to have a few words with him before letting him go. After examining his elbow, I asked,

"Are you happy with your elbow now?"

"Yes. But, can you get me a job?" he asked.

"Why do you ask that?"

"Because now that my elbow is fixed, what do I show to people to get them to give me some money? I am useless!"

I was dumbfounded. I stared at him for a few long seconds in sheer disbelief. The look of incredulity on my face mixed with a tinge of amusement must have been glaringly obvious – and all because I had never, in my wildest dreams, expected such a response. Here I was, thinking I had done this young boy and his family a huge favor by correcting his elbow deformity, and here he was, giving me a lesson on the harsh 'economics of poverty'.

As sad and unfortunate as it all was, personally speaking, it was a reality check for me. I do not know whether or not that boy went back to begging after his surgery because I never saw him at that intersection again. And even if he was there, I am sure he would have made it a point never to come up to our car ever again. Or perhaps he and his mother moved to a different intersection. Who knows? But, then again, with his elbow all fixed, he could very well have gone back to actively helping out his family. He must be a grown man now, with a family of his own, and I do hope he is leading a decent life somewhere.

A Piece of Paradise

I did not seem to be the only one leading a hectic professional life at CMH Chittagong. Being the lone pediatrician at the hospital, as well as being the on-call pediatrician every day, Samina too had her share of a frantic – and a rather chaotic – lifestyle. Moreover, when it came to children, infants and neonates, it was rather imperative that a more intense and meticulous care and attention be provided, which therefore kept her involved through almost every hour of every day, and at unpredictable hours of almost every night.

Despite all that, we endeavored to make the most out of our days at Chittagong. To begin with, the community of army officers at Chittagong Cantonment was small and tight-knit, which obviously led to closer, more intimate and therefore more enjoyable friendships and relationships.

In the midst of it all, we discovered a cousin of mine, Mahmud Hossain Murad, an individual full of life, and his wonderful wife, Zarina, a lady full of charm, who lived only about half an hour's drive from our house in the cantonment. We spent countless evenings, either going out to dinners together or simply chatting with them – which went a long way in infusing a measure of relaxation and enjoyment in our otherwise hectic way of life.

And then, one weekend afternoon I was at a gas station just outside the gates of Chittagong Cantonment, when I spotted a gentleman there, who looked oddly familiar.

It felt as if I had seen him somewhere before, and had this strange hunch that I knew him well too. And so I decided to introduce myself, lest we found a connection. While I was walking up to him, my mind began to race through the days of yesteryear, trying desperately to place this gentleman. The same thing must have been going through his head too, because he started walking towards me at almost exactly the same time. And as soon as we were close enough to shake hands, it occurred to us both, almost simultaneously, that we were friends from high school from some thirty years ago, and we hugged each other – because a handshake seemed rather inadequate for the occasion!

I was amazed at how little my old school friend, Jamil Razzak, had changed, and which was probably the reason I was able to place him this quickly. On our first visit to Jamil's house a few days later, his little seven-year-old daughter seemed visibly disappointed while meeting me. Having been told that one of her dad's friends from the time that he was about her age was visiting them, she was expecting to see someone her size! She had to be explained that people grew!

The hectic hours at the hospital notwithstanding, I must admit that both Samina and I spent a rather enjoyable time in Chittagong. Relaxing and carefree evenings were spent with my cousin Murad and his wife, with my friend Jamil and his family, or the families of other officers of CMH Chittagong. On some weekends we went on trips to the various exquisite hill towns of Kaptai, Rangamati,

Bandarban, Khagrachari or Alikadam – either just the two of us, or with the other families.

Every hill town, big or small, had a cantonment commensurate with the size of the town it was located in, and which was also quite strategically placed in the midst of a most picturesque setting. The Officers' Mess at each of these cantonments, moreover, was located particularly and purposefully to be able to witness the best that Nature had to offer. It was always a treat for the eyes, and of the mind, to simply lounge in the balcony of the mess and to either look at the green rolling hills all around, or soak in the sight and sound of a nearby river rushing rapidly downstream.

Most enjoyable were the drives through Bandarban, known for its high hills and mountains, where the winding roads hugged their sides that were thick with dense green foliage. During the drive, the Sangu River could be seen winding its way like a sparkling ribbon along the deep valley below. Looking down too, it was a sight worth a million dollars to behold misty clouds floating and racing along below between the hills and the mountains.

On way to Bandarban was a scenic site called *Meghla* maintained by the district administration of Bandarban, which showcased a waterfall called *"Shoilo Propat"* (meaning "mountain waterfall"). This was basically a rocky area where the water, clear as crystal, tumbled over the edge of a high hill, and made its way down and over the rocks below.

Over the years, the constant flow of water had eroded into the rocks, revealing layers which perhaps dated back millions of years. An observation platform had been built downstream of *Shoilo Propat*, and adjacent to the falls. This platform, standing on massive metallic supports, was nestled on to the steep rocky face of the hill, and from which a metal stairway went all the way down, close to the base of the falls. Where the stairway ended, the falls became a stream of clear water flowing over a rocky surface. This area, though still fairly steep, could easily be negotiated. Nevertheless, one had to be careful, since a good portion of this rocky terrain on either side of the clear flowing stream was covered in slippery and slimy moss.

At *Shoilo Propat* in Bandarban

It was during one of our visits to *Shoilo Propat* with a colleague and his wife one time that we were down on the rocks below to take pictures, which always came out attractively well because of the scenic surroundings. That was when our colleague's wife stepped where she should not have, and in an instant was starting to slide down the slimy gradient. Fortunately, I was close enough to be able to grab her by her hand, though I had to look for enough purchase myself at the same time, in order not to slide down along with her!

Most thrilling, however, was the drive up to *Chimbuk-Thanchi*, one of the notable peaks of the country, about 3000 feet high, located also in Bandarban.

On way to Chimbuk-Thanchi

One had to be skilled and somewhat brave to be able to drive up along the narrow, steep and winding road which led up to the summit. The very top had been shaved off and flattened to accommodate tourists and visitors. There was also a small and cozy rest house there, with a verandah in front, where one could rest and regale in the surrounding beauty. But the real sight – and the sight which was most thrilling – was from the very edge of the summit, from where one could gaze out as far as the eyes could see, at the breathtaking panorama. Looking down at all the other peaks below, which protruded out of a surreal carpet of white mist for miles around, one felt like a god watching over Earth!

Prior to one of the trips to Bandarban which Samina and I once made, we had informed the Officers' Mess there, of our arrival that afternoon. The scenic drive from Chittagong Cantonment to the cantonment in Bandarban usually took anywhere from two to three hours, depending on the number of stops one made along the way, to marvel at the surrounding natural beauty.

When we finally arrived at the officers' mess in Bandarban Cantonment, and were driving up to the front entrance, several junior officers came out on to the front porch to receive me and my wife. I was visibly surprised by this, since there was no way these officers could have known that we would be arriving at exactly that time. From the time that we had left Chittagong Cantonment till we arrived in Bandarban, there had been no communication between us and anyone else. It is worth noting too, that the use of mobile phones was not as widespread then, as it is today, and we did not own one either.

Obviously therefore, one of the first things I asked the gathered Officers right after having exchanged our preliminary pleasantries was "How?" Only then was it revealed to me that from the moment our car had entered the Bandarban area, it was being continuously tracked by the numerous army observation posts that dotted the route – and unbeknownst to us, our progress was being constantly relayed to the officers at the mess at Bandarban!

Though it was most gratifying to see that the officers at Bandarban cared enough to go to such lengths to be able to welcome us properly, it nevertheless made me a bit queasy knowing that powerful binoculars had perhaps surreptitiously followed us as we drove along the winding roads to Bandarban, or strolled among some of its breathtaking natural surroundings.

There were also times that we went on fishing trips with our friends to the many beautiful lakes which dotted the hill region. And during such trips, being with delightful company and simply having a good time seemed far more important than the number of fishes we actually caught.

It was indeed gracious and generous of the surgical and the medical specialists at CMH Chittagong to have kept an eye on the orthopedic and pediatric cases respectively, for the short period we were away on such trips. Fortunately, they too realized how intensely involved we had to remain with our work and with our patients day in and day out, especially with no one else in our specialties to fall back on. Nevertheless, both Samina and I were all too aware of the fact that we could not afford to venture too far for too long, because in case of the arrival of a patient too complicated for others to handle, our presence would be required almost immediately.

There was also this standing order from both our Commanding Officer and the DMS that both Samina and I should be reachable over the phone, wherever we may be, so we were at least able to assess the severity of a newly-arrived case and, if necessary, dictate the initial critical management while we were on our way back.

As I had mentioned earlier, this was an era when mobile phones had not yet arrived on the scene, and the very few that were around were not only as cumbersome as the walkie-talkies of World War II, but were outrageously expensive as well. The one thing which saved the day for us was our discovery of a commercial pager service in Chittagong, with the only inconvenience being that we had to rush to the nearest land phone whenever paged. Nevertheless, this seemed like a fairly acceptable solution since we always ensured that we were never too far from a land telephone, and that none of our patients ever suffered at any time as a result of such an arrangement.

In the meantime, both Samina and I fulfilled all the criteria for becoming “Classified” specialists, both in terms of length of service as Graded Specialists and the publication of scientific papers. This paved the way for us to be promoted to the rank of Colonel and beyond, with the potential of becoming departmental heads in the future – both of which, at that point in time, and in reality, seemed ridiculously distant.

The Enigma of Empowerment

> *"The problem isn't the abuse of power; it's the power to abuse" – Michael Cloud*

It is at this point that I feel I must briefly discuss a couple of issues, for want of a better place to mention those.

The first is the processing of articles submitted for publication in the Bangladesh Armed Forces Medical Journal. This journal, as its name implies, is a medical journal published periodically by the Bangladesh Armed Forces containing either original articles on medical research conducted by doctors of the Army Medical Corps, or reports on medical observations made by them. The publication of this journal, which was fairly highly regarded at a countrywide level, was the responsibility of the Armed Forces Medical Institute (AFMI).

The process of submission of articles for publication, which I am about to elaborate, is what used to be practiced at the time that I was a part of the institution. Whether or not the same procedure is still in practice today, I do not know. If it isn't, I will have to admit the process has finally been able to make strides in the proper direction.

To begin with, an author had to submit an article intended for publication to the "Research & Publication" wing of the AFMI. This department, after ensuring that the submitted article conformed to specified guidelines, forwarded it to the head of the respective specialty for further perusal in terms of scientific validity. Up to that point, however, everything was according to how it was supposed be, particularly in terms of how a scientific article, meant for publication, ought to be dealt with and processed. But what happened next was a puzzle I have not been able to solve to this day.

The article then had to be sent to those who dealt with military intelligence – and please don't ask me why, because I wouldn't have an explanation worth a shred of logic. Perhaps it was in the profound sagacity of those who were trained in the art of warfare that they felt they should have a say in matters of medical research. Or perhaps it was in their laudable attribute of vigilance, suspicion and mistrust that they felt that vital secrets were perhaps being covertly given away to 'undesired quarters' in a coded format through medical research publications!

In reality, such medical articles dealt with highly technical and complex medical topics, sometimes near-incomprehensible even to someone from another sub-specialty. And non-medical individuals vetting such articles perhaps whetted certain unfulfilled desires in some, or maybe instilled in them a sense of being in control. Who knows?

The other matter which I feel I am obligated to discuss at this point relates to the intangible web formed by rank, seniority, qualification, proficiency and experience, and the dynamics between those.

Suffice it to say that rank and seniority, especially in the context of a military organization, are always given precedence over qualification, proficiency or experience. They practically form the backbone of institutional functionality, and are the undisputed denominators of success and progress. And why shouldn't they be? Every such organization on the face of this earth survives on the framework of a rigid hierarchy, and the indisputable pecking order of dictatorial seniority, where a command is considered more scared than the scriptures and its disobedience more apocalyptic than Armageddon itself.

There is no denying the fact that seniority alone is the lifeblood for promotions, provided the record of the officer being promoted has no blemish, or the minds of those who give the promotion nurture no bias. And no amount of merit, proficiency, qualification or experience is ever considered enough to be able to upstage or surpass the worth of seniority. Rather, those are always viewed as rank outsiders, trying to force their way in and spoil the fun and, therefore, always looked down upon with a certain degree of skepticism, disdain, and sometimes even animosity.

However, I consider it rather unacceptable that denominators like merit, proficiency or experience are so totally out of context with regards to progress in this or, for that matter, in any other establishment. This I say even at the risk of being judged somewhat harshly by those who are otherwise accustomed to the more traditional and time-honored precepts and practices of organizational setup and functionality. And

I am also likely to raise eyebrows for questioning and suspecting the validity and reliability of these long-held determinants of advancement in any organization.

Nevertheless, I am also hopeful that a good number of my readers will, after having gone through what I have to say, see the substance in my argument as to why merit and proficiency too, ought to figure equally, if not more, in the overall modus operandi of an organization. While providing my viewpoint, I will be alluding to situations only in the medical corps because I am not in a position to be able to make qualified observations regarding the arms and other services – though I would give myself to believe that perhaps matters weren't much different there either.

Let me begin at the stage where doctors of the medical corps become specialists. It might seem as if my argument is taking off at a rather imprecise and irrelevant point in the evolving history of an officer of the medical corps. But that, in fact, is exactly where the crux of the contention lies, and which, therefore, I feel obligated to discuss. It is precisely at that point – at the locus of the transformation of a medical officer into a specialist – where an improper and unfair concept and criteria for individual advancement within this establishment seems to reside, and which blatantly disregards the worth of merit and proficiency.

And, this is how.

For the purpose of post-graduate courses and qualifications, officers of the medical corps are deputed to recognized apex institutions of the country which conduct the courses and finally confer the degrees. However, within the corps itself, a process of selection is in place whereby the authorities choose those most likely to succeed in such courses, and have the potential ability of completing the course within the stipulated time.

Nevertheless, there have been instances when it has taken an officer much longer than normally expected, to obtain a post-graduate degree or qualification. And there are two reasons for that.

First, an officer will perhaps repeatedly fail the selection process, but will nonetheless keep trying every year, till some eventually succeed. Therefore, with much time lost in this effort, that officer will obviously be starting the post-graduate course much later in his or her career. And second, even when selected, some will take longer than normally expected, to complete the post-graduate course – and I think we all know why.

But, whatever may be the reason for having taken longer to succeed, that officer's appointment, always decided upon by seniority, will remain preserved, to be immediately repossessed upon returning to the armed forces, whenever that might be. In fact, that officer will right away surge ahead of a colleague junior by even a day, but who might have obtained the same qualification years earlier, and perhaps more proficiently. What more, if that 'late-returning officer' happens to be the senior-most in a particular department, the coveted appointment of departmental head is always there for the taking upon return, regardless of any apparent academic inadequacies demonstrated during the post-graduate course. Obviously therefore, seniority – and not merit or proficiency –is the premise for progress, and the determinant for critical appointments. I do not really know how others feel about this, but in the weighing scale of fairness and objectivity this, to me, always seemed most improper, imprudent, undeserved and unfair.

I can understand that rank, seniority and length of service are rigid and tangible parameters on the basis of which an individual can move forward in any kind of an organization. But, what I do not understand is how rank and seniority alone can be any more of a tangible parameter for further promotion and progression than the indispensable qualities and qualifications of merit, proficiency, knowledge, intellect and expertise. I do not know what shapes the functioning principles of an establishment that promotes and practices such a restricted and regimented model. I also do not claim to have a full comprehension of the standards set by such establishments, including the yardstick by which it measures the qualities and qualifications of its personnel.

The strength, standing and success of any organization actually depends on the caliber and the capacity of those who hold its helm. And needless to say, good caliber and capacity are the direct and obvious outcome of merit, proficiency, knowledge and expertise. In fact, throughout our formative years, starting from kindergarten all the way through to graduation, the pursuit of proficiency has been the formula for success and advancement that was inculcated in us, and on the premise of which we always toiled for excellence.

But then, when we eventually step into the world of our professional pursuits, we are slapped into the realization that our lifelong concept for progress and advancement had always been flawed! We wake up, all flummoxed by the fact that our hard work and academic achievements actually has no place in the grand scheme of things – that seniority, and not merit and proficiency, happens to be the quintessential element for a person's progression and promotion in any organization.

What then, I ask, is the whole point in providing grades during an examination? What is the purpose in classifying a group of students as being better than the rest? Why are students who do not measure up to the requirements of a curriculum, made to lose an academic year? Why are more accomplished students provided with a scholarship? And, how would it look if a student who had earned a failing grade was awarded a scholarship for meritorious abilities?

If merit and proficiency has nothing to do with selection for the purpose of advancement and progress, then we might as well abolish the system of grading during examinations. Or perhaps abolish examinations altogether. Or maybe even abolish education!

It is not entirely fair that organizations and establishments continue to maintain that seniority – and seniority alone – should be the yardstick for governance and guidance. I believe there should also be a system capable of replacing, at regular intervals, the ignorant with the learned, the incompetent with the efficient, and the lethargic with the enthusiastic – irrespective of seniority –for the sake of the survival and success of any organization.

In the setup and context of a medical institution in particular, there ought to be a policy and a process in place by way of which the knowledge, proficiency and ability of a specialist can be judged, and only the more competent allowed to progress regardless of seniority. Only then will a department, a faculty, an organization or an establishment be capable of moving forward on the basis of innovative ideas, meritorious contributions, and laudable achievements, and be spared the redundancy, the degeneration and the deterioration so often witnessed.

The Elements of Mistrust

> *"Suspicion is a heavy armor and with its weight it impedes more than it protects"*
> *– Robert Burns*

It was in the very nature of certain elements to constantly keep the medical institution in the cross-hairs of their gun-sights, and to let off a thunderous volley at the slightest hint of what, in their opinion, was a lapse in performance. That there could be perfectly valid and verifiable explanations didn't quite figure in the equation. What perhaps worried some in certain lofty offices was the chilling realization that whatever was going on in the medical functionary was mostly beyond the power of their comprehension – and which perhaps made them uncomfortable. Therefore, in an attempt at exerting an influence over all that lay within the sphere of their control and authority, the powers-that-be gave themselves the license to interfere, often quite unnecessarily, in certain medical matters.

We have seen how a non-medical individual had quite unilaterally dictated the distribution of manpower and equipment for the second largest and the second busiest military hospital in the country. We have also seen how a tried and tested innovative orthopedic procedure was most perfunctorily brushed aside as being useless – thanks to the commendable medical understanding of a non-medical individual, adequately endorsed and complemented by a medical officer at the local headquarters who, in all likelihood, was looking out more for his rank and position than anything else.

However, laying a wholesale blame on some in the higher offices alone for their propensity to meddle in matters of the medical institution would not be entirely fair and justified either. Looking at it from an objective angle, such interferences were perhaps a necessity, given the way the medical functionary often managed – or mismanaged – its affairs. Because quite often, elements of the medical hierarchy, either by way of ignorance, imprudence or both, did help to create a status quo which called for such interferences.

Disappointing as it was, I will have to admit that even that was not where the actual problem lay. The actual problem arose when an inch was given by the medical establishment through their occasional shortcomings and shortsightedness, and a mile was taken by some in the higher non-medical offices through their interferences. And these, unfortunately, were oftentimes disproportionately intense and unnecessarily in excess. That, actually, was when mutual confidence and credibility were shattered, paving the way to reciprocal mistrust and disrespect.

Regrettably, when it came to such interferences, most at the helm of the medical establishment, despite their full knowledge of medical science and their complete comprehension of the functionality of the medical institution, often chose to abandon their judgment and assertiveness, and served as a doormat to anyone with a craving to meddle, intrude and impose. Why, I don't know. It could be that some guardians of the medical corps feared their position and prominence would perhaps be compromised as a result of the ire of the high command, and were therefore willing to go to any length to prevent 'kingly feathers' from being ruffled.

In this regard, I would like to relate an incident which adequately illustrates my point. It involves a cadet from the nearby Bangladesh Military Academy who was brought to me at CMH Chittagong for orthopedic treatment.

But, before I get into that, I would like to give my readers a brief description of the area in and around the Bangladesh Military Academy (or BMA). Though this has no relevance to the events I am about to relate, I feel obligated to give the readers an overview of the locale because the natural beauty of this area was too breathtaking not to be mentioned.

The Bangladesh Military Academy (or the BMA), a sprawling training complex meant to transform raw cadets into officers of the Bangladesh Army, was located hardly twenty minutes from CHM Chittagong. It was neatly nestled within the hills of Bhatiary, which was adjacent to the insanely busy Dhaka-Chittagong Highway – which served as the only artery between the capital and the port city of Chittagong. The portion of that highway running through the Bhatiary and the adjacent Faujdarhat areas was rather picturesque, with hills on one side of it, and the Bay of Bengal on the other. The complexes of the BMA, though facing this highway, were set far enough away from it not to disturbed by the vehicular commotion.

Though Chittagong Cantonment was set further inland, it was connected to the Dhaka-Chittagong highway by a road that ran over the hills to Bhatiary, approaching the BMA from behind. This road cut down travel from the cantonment to the highway quite substantially, and was the preferred route during our road trips to Dhaka or back. Had that not been the case, one would have had to take the longer and more time-consuming route through the heart of Chittagong and through some difficult traffic, to be able to get on to the Dhaka-Chittagong highway.

The drive from Chittagong Cantonment through Bhatiary, and to the point where the road joined the Dhaka-Chittagong highway, was one of the most scenic. The winding road threaded its way gracefully over and along the hills, while stunning lush green foliage and clear lakes adorned the route. Quite often, in the evenings, Samina and I would go out on a leisurely drive along this road, either to simply soak in its stunning beauty, or to fish in one of its lakes. At times, we would simply sit on one of the hilltops – particularly one called 'Sunset Point' – and watch the huge red ball of the setting sun sinking into the Bay of Bengal, coloring the infinite sky and the endless ocean in an incredible splash of red and orange.

At *Sunset Point*, Bhatiary, with the BMA (Bangladesh Military Academy) in the background. The Bay of Bengal lies beyond the tree-line behind. The hull of two ships can be seen in the ship-breaking yard on the Bay

Cadets from the BMA were my regular patients, having frequently sustained injuries during training. Such injuries ranged from minor sprains and strains to major fractures.

One such cadet, who had fractured his femur – the thigh bone – during training, was brought in for treatment. The approach to treating such a case is quite standard and straightforward, and was something I had done countless number of times. Surgery for a fractured femur, when required, is so basic, that it is one of the first solo surgeries a student in the Masters Course is allowed to perform. Moreover, this was a surgery I had also frequently taught other junior surgeons to carry out properly.

If the fracture line ran obliquely or in a spiral manner, the two ends of the bone would obviously not stay together. That was when surgery was required in order to put in a metallic rod to keep the unstable fractured ends in place so it could heal. However, like anywhere else in the body, the muscles around fractured bones in the thigh go into spasm (a state of sustained contraction) as a natural response. But anywhere else in the body, this is not as big a problem as it is in the thigh because the muscles around the femur – being the most massive in the body – go into a spasm which is quite considerable. As a standard practice therefore, the thigh needs to be put in traction with weights for anywhere from thirty six to seventy two hours to overcome this enormous contraction. This also allows time for the inevitable injury to the surrounding tissues to settle so that the surgery, when performed, would be less difficult and less traumatic. Minimizing trauma is one of the prime objectives of any surgery. Otherwise debilitating scar tissue could form upon healing.

On the other hand, when traction alone is sufficient to bring the two fractured ends together and keep them in place, then a conservative mode of treatment – precluding the need for surgery – can, at times, also be considered. However, without going into the technical details, suffice it to say that the uncertainties involved in such a mode of treatment are multifarious, and the duration of treatment and of immobility, also prolonged. However, when it involved cadets from the BMA in particular, a rapid turn-around was imperative, and for obvious reasons. And therefore, for such patients, an operative treatment was the preferred option irrespective of the type of fracture.

This cadet had a spiral fracture, and as a standard procedure, his limb was put on traction, and all necessary medications prescribed. It was at that time that due to certain unavoidable reasons I had to be away from CMH Chittagong for two days. All that was required for the patient during that period was the proper administration of medications, and the monitoring of the traction apparatus which, as mentioned earlier, needed to be maintained for anywhere from thirty six to seventy two hours prior to surgery in such cases. And my team of orthopedic assistants and the nursing staff were more than adequately proficient in that regard. The other doctors too were apprised of the situation, and knew very well how to keep an eye on any such case awaiting surgery.

It so happened that during the two days that I was away, a friend of the patient's – another cadet who incidentally was connected to 'high places' – paid him a visit. That was when the patient complained of some pain in his leg. This, of course, was not quite uncommon for a case such as this, and for which there were medications aplenty, as were qualified doctors and nurses who knew exactly what to do. It was not as if this patient was being neglected or being left unattended. But that was exactly how it was made to look like, as news of the patient's passing discomfort percolated up to the local area commander himself – and questions began to be asked. Why is the patient in pain? What are you doing about the fracture? Where is the orthopedic surgeon?

Any and every doctor in this hospital who mattered – most of all the Senior Surgeon and the Commanding Officer – had very sound and reasonable answers to these questions. But surprisingly, they decided not to provide them.

The Senior Surgeon probably did not want to concern himself with it because it was a matter of orthopedic surgery, and he was not an orthopedic surgeon. That was besides the fact, however, that whenever it suited him, especially when it came to taking advantage of a particular situation, he would like to exert control over the orthopedic specialty, including imposing extra on-call duties on the orthopedic surgeon or snatching away floor spaces earmarked for orthopedic surgery.

The Commanding Officer on the other hand, was perhaps going into convulsions at the thought that his coveted rank, appointment and status could be at serious risk because of this. So, rather than give the obvious logical and professional explanation, he decided to go with the flow, much like a dead fish floating belly-up in the murky waters of a river draining into an ignominious ocean of confusion, fearfulness and insecurity. For him, it was perhaps a choice between preserving his own rank and appointment on the one hand versus sacrificing not only the value and worth of one of his specialists, but also abandoning his own knowledge of the time-honored principles of surgical practice.. And true to the spirit of the faint-hearts of the medical institution, he promptly forgot who, or what, he actually was, and then proceeded to sacrifice the merit and dignity of his specialist at the altar of cowardice and depravity.

I was confronted by my Commanding Officer immediately upon my return. From his overall disposition I could tell that he was rather convinced that the carefully orchestrated world around him, which he had fine-tuned to perfection over the years, was on the verge of crumbling into a worthless heap. I was informed by him of the questions being asked, and I could sense a desperate urgency in him to rush to the area commander without further delay, and do everything necessary to retain the brass on his shoulders and the uniform on his back. At that very moment, I could see that my Commanding Officer had switched into what could be termed a 'salvage mode for the purpose of survival'.

And in the resultant exuberance, he perhaps got a bit ahead of himself and suggested that I should also bring along my textbooks, to the office of the area commander. He probably wanted to prove to the latter that the treatment I had instituted was in accordance with what was also in the orthopedic texts – which, in fact, it was. But what both angered and disappointed me at that point was that it did not seem to be quite enough for my Commanding Officer that I was an adequately qualified orthopedic surgeon with years of experience to back me up, that he wanted the textbooks along as well. This was the kind of confidence the medical institution had on its specialists, and such was the frivolous nature of some of those who steered it.

No sooner were we seated across the table from the area commander, my Commanding Officer launched himself into a discourse on the case, adding hastily that we had textbooks with us to prove our point. Interestingly, the area commander cut him off rather off-handedly, saying, *"I do not want to see your textbooks. I only want that proper care be taken of the patient."* The look on the face of my Commanding Officer, at that moment, was worth a million dollars.

If what my Commanding Officer had been doing all along was bordering on being 'comic', the phrase that I had just heard was rather tragic. *"I only want that proper care be taken of the patient"* – For this to have come from someone sitting as high up in the hierarchy as an area commander was like a branded collective expression of the mindset of some individuals in this establishment. It was as if I, being a Classified Orthopedic Surgeon, was not taking proper care of my patients, and therefore needed to be reminded of that. That was when the lack of confidence of some in this establishment on its specialists finally cracked across my cheek like a slap of shame and disgrace. I found it most degrading that the area commander felt it even necessary to haul a specialist into his office and play Hippocrates with him. As for my Commanding Officer, he seemed overly eager to make as hasty an exit as possible, with his rank and appointment intact.

I carried out the surgery the next morning, as was originally scheduled, and it went well. Over the next few weeks the patient was on the road to a swift and uneventful recovery. But, whatever transpired regarding his case must have somehow reached the ears of the young patient, for one day when I went to see him, he looked squarely and sincerely into my eyes and said, "Whatever happened, I'd like you to know that I personally think my case was handled very well right from the start."

But apparently, not everyone seemed to have thought so. I do not know from which disgruntled quarter of the establishment it was initiated or instigated, but Colonel (later Brigadier-General) Fazle Rahim was soon flown in to verify that I had been able to properly handle a most basic orthopedic situation. He went over everything with a fine-tooth comb and finally expressed his complete satisfaction with the way the case had been handled. He left with a smile that seemed to say, "I know why I was brought here."

While, in the meantime, I was left wondering, *"What, in the name of Heavens, am I doing here?*

> *[It is with a heavy heart that I would like to mention that Brigadier-General Fazle Rahim has sadly passed away. I will always remember him as the person who had stimulated and supported my interest in orthopedic surgery and one who had guided me skillfully through my initial years as an orthopedic surgeon. I pray for the Heavenly salvation of his departed soul]*

Chapter 9
A FAREWELL TO ARMS
The tribulations of disengagement

> *"A bend in the road is not the end of the road ... unless you fail to make the turn."*
> *– Anonymous*

"What, in the name of Heavens, am I doing here?"

That, perhaps, was one question I should have asked myself much earlier on in my career. But how many amongst us have asked the right question at the right time, let alone do the right thing at the right time? Sadly, when we fail to do either, we transform ourselves into being a slave who, for the rest of our lives, bears the burden of questions unanswered, of aspirations unfulfilled, or of dreams that either remain just a dream – or often turn into a nightmare.

Should I have asked that question when I forced myself to guffaw along with others at my Commanding Officer's distasteful jokes, or when his divine flash of brilliance sent me on a grueling Route March even before my basic military training?

Should I have asked that question at the end of my very first day as a Duty Medical Officer, or when my application to proceed for surgical specialization was rejected because I fell short by a mere twenty four hours, and the authorities therefore felt I needed six more months of military activities to prepare for it?

Should I have asked that question when I was forced out of the opportunity of a post-graduate program abroad perhaps because others with 'connections' felt they deserved it more, or when I was compelled to engage in discourses on military history and strategy during the Study Periods, instead of being given the opportunity of learning more of medical science?

Should I have asked that question when my surgical mentors seemed more inclined to partake to deafening tirades over petty nonsensical matters rather than teach us surgery, or when I was forced to dispense medications to apparently healthy individuals because it would ensure permanence of rank, status and appointment for some?

Should I have asked that question when a well-accepted surgical procedure, which was my thesis, was branded as being 'experimental' and therefore banned, or when a scholarship in orthopedics offered to me by a prestigious institution abroad was blatantly ignored by the authorities on the premise of flimsy and baseless bureaucratic excuses?

Or should I have asked that question when, finally, justice failed to prevail, and the very fabric which made me what I was, was ripped out of me by certain demons in disguise?

These are questions to which I wish I had some answers. But, these are questions to which, perhaps, there *are* no answers, for the simple reason that the essence and embodiment of what we call *Life* is an existence, and what we call *Fate* is an acceptance, both so intimately weaved within the fabric of a grand scheme that we often accept both as being one and the same. We often seem to overlook the fact that while an 'existence' can have meaning, an 'acceptance' can have alternatives.

Quite often the 'balance sheet' of our total existence reflects the Fate that was unfairly imposed upon us, and which we were compelled to accept, rather than being able to do what we desired to do with our lives. It is much like a bank statement where the column of 'credits' are the aspirations and the abilities we bring with us, while that of 'debits' is what we are sometimes forced by Fate to accept. And, like many things in life, when debits outweigh credits, the story doesn't have a particularly happy ending. My acceptance of whatever was forced upon me as I walked in through the imposing and inspiring gates of an establishment was filled with the hopes of being able to nurture and enrich a confluence of my desires with the demands of the establishment.

But unfortunately, and quite unknowingly, I had walked into an arrangement which did not seem quite rooted in rightfulness and righteousness on the part of certain individuals, and perhaps was never intended to be – and which took me a while to realize. And when I did realize it, I was left wondering whether or not it was already too late. Naïve as I was, I kept trying to convince myself that that was not actually the case; that it was perhaps a matter of simple oversight, and not of design; that this was an exception and not the rule. Nevertheless, however much I tried to put faith and trust in my convictions, the more it became obvious that my passage forward was actually a one-way trip to oblivion.

Despite my usual natural inclination of being one of the last to abandon a lost cause, there came a point in my journey when I knew, in the most trusted depths of my heart, that my great 'titanic moment' had actually arrived. I knew that time was ripe for me to jump off of a sinking ship if I were ever to give myself a fighting chance of reaching the shore, where I could at least feel the firm ground of purpose under my feet, and ignite the hope of a meaningful existence in my heart.

Yes, I may have silently tolerated more than my fair share of sea-sickness during this voyage, and yes, I may have drifted far from my dream destination into uncharted and unknown waters. But I was certainly not willing to stand on the deck of a sinking ship any longer, and be its companion on its way down to the deepest and darkest depths of misery and malevolence. That way, my conscience would at least be at peace with the fact that logic came before misplaced loyalty, that hope took precedence over hollow promises, and that the endeavor to continue to live a meaningful life was certainly more desirable than being a martyr to a cause that was as distorted as it was devious.

There are basically two ways of living one's life. Firstly, it can be lived the way it unravels – being uneventful, lackluster and rather ordinary. On the other hand, it can also be lived the way it ought to be lived – with grit and gumption and the resolve to turn things around in one's favor. It all boils down to how one looks at Life itself, and how one wants to live it.

True perception of Life, in my opinion, and perhaps the most fulfilling way of living it, lies in our ability to steal a glance beyond the crests of the waves of our daily struggles, to catch a glimpse of Fate and Destiny beyond – before those waves come crashing down on us. Whether we are eventually able to ride those waves, or unceremoniously drown in it, is dictated not by skill alone, but also by our resolve to live.

And nothing can be more tragic or heartbreaking than when one reaches a point where the fine line separating these two situations gets blurred to the point of extinction – thus ushering in the glorious conclusion of the diabolical designs of some. That is when one gets converted into being exactly what that person was 'conceived' to be, rather than what he or she was capable of being.

I realized only too late that that was, in fact, nothing less than a matter of covert intent crafted meticulously by some, in trying to hold on to certain self-serving and selfish needs. And sadly, at the end of the day, you become the firewood on which feeds the flames of deceit and deception, and which reduces you to the ashes which form the foundation of a memorial dedicated to your valiant, yet futile, efforts.

So, about eleven years after we began our search for the proverbial “Promised Land”, Samina and I finally realized we were actually trudging along on a barren and inhospitable desert. We seemed to be continually climbing sand dunes of institutional insensitivity, braving sandstorms of institutional impropriety, and evading the quick-sands of institutional imprudence. In fact, we seemed to be chasing one mirage after another, only to find displeasure in place of delight, vice in place of virtue, sacrilege in place of sanctity, falsehood in place of fairness, and dishonor in place of dignity.

This is not to say that there weren’t any occasional oases scattered along the way. But those, besides being few and far between, always seemed to have been occupied by travelers who were never meant to have survived this long in the first place, not to mention having come this far. However, it did not take us too long to realize that a good number of those fortunate travelers actually got there by riding on the backs of camels unjustly gifted to them, and were surviving on provisions bestowed unto them through the blessings of ‘connections’.

And thus did Samina and I decide to resolutely ride out that proverbial wave into a realm in which we could hold the helm, choose our path, and chart our lives, unencumbered by imposed institutional barriers. Most of all, we were yearning for the freedom of making our own life, by making our own *choices* in life.

But it was soon obvious that the wave we were planning to ride out was not a wave at all – it was a horrendous tsunami. It was a wave which dwarfed and decimated everything around it with the might of its monstrosity and the height of its arrogance. It was a mammoth wave with the power and the potential of destroying anything it encountered, and crushing everything that stood in its way – leaving behind a trail of denied opportunities and shattered dreams. And as it turned out, Samina and I had an appointment with it.

The behavioral code of social conduct of almost every race, clan, community, group, institution and establishment requires that its precepts, principles and practices focus on the preservation of self-worth and the application of built-in values. Conflicts arise when well-established belief systems, well-practiced conventions, and long-serving self-interests are threatened by hitherto unknown forces, unforeseen circumstances, and unexpected occurrences.

And the world around me seemed no different. Notwithstanding the fact that some of its precepts, principles and intuitive values appeared to be sitting on a foundation that was somewhat flawed in concept and archaic in value, the instinct for self-preservation, nevertheless, of some around me was rather intense. Regrettably, it also seemed to be based on the flagrant assumption that vested institutional interests took precedence over essential individual priorities, needs and desires.

Central to this posture was an innate instinct to resist anything and everything they were perhaps unacquainted with, or were unprepared for. This obviously stemmed from an oddly confounding and a largely unfounded fear of losing authority and credibility. It was as if they were averse to deviating from a path which they had trodden over the years, happily trampling on anything which did not seem to fit into their grand design. And anything, or anyone, straying ever so slightly from that beaten track needed to be flayed back into the strict and restrictive confines of their dogmas and doctrines.

Not surprisingly, therefore, our endeavors to voluntarily take leave prematurely were met with a kind of resistance which, from the very outset, was mentally distressing, morally disheartening, and sometimes even personally abrasive.

According to regulations, specialists were required to render their services for at least five years following post-graduation. The day that Samina and I submitted our letters of resignation for a voluntary pre-mature retirement, we had both served much more than that.

However, from the moment that our resignation papers reached the high offices, some seemed to think that they have suddenly had a severe shortage of both orthopedic surgeons and pediatricians. That was when, perhaps, the imprudence of not having had enough of such specialists in this institution – particularly orthopedic surgeons

– finally hit home. Therefore, from the perspective of some sitting in the high offices, it seemed like a foregone conclusion that we could not be allowed to leave under any circumstance, mainly because of an alleged shortage of specialists available to fill the void which would purportedly be created by our absence. Amusingly, such a posture actually ran contrary to one of the most frequently and passionately repeated proclamations of this institution: "No one is indispensible" – with which, this time at least, I genuinely and whole-heartedly agreed.

One of the reasons, obviously, for such a stance was the situation of suddenly being faced with the not-quite-predicted prospect of losing two qualified specialists at the same time. Not that voluntary retirement was unheard of, but this time it probably caught some people off-guard, and in the midst of a profound slumber.

This was perhaps the slumber of being secure in the assumption that their well-oiled wagon, however antiquated, presumptuous or overbearing, was trundling along quite smoothly and contentedly in a manner which suited them well. Undoubtedly, our letters of resignation were making that ride a bit bumpy, squeaky and uncomfortable. Though the foundations were by no means shaken, it was something that was perhaps felt as an unnecessary thorn on the side. Needless to say, therefore, the overall attitude of casual dismissal of our resignation letters was a response which was obvious and expected.

To begin with, our applications, on initial submission, were immediately put away by the unit's Second-in-Command into a corner of his desk which usually demanded the least of his attention, and piled along with a stack not usually meant to make its way into the Commanding Officer's room. Foremost in his mind was perhaps the guaranteed resentment of the Commanding Officer for having been handed an unnecessary annoyance which would most certainly disrupt the finely orchestrated tranquility of his peaceful world.

However, after the Second-in-Command had garnered enough courage to pass on our applications to the Commanding Officer following our repeated reminders, the latter held those up again. He simply refused to send our applications along to the higher offices on the pretext that we were not to throw our so-called 'promising careers' away, and that we needed to reconsider our decision.

In reality however, both the Commanding Officer and the Second-in-Command were unwilling to ruffle feathers in the high offices by handing them letters of resignation from two specialists, and that too, at the same time. To be very honest, they were actually more concerned with their own standing with the lofty offices, where careers were routinely made, broken, or frozen with the casual stroke of a pen. That our letters of resignation could easily be construed as evidence of inept command and a lack of control was a frightening prospect, especially for the Commanding Officer. After all, the last thing one would want, having risen to such dizzying heights of status and prominence, was a blemish in a career to which self-serving spit-and-polish had been applied over the years. It was only after we pointed out to the Commanding Officer that it was well within our rights to demand that our applications be sent along, that he most reluctantly relented.

Not surprisingly, however, the initial response of the lofty offices was one of indifference and outright rejection.

Just as ignoring a problem is the most time-honored way of pretending it does not exist, the powers-that-be probably felt that their most recent 'inconvenience' would simply disappear if they kept silent and did not respond. But the more they tried to distance themselves from what they probably felt was a nuisance, the more we persisted in our efforts to be heard by way of reminders and requests for a response. Eventually, it was conveyed to us formally, and through an official letter, that our application for a premature voluntary retirement had been summarily rejected.

This was most distressing for us. Though Samina and I continued to provide our day-to-day services at the hospital to the best of our abilities, we seemed to be otherwise consumed by the 'whys and wherefores' of the issue. Central to our preoccupation at that stage, obviously, was the search for an avenue of egress. We felt we had every right to leave, since we had served our mandatory periods. That obviously meant that we were now beyond any official obligation to serve any longer, and beyond the need for any further association that could be considered mutually productive. As far as we were concerned, we had reached the end of the line – like runners who had run their distances to the best of their abilities, regardless of the nature of the track. Whether or not we came out winners, was no longer the bone of contention. What mattered now was whether chewing on that bone any further was going to yield any fruitful results. And we could clearly see it wouldn't.

Therefore, in spite of our applications being rejected, we continued our relentless efforts. This was either in the form of seeking an audience with those placed high enough to matter, by indicating to the relevant authorities at every opportunity of our intention to leave, or by reminding anyone high-ranking enough whom we came across, that our applications were collecting dust somewhere in the high offices.

It seemed our efforts eventually paid off because, finally, some seemed willing to listen. Though we had no way of telling how sincere this response was but, given our previous experience, we suspected it could very well have been a way of simply buying time. And as it turned out, it was! Sculpted by a culture which was both insensitive to the needs of others, and self-serving to the extent of being obdurately arrogant, some in lofty offices came up with a trade-off proposal.

Nonetheless, there was a glimmer of hope in it. Because when a posture changes from one of 'no response' to that of a 'proposal', it perhaps means that the outer fortification of the citadel has perhaps been breached. And that was progress, as far as we were concerned! Unfortunately, however, there was also the flip side to the situation that also needed to be taken into cognizance. Because when a proposal is made when there is, obviously, no need for making one, it can mean only one thing – that the infamous Pandora's Box of endless delaying, and perhaps even fear, tactics was going to be unlocked very soon.

The opening salvo landed on the desk of my Commanding Officer one morning, and I was summoned to his office to be informed of it. It was a letter from the high office in Dhaka stating that Samina's application for pre-mature voluntary retirement would be accepted only if I was willing to provide a written undertaking to serve for another ten years!

Perhaps this was an attempt at buying time; or perhaps this was a way of dissuading us from pressing ahead with our intention to retire; or perhaps this was the way things were done around here. Sincerely speaking, I did not know which it was. But, if you ask me, it looked more like a banner on which was written, "We know you won't accept such a proposal because you don't want to serve another ten years. So, please stop being such a pain in the neck, and go back to work. But remember, we did make an offer – which you refused!"

At that point, I found myself pitying the plight and the shameless desperation of the powers-that-be. This letter was a brazen exposure of a deep-rooted frailty and a pathetic vulnerability. Here was a demonstration of how some individuals within an organization that was otherwise known for its strict adherence to rules, regulations and righteousness could, for reasons which served their own purposes, resort to a practice so improper and imprudent. Nevertheless, this came as no big surprise since our trust and confidence on the ethical and moral complexion of some within this establishment had, by now, already gone past the point of no return.

That day, I left my Commanding Officer's room, having explained to him the ambiguity and the absurdity of the proposal. I had not the slightest doubt that certain enlightened minds sitting upstairs were actually trying their best to create a face-saving status quo. And I found it ludicrous and lamentable that this was what the finest brains could come up with. I had joined this organization under the impression that it was guided by brilliant minds, served with the realization that not everyone was perfect, but was now convinced that some of those minds actually needed help. It irked and bothered me that they had lowered themselves to a level where they were now playing the card of our marital status against us, in their bid to win this battle.

I had to explain to my Commanding Officer that Major Samina was an officer of the armed forces much like me, him, or any other. From that standpoint, I asked him whether he would be willing to provide a similar undertaking for her, if demanded of him. The perplexed and exasperated look on his face was all the answer I needed. I do not know exactly how the reply to the lofty offices was worded by my Commanding Officer, and frankly, I didn't care. It was enough for me that this time, at least, I had not cowered under the crushing weight of the authoritarian heavy-handedness of some in the lofty offices.

A lengthy silence followed. This meant that perhaps the next preposterous move was being planned, or that there was this impression that ignoring us once again would somehow make us go away like magic. The plan, it seemed, was to either tire us to the point of frustration, or intimidate us to the point of submission. But as far as we was concerned, the pebble was already on its way down the slope, and if anything, it was destined to snowball soon into a huge boulder of resolve and resilience.

And so, our relentless quest for the elusive utopia continued, mostly in the form of persistent and sometimes obstinate reminders to anyone with enough brass on their shoulders and medals on their chests about our applications, on which the high offices seemed to be sleeping. By now however, most of the top brass, especially those who walked the Corridors of Power, knew about our applications to retire, and my appeal to them was for a fair, rational and considerate response.

But, every door we knocked and every audience we sought were met with exactly the same well-known set of responses: Intent and sober attentiveness and nods of meaningful understanding – all culminating to solemn assurances of help and cooperation. But, unfortunately, those were invariably followed by a silence synonymous with that of a graveyard. Nevertheless, we persisted, even if it meant placing a 'bouquet of appeal' at each and every tombstone.

An Appointment with the Angels

> *"Sometimes serendipity is just intention unmasked." – Elizabeth Berg*

It was during this drawn-out and exasperating 'battle' that I got the impression that some sort of a divine power from somewhere was perhaps also lending us a hand – in a most subtle and surreptitious way – to further our cause.

I have often questioned my inner self as to whether all this could have been the conjecture of a predisposed psyche, or whether in fact, it was all too real. Call me naive or gullible if you will, but as far as I could see, such interventions seemed rather tangible and unmistakable to me. They seemed to have the subtlety of the divine, and a hint of the supernatural. Yet they were somewhat also elusive. So elusive that they could easily escape notice, if not sought with faith in the Power of Providence, or the proverbial 'third eye'.

To begin with, the very fact that we never lost heart and hope throughout our endeavors, and faced insurmountable odds with patience and resolve, was proof enough of the fact, at least to me, of some sort of a divine intercession and inculcation. This, I must admit, proved to be our Guardian of Guidance throughout the entire ordeal, and proved to be the strength and support we needed at our times of need.

Besides, other incidents every now and then during that period more than convinced me that we were perhaps not entirely alone in our struggles. On the one hand, such incidents were very real, and had a definite impact on the sequence of events that were unfolding. On the other hand, such incidents had a rather mystical connotation, as if they belonged somewhere just beyond the edge of human comprehension and cognizance.

And, this is what I mean.

The Director General of Medical Services (DGMS), a Major General by rank, and the number one person of the Army Medical Corps was on a goodwill visit to Chittagong.

Both Samina and I knew that the DGMS, from the very outset, was not particularly keen on having us leave, and that in this matter, as in most others, he usually toed the line with some of the enlightened minds in the lofty offices. Nevertheless, singularly on the basis of his rank and appointment, we felt that if there was anyone with the power and the potential to be able to impress and perhaps also convince those who mattered to release us, it would probably have to be him. Whether or not he would actually advocate on our behalf was quite another matter, and which could admittedly be compared to a coin spinning in the air. Even so, meeting with him and trying to make a case of our intention to retire was a gamble I was willing to take. All I needed to do was to try my best to convince him, lest it worked.

I contacted the *Aide de camp* (ADC) to the DGMS and informed him of my intention to meet with the latter. The ADC, after consulting with the DGMS, conveyed to me that he had agreed to give me an audience at 7 p.m. of the following day at BNS Patenga, the naval headquarters at Chittagong, where the DGMS would be staying that night.

BNS Patenga, situated on the shores of the Bay of Bengal, was about a 30-40 minute's drive from Chittagong Cantonment. There were two ways of getting there. One was along a proper two-lane road which everyone used. The other was a narrow strip running along the shoreline of the Bay of Bengal, and which could be considered a little more than a glorified trail. This second route, though used sparingly, was considerably shorter, and cut travel time from Chittagong Cantonment to BNS Patenga by at least about ten to twelve minutes.

I was hardly a few minutes into my trip when I realized I would be late for my appointment if I took the more frequently-travelled route. So I immediately turned my car around and set off along the less-traveled narrow strip running along the shoreline. By now the sun had already set and darkness had descended. And on an unused and unlit road such as this, the darkness was even more obvious – perhaps a bit ominous as well. This was a kind of road on which hardly anyone drove during the day, let alone at night. And moreover, with the nearest habitation being miles away, this road was also devoid of any human presence. My car, with its lights literally cutting through the thick darkness, was the only moving object on that road that night.

I soon realized that I was actually going to be able to cut down on my travel time which, considering the fact that

I was running a bit late, was a huge relief. But hardly about 5-7 minutes from my destination, my heart sank. Caught in the headlight beams of my car were three humongous boulders sitting right across the road, with no room for my car to go either through or around those.

And there I sat in my car, wondering what to do. Those boulders were so huge, there was no way I was going to be able to move them, even with someone's help, let alone by myself. I was now contemplating turning around and somehow getting on to the proper roadway. But that road was miles away, and I was not quite sure how to get to it from where I was. Nevertheless, I decided to try. Though I knew I would now surely be late for the appointment, it was a chance I was willing to take, mainly because I was in no mood of turning back now and going home – not after having come this far.

Just as I was about to put my car into gear, I sensed a movement beside the road. It was more of a weird warping of the blackness outside, which caught my attention. As I squinted and tried to focus, a figure emerged, as if out of nowhere, and stood in my headlight beams. It was a man of medium build wearing a vest and a traditional *lungi*. I was totally perplexed, not as much by the fact that he was there, as it was by the question of how he could possibly be there. To see someone here at this time of the night, with no human settlement for miles around, was an incredulity that was still in the process of sinking in, when I heard the question, "You want to go through?" floating to my ears. And when I answered in the affirmative, he proceeded to move those boulders as if they were made of nothing more than Styrofoam. Within moments he had made a way for my car to go through, and said, "Now you can make it". I was left totally mystified and stunned by the drama that had just unfolded in front of my eyes. And as I drove off, I remember having mumbled my profuse thanks while still in a state of trance and disbelief.

Amazingly, I made it in time for my appointment, and did get the opportunity of conveying to the DGMS in person, of our intention to retire and to request a favorable consideration of our case. Though I did get a patient and an apparently sympathetic hearing, I had my doubts whether, at the end of the day, it would really amount to anything. Nevertheless, I had the satisfaction of having tried. Whether or not my efforts were going pay off down the road, was a different matter altogether.

It was actually on my way back from BNS Patenga, relaxed now after a frenzied trip and an apparently satisfactory appointment that I began to reflect on the events that had unfolded on my way there.

I do not believe that divine interventions, such as the parting of the Red Sea or of a rod turning into a serpent, happen anymore. Those were different times, when God had a different kind of an agenda for Humankind. And those interventions were clear and obvious, with the power and the potential of changing the Fate and Fortune of Mankind. Not anymore. But, this is not to say that heavenly guidance and interventions do not take place these days. In my opinion, they do, but are more subtly integrated into our day-to-day life, and are not as obvious. It would be something akin to the imperceptible growth of a tree, for example, which would not be noticeable from one day to the next, but the progression of which would be the result of little everyday-miracles which sustains that tree.

Hence I would not like to be so reckless or so naive as to even contemplate the sudden appearance of a stranger on a dark and deserted road – who so effortlessly removed boulders from my path so I could go through and be in time for my appointment – to have been some sort of an outrageous and manifest display of divine favor. Not unless I was willing to carry both the stigma of fickle-mindedness and the burden of ridicule on my shoulders the rest of my life! Nevertheless, however much I tried, till to this day I have not been able to explain whatever had happened that night on a dark and deserted road to Patenga – not at least in terms of conventional perception and common everyday comprehension. But in the depths of my subconscious awareness I am convinced that that event was, in some way or the other, a contributor to shaping my future.

Deeds of Desperation

> *"There are no desperate situations. There are only desperate people." – Heinz Guderian*

It seemed our persistence and perseverance eventually paid off, at least partially, as Samina's application for retirement was finally – and I believe most reluctantly – accepted.

The decision-makers, at length, seemed to have decided they were perhaps better off not having both the irritating birds together in the same cage, chirping away to the point of intolerance. It was therefore probably a calculated move on their part, made on the premise that the freedom gained by one would not only reduce the overall noise level in the vicinity, but that the other bird – out of sheer gratitude – would perhaps also cease to be so irritating and bothersome. It also seemed like a desperate attempt by some in lofty offices at salvaging one specialist while, at the same time, not making it look like they were giving in entirely to our perceived recalcitrance.

Retiring Samina only was understandably a distressing inconvenience for me. But what the authorities had not predicted was that as far as I was concerned, it was like waking up short of my dream reaching a pleasant and fulfilling conclusion, because that was not the kind of closure I had in mind. As a matter of fact, I was willing to go to sleep a million times over, if need be, with the singular intent of reaching a conclusion more acceptable than this. Moreover, I was so far gone down the road of disenchantment, discontentment, disappointment, and perhaps even bitterness by now, that I was left consumed by a single-minded recklessness and a burning desire for a premature retirement for myself as well.

In hindsight, it seems the decision-makers did themselves a huge disfavor by allowing only Samina to retire because their plan and prediction had failed to foresee the fact that it would only serve to rekindle my intent and endeavor to take leave.

So, as the two sides once again got down to jockeying and jostling to gain the upper hand at the negotiating table, another volley landed on the desk of my Commanding Officer. I was informed that if I submitted a financial 'compensation' to the tune of Taka 13 lacs – approximately equal to USD 32,500, at the rate of exchange at that time – I would be allowed to go on retirement.

I could clearly envision some of the enlightened minds being immensely pleased and satisfied at the ingenuity and the novelty of this latest momentous proposition of theirs. But, of all the absurdities that I have ever encountered in my lifetime, this had to be, without a doubt, the most dubious, demeaning, and decadent ever. And, if truth be told, I never expected anything better from those who had proved, time and again, to be professing a philosophy which was as conceited as it was contemptuous. So here I was again, being asked by a gargantuan entity to pay an astronomical sum of money when there was absolutely nothing that I owed it. It was as if I was being told to my face, "So, you want freedom? We sell freedom. Buy it". Had I looked around more attentively, I would perhaps have seen the shadow of Shylock lurking somewhere in the dark alleys around me!

If all was fair in love and war, it seemed well within my rights to fight fire with fire, especially for one pushed to such exasperating limits as myself. In a way,

I was being compelled to always stay a step ahead in this unnecessarily drawn-out and frustrating drama of deceit and deception, and which I was partaking to most unwillingly. And, from the way it was unfolding, I could foresee that the smoldering ashes of the aftermath would turn into an epitaph of bruised egos and battered mutual respect. But frankly, I was well past caring by now.

So I set about attempting to make some sense of the financial stipulation placed before me.

To begin with, it made no sense. There was actually nothing that I owed anyone at this time: not after having served the requisite number of years following my post-graduation, and certainly not after having given more than fifteen years of mostly thankless service. It was up to me now, therefore, either to give in to such a demand, which was as confounding as it was reprehensible, or to try to reason with the mindless. But I had my doubts whether reasoning would succeed because over the years it hardly ever seemed to work. Nevertheless, and against all odds, I decided to give it a try.

It needs to be mentioned at this point that in exchange of a fixed salary, which was paltry by any standard – especially where it concerned specialists doing highly 'specialized' work – we performed our surgeries regardless of their number and complexity. From the perspective of those who governed, those were deemed to have been paid for out of the paltry salary we received. This was besides the fact that the average charge for a single complex surgery at any civilian institution at that time would have been approximately equal to the entire salary we received in a month, or maybe even more. Nevertheless, even that was something we were willing to live with.

However, I now reasoned that if the some in the high offices felt it was within their rights to demand an astronomical 'penalty' from me when there was nothing that I owed them, it was well within my rights too, to demand payment for all the so-called 'free surgeries', that I had performed over the years. If this seemed anything like an unfair demand, then in my opinion, the definition of fairness and justice would need to be revisited and redefined, particularly for the benefit of those who regularly decimated it with an attitude of detached dismissal.

So I got down to doing my calculations which, in fact, was pretty simple and straightforward. Eventually and interestingly, it turned out that if I had to be paid for all the surgeries I had performed literally free of cost, it would actually add up to more than twice the amount being demanded of me as the so-called 'compensation'. My solution, therefore, was outrageously simple. Out of the amount owed to me for all the surgeries I had performed over the years, they were at liberty of keeping for themselves their 'compensation', and pay me the rest – and I would happily go home!

Here was a lone individual – who, in the eyes of some in this gargantuan organization, was worth nothing more than a mere obscure number – staring them squarely in the eye and insisting that matters be sorted out on a level playing field. Very rarely have they, otherwise always so secure within the sanctuary of their might and megalomania, been challenged. It was like David walking up to Goliath, slingshot in hand, taking aim at his forehead!

And Goliath must have been felled.

He must have been felled because there was this famous deathly silence once again, following my counter-proposal. It was as if too many confounding numbers had been fed into a computing machine, slowing it down, as it tried to crunch integers it was not designed to deal with. I could sense some of the illustrious minds sitting upstairs not being particularly impressed with all this, and perhaps starting to consider me a lunatic by now.

What military officer, in his sane mind, would ask his commanding officer whether or not he was willing to serve ten more years so his wife could retire? What craziness would prompt an officer to demand recompense from the mighty and the powerful, when asked to pay a penalty? Long-presumed reliable logic was being decimated mercilessly and with casual disrespect. Tried and tested strategies, proven effective till now, were being undone effortlessly with simple reasoning! Under the circumstances, my name was undoubtedly reaching more ears at the high offices now, than it should – which was probably not a good thing. I began to have this uneasy feeling that, perhaps by now, I had more enemies within the Corridors of Power, than friends.

At that point, the powers-that-be probably decided not to hem and haw any further and confront me. They dug in deep with finality and seemed unwilling anymore, to entertain even the slightest hint of my retirement. Inquiries into the status of my application were either shrugged off or totally ignored. Ardent appeals to the person at the very top of the hierarchical pyramid fell on a set of deaf ears. Concerned quarters now seemed to have adopted a posture of total disregard and indifference towards my cause.

By and large, certain elements within this otherwise righteous and distinguished institution seemed so preoccupied and so single-mindedly engrossed in their skirmish with a lone officer, and so elaborate and innovative in their endeavors to thwart his quest for freedom that their true nature, weakness and self-serving intent actually lay mercilessly exposed. And therein lay my true satisfaction: In the fact that I was able to bring out the worst in them. Needless to say, the worst is always revealed when it hurts. And it hurts when something, or someone, is being taken seriously. And that, in itself, was proof enough of the fact that the matter of my retirement was perhaps not quite dead yet!

It is regrettable, however, that when push finally came to shove, some people bared their fangs and spat their venom like an angry wild beast bent on preserving its territory – and then proceeded to make a 'dog's breakfast' out of a perfectly simple, legitimate and straightforward proposition. It hardly mattered to them that the means to that end was unfair, unconventional or irrational.

Neither did it seem relevant to the issue that, in doing so, the otherwise righteous, honorable and respectable image of this establishment was at a risk of being tarnished. Rather, the strategies and methods exercised and employed by them in this lopsided skirmish seemed like a distorted and preposterous reincarnation of good sense and sensibility. And, at the end of the day, all that transpired, and all that was inflicted upon and endured as the result of their arrogant and obdurate obstinacy was like a chisel engraving the epitaph over the grave of their famed and flaunted 'orderly conduct'.

If truth be told, both the matter of me wanting to retire prematurely, as well as the desperate attempts by some in high places at thwarting my efforts perhaps qualified as a 'disorderly conduct' – which, presumably, is one of the most frequently-used phrases in the manuals of military law around the world. And as to whether I or the other side was actually guilty of this disorderly conduct depends on whether one believes a zebra is a white animal with black stripes or a black animal with white stripes. It all depends on where allegiances lie, the way belief systems are born and nurtured, and the kind of institutional convictions and practices that take root over time.

But, what actually concerned me was the way the situation deteriorated rather rapidly like a runaway wildfire to an unpleasant, maligning and abrasive level. If anything, and as far as I could see, it had actually deteriorated to the level of being more appropriately labeled as a 'Disorderly *Mis*conduct' – assuming such a phrase even exists, and hoping it is capable of conveying the actual magnitude of the matter. And while both parties were perhaps equally guilty of it, one brandished it out of a need for survival, while the other brandished it out of sheer obstinacy, egocentricity and perhaps even animosity.

If this was any theatrical show – which essentially it was, then it would have to have a climax and a culmination – and which indeed it did. But that was not before a final act of insensitivity and intolerance was played out by a star-studded cast.

It was a dinner night at the Tiger Mess in Chittagong Cantonment. The Tiger Mess is the flagship mess of the East Bengal Regiment, or the Bengal Tigers, as they were so gloriously called – and hence the name. Quite understandably therefore, the mess was big, posh, plush and glitzy.

Though I do not quite remember the occasion, it had to be important because I was literally dazzled by the high-ranking glitter and sparkle which saturated the premises. And, strangely enough, the fact that almost everyone who walked the Corridors of Power was gathered at one place actually made me feel like a kid in a candy store. Included in the eminent gathering were those who knew about my letter of resignation, as well as those who had actually dealt with my case. And in a moment of playful imagination I fancied myself as a shark circling its prey, as I swam amongst the gathered nobility, and waited and prayed for an opportunity to strike, to be able to make my case, even though it would obviously be out of situational context. Because right then, I was not only an 'angry young man', I was also a 'hungry young man'.

I was angry because I was being denied a legitimate right and deprived deserved liberty through the insensitivity and egocentricity of a handful few. And, at the same time, I was hungry with the desire to be able to decide for myself what to do with whatever remained of the one Life I had, and not have someone else decide that for me anymore. And right then, all who mattered and all who figured prominently in the overall equation were there in the tiger's den – all in one place. The setting and the situation couldn't have been timelier or more appropriate than this.

Just as Fortune had smiled upon me at other times in my lone struggles, Providence once again stepped in and literally gifted the prey to the shark.

It was in the form of a group of officers, glittering with seniority, who called me aside. My gut instinct told me that my perceived 'lunacy' was soon going to be discussed, and most likely dissected – because, as far as some were concerned, I was the hallmark of discontent, dissension and, to a certain extent, rebellion.

Needless to say, I was salivating at the prospects of the approaching encounter. This moment had the potential of making it the turning point in my efforts to retire prematurely from the establishment; this was perhaps going to be my Battle of Midway, and my landing on the beaches of Normandy. But, if nothing at all, this was where I was at least going to be able to express my views, vent my frustrations, and stand my ground – yet once again. And, with an important segment of the 'makers and shakers' in one place, I had to make it count.

"I hear you intend to retire?" was the opening volley.

"Yes sir, I do".

And then I was totally broadsided by, *"Well, if you are so keen on retiring, then why did you join in the first place?"*

I found myself visibly taken aback by the sheer absurdity and the palpable lack of intellect overflowing from a question such as this. It not only surprised me, it confirmed my long-standing suspicion that an army not only "marches on its belly" – as Napoleon had so famously said – but that some characters in it also often flopped around on that belly like some lowly, miserable aquatic life-form wallowing in a pathetic pool of self-created grandeur and pompousness. If this very senior officer was any representation of the kind of institution I was still a part of, it easily qualified as one of the leading reasons why I was so desperate to relegate it to my past.

After all these years, I am not quite sure of the exact words I used in even dignifying such a question with a proper response. However, I do recollect having mentioned that under the circumstances which had existed for me at the time of my joining the medical corps, it was the best decision for myself, and that none had the right to stop me from having done so.

The grim and heavy silence which followed was an initial confirmation of the fact that such a response was not quite expected, and that Truth had been told. I went on to explain how, over the past fifteen years or so, the mechanisms around me, which was otherwise supposed to support and supplement my expertise had failed to keep up with my transformation, both in terms of professional attainment and technical evolution. I informed the group that I had probably 'outgrown' the confines of my environment in the context of its existing and ongoing agenda and philosophy. I further mentioned that with the way things were at that stage, it seemed that the institution, due mainly to the shortsightedness of some, lacked both the vision and the intent required to be able to properly utilize whatever I was capable of delivering as an orthopedic surgeon. I concluded therefore that that establishment probably had no further need of me, as much as I had no place in it anymore.

The air was so thick with silence for the following few agonizing seconds that one could possibly reach out and touch it, or perhaps even cut it with a knife. If Time had ever stood still, it certainly was now. And as the train of empty seconds ticked by, it seemed as if this so-called 'motionlessness of Time' was being stretched to its absolute limit of awkwardness and distress. And standing there, in front of a collection of apparent incredulity, annoyance and perhaps even indignation, I was overcome by a premonition that this singular moment had the potential of either an outburst of cataclysmic proportions or a composed and rational response of dignified reasonableness.

Surprisingly, it was neither. The eventual and abruptly dismissive "You may go now" that was delivered with a presumably intended tone of condescension sounded as if this was a training ground and I was a lowly recruit drafted into the establishment only yesterday – and not a Classified Specialist of the corps with fifteen years of dedicated service behind me. That, in itself, was a clear expression of a deep visceral perception of some in this establishment, of the worth and dignity of a specialist. But, that aside, it was more important that I did not hear any vocal explosion or any demeaning expletives. And given the predilection of some around here, I found that rather strange, perhaps even inappropriate and, I daresay, disturbing as well. Obviously, the computing machine had slowed down once again as it battled to make sense of the arguments presented. Though I most respectfully moved away, feeling quite content with myself for having made my point, I had my misgivings. Had I wasted my breath? Was this something I should not have done? Was this going to destroy whatever chances I had of making it out of this establishment? Was I needlessly trying to hammer a nail into some sort of a fossilized rock made impregnable by preformed precepts and an obstinate mindset?

The Last Port of Call

Whatever happened that night probably had a role to play in the events which unfolded over the next few months.

The so-called 'fraternity of the obsessive and the obstinate' probably came to terms with the fact that a horse could certainly be taken to the water, but making it drink that water was quite another matter. It is not that unwilling horses were never made to drink against their will, but this time it was somewhat different. This time the horse, having already tasted that water earlier, knew how polluted it was with guile, presumptuousness, dogma and diktat. So, this time the horse was bucking and kicking. And it was therefore felt wiser to let go of the restless beast than have hands abraded any further in a bid to rein it in.

Finally, four long and arduous years after having submitted my application for premature voluntary retirement, the authorities relented. It was four years of denial and antics on the part of a handful few in the hierarchy and four years of struggle and strife on my part – all of which ultimately culminated in this final concession. Allegedly, even the person at the very top had to be reminded most bluntly by his own Military Secretary that no further attempts be made to retain me in the establishment because of its potential futility.

What amazed me was the tremendous tenacity with which some of the men and the machinations always prevented me from getting what I wanted – from the moment that I joined with hopes of making a future for myself, to the moment that I wanted to leave, hoping to make a life out of my future. They literally fought tooth and nail to the last ounce of their institutional strength to keep as their own what they wrongly thought they owned. And in doing so, they dug deep into their never-ending reserve of cunning, connivance and craftiness which they carried around in their bag of institutional tricks.

In retrospect, it is plainly obvious that it is in the very nature of some within any establishment to pamper ranks and appointments as if those were nothing less than godly attributes and qualifications. And, with the same sweep of the hand, they use their own ranks and appointments as a tool to subjugate those lower down in the chain of command to render them overly subservient. There are also those who, at times, take selfishness and self-gratification to levels beyond basic decorum and decency while, with the same self-serving sweep of the hand, they dismiss values, virtues, merit and proficiency like they were some kind of a stumbling block on the road to whatever was their mandate.

Furthermore, individuals in any establishment get molded with time along the lines of the ideologies, beliefs, values and the isms that are 'homegrown' in that particular establishment. But, whether that is for the better or for the worse for those who serve in it is sometimes debatable. At the end of the day, it is all about the methods employed in pursuit of the acquisition of attributes and the inculcation of ideologies. And sadly, in some cases, there seems to be an overall slow and somewhat deliberately-enforced transformation which distorts ethics, morals and principles in order to legitimize certain aberrant values, misguided concepts and peculiar practices. This, unfortunately, jeopardizes the inherent good name of any establishment and taints the reputation of those devoted souls who serve it with dedication and diligence. I was perhaps one of the fortunate few whose conscience and consciousness could not be drugged into accepting such a transformation.

As far as I was concerned, this was a new dawn and the beginning of a bright new day, much like the one more than fifteen years ago when I had approached CMH Savar for the very first time.

Peering out the window of the car I had been impressed by a sight full of promise and opportunity. I was excited by prospects beyond all expectations, and buoyed by hopes beyond my wildest dreams. But unfortunately, I had no crystal ball with me that day, to be able to see through a prim, proper and promising facade. There was no way that I could have foreseen some of the improprieties within, and which unraveled gradually over a good part of the fifteen years of my service.

And all through those years I was waiting in eager anticipation for a Utopian culmination of my dreams and aspirations – in much the same way a caterpillar evolves gradually into a beautiful butterfly. But, I looked on in dismay and disbelief as some of those caterpillars turned into monsters instead, and confronted me. The last four years of my service were spent fighting them

– a process which very nearly transformed me into the very demon they were. It left me with scars which bore testament to the fact that certain institutional injustices can inflict injuries so deep and long-lasting that one half of the soul carries them as a legacy, while the other half keeps getting haunted by it for the rest of one's life.

But for now, I had won. I had won my Battle of Midway, and I had landed successfully on the beaches at Normandy. Though shell-shocked and battle-weary, I finally stood on the beach with firm ground under my feet, a clear view of what lay ahead, and with a euphoric sense of achievement which comes only after a protracted period of abrasive conflict.

Finally, I was free. I was free to take control of my own life and not scamper mindlessly after a 'stick' thrown by certain 'masters' consumed by an overpowering appetite for self-gratification. I was free not to have to guffaw along with a senior officer's tasteless jokes whether I liked those or not. I was free not to have to worry about not having saluted a senior officer inadvertently, and thereby suffer appalling consequences. And, I was also free of the need to look over my shoulders every now and then to see if any whim of the lofty offices was chasing me in the form of a charge-sheet.

But most of all, I was finally free of the sense of 'belonging' – not the kind of belonging associated with any sort of prideful affiliation, but the kind associated with a slave belonging to a master. It was a release from a bondage which would have made Abraham Lincoln proud and Nelson Mandela smile.

All that was left for me now were the formalities for terminating my service with this establishment.

Though a part of me felt ecstatic, I must admit that a special corner of my heart was, nonetheless, sad. This was the sadness at realizing that I would be leaving behind a part of myself in the trusted hands of a few wonderful friendships and relationships which took birth and blossomed during the fifteen years of my service. Those who know who I am talking about can take heart from the fact that they are not forgotten – and never will be. I, in turn, have taken away with me a part of their warmth and caring which I shall always cherish. I only wish the same could be said of a certain group of individuals in any establishment.

Preparatory to my release, I was attached to CMH Dhaka for the last few days of my service.

This was the same hospital where I had done my Grading Course in Surgery. But, this time, there were no screaming, child-like surgical mentors to contend with or flee from, no duties as a DMO to wear me down to the last ounce of my physical and mental strength, or no whimsical official inquiries waiting to strip me down to the last vestiges of my dignity. Quite surprisingly, for those last few days, no one bothered me. I was left alone, and that seemed rather strange. I would give myself to believe, however, that as far as this establishment was concerned, I had already ceased to exist, and that I was of no further use to it anymore. I was probably of no more value now than a used and useless piece of paper napkin which deserved only to be tossed most offhandedly into the waste-basket. And it was exactly with that kind of an unmindful, neglectful and dispassionate attitude that some who represented this establishment, finally and officially, bade me farewell a few days later.

Hosting a farewell dinner for a retiring officer, with all the trappings of military formalities, was a matter of institutional etiquette, decorum and tradition. It was considered a mark of respect for the standing of an officer, recognition of the services rendered by him or her, and an expression of gratitude for contributions made.

But, in my case, a segment of the establishment chose to ignore it all, and failed to rise to the occasion. It did not have in its fabric the decency of hosting a proper farewell dinner for an officer who had served for more than fifteen years with total devotion and unwavering dedication against all odds, be those incidental, consequential or man-made. It neglected to respect my standing as an officer who had served with selflessness and with integrity. It chose to ignore the contributions, however small, that I may have made, which had perhaps left this institution slightly richer than when I had joined. And I wish there was some way of carrying all of that to the 'Court of Conscience' for a fair verdict.

Sadly, what some in this establishment failed to realize is that by denying me the privilege of a decent send-off, they had exposed their own decadent mentality and selfish nature. If truth be told, it actually amounted to a visible demonstration of their frustration and fury in not being able to break the will of one individual. It exposed the angst of the powers-that-be with what they had to swallow against their wishes.

From my perspective, however, all this proved to the world that smaller minds did exist which neither understood the worth of selfless devotion, nor appreciated the value of useful contribution. But, to be very honest, I doubt if any of this was even remotely comprehensible to those who regularly abused this glorious institution's values and viewpoints, plotted its self-destructive path, or seemed to nurture the notion that there was no difference between a *lawful command* and the *exploitation of command.*

My farewell dinner was about fifteen minutes one morning in the Commanding Officer's room with a cup of insipid tea and a few second-rate biscuits from the cafeteria sitting in front of me. Moreover, not one individual from the upper echelon of the Army Medical Corps felt it was necessary for them to be in any way involved in this pitiable exercise. Tragically too, the Commanding Officer himself, sitting behind a mammoth desk with an impassive face, made no attempt at hiding an expression of detached disinterest, impatience and boredom in having to accommodate me in his daily schedule. It was as if I was an uncalled-for interference in his work, which he would like to get back to, as soon as this charade was over.

A solemn sermon of institutional gratitude for the fifteen years of my dedicated and selfless service was mumbled out by the Commanding Officer in hardly two sentences, much of which I don't even remember, mainly because they were not sincere or momentous enough to be remembered. They were certainly not the same kind of words I had heard spoken about me by the Commandant of the AMC Training Center some fifteen years ago – words which I still carry in my heart with pride and fondness, and which I shall do so for the rest of my life. And while those were spoken only after twelve weeks of attendance at a training center, this was after fifteen years of affiliation with an establishment!

Interestingly enough, even CMH Chittagong and the Department of Surgery at CMH Dhaka had given me a much better send-off than that. Understandably, the first was a farewell from the hospital where I had last served, and the second a farewell from the department of which I was a specialist.

At the farewell dinner hosted by CMH Chittagong
(The author is in the front row, 2nd from left)

At the farewell lunch hosted by the Department of Surgery, CMH Dhaka (The author is sitting 2nd from right)

The author (3rd from left) with Brigadier-General Fazle Rahim (2nd from left) and other surgical colleagues after the farewell lunch hosted by the Department of Surgery, CMH Dhaka. This is the author's last photograph in service

And if the overseers of the Corps felt that that was enough, and that the Corps itself had no further obligations towards bidding one of its specialists a fitting farewell on behalf of the Corps, then I have nothing to say. Justifiably therefore, I was left with the impression that the two pieces of brass bearing the initials "A.M.C", which I had so proudly carried around on either shoulders for fifteen long years, and which I had always endeavored to ensure be viewed with respect and dignity, were actually nothing more than what they already were – two random and meaningless pieces of brass!

And, as if to reinforce the fact that certain petty matters were oftentimes of greater significance to some in this institution than the bigger picture, the ten to fifteen minutes that I was with the Second-in-Command, waiting to be ushered in for my momentous 'farewell celebrations' with the Commanding Officer, was spent in the Second-in-Command berating me for my hair, which he felt was slightly longer than he would have liked. Pathetically, on the very last day of my five thousand six hundred and seventy two days of service, the length of my hair – and nothing else – seemed to be of utmost importance to him.

That was my 'farewell dinner'. That was how this institution and this establishment said goodbye to me.

To be rudely honest, I didn't care. I didn't care because I was now at the finish line of a marathon: a marathon that seemed to have more miles than I was prepared for, and more surprises along the way than I had anticipated.

It was a marathon which was painful through every mile, and disappointing to the very last yard. It not only sapped all the energy with which I had joined, it also stripped me of most of the substance that made me who I was. The emaciated specimen left behind as a result, was a symbol of the overwhelming success of the motto, motive, and mantra of some in this establishment. And in the process, it destroyed any respect I had for them.

Nevertheless, everything paled into worthless insignificance compared to the feeling of achievement and freedom which flowed through every vein of my being as I finally stood on the victory stand to receive my coveted medal from none other than Providence Himself. I said a silent prayer of gratitude to the Power in Heaven above for having held my hand with compassion and for having guided me through some dark and suffocating rat-holes. I thanked Him for having ignited the light in my heart that helped me fight the darkness, for having granted me the foresight and the fortitude of choosing the right fork in the forest at the right time, and for having given me the strength to break my shackles and choose my path.

Finally then, this is one more insignificant stitch in the mighty fabric of the Human chronicle that has been sewn: one stitch which I hope can hold that fabric a bit tighter, and make the epic of the Human journey a bit more meaningful, be it by an imperceptible degree. At the very least, I can take satisfaction from the fact that my efforts, however small and insignificant, will perhaps be able to contribute to the integrity and completeness of the Human chronicle.

Finally now, I can put to rest a conscience which has otherwise been somewhat perturbed all these years. And that has been possible through accounting the successes and the sufferings of a human who walked this Earth, and through recounting the injustices and prejudices of certain personalities – the likes of whom often threaten to destroy whatever Humankind knows is right and proper, and therefore holds dear. I cannot take back what has so casually and mindlessly been taken away from me over the years. But at the very least, I can expect my recollections and reflections within these pages to not only serve as a contributive treatise for those who are suffering or will suffer the consequences of institutional injustice and the insolence of some within it, but to also be a monument dedicated to those who already have.

I know what I did was right. My protests, my struggles and my strife with certain depraved segments of an entity, and the expression of those within these pages, was the logical outcome of a need to preserve human dignity, define moral ethics, and underscore the need for fair institutional practice. It was a quest for rightful liberty, which was often curbed. It was a demand for deserved justice, which was often denied. And for all of which I very nearly rebelled openly.

It is not a question of whether the *'disorderly misconduct'* was mine or of some within the establishment. What matters more is a consideration of what constitutes the morality on which the principles of an institution are based, and the way those principles influence the moral and ethical basis on which that institution is served. Obviously, in a world of relative considerations, either could be at fault. It all depends on where one sits on the scale of moral and social norms, ethics and responsibilities.

I know what I did was right because I did it not for myself alone. I did it also for those who can take heart from the fact that in spite of all the misguided principles, distorted philosophies, demeaning prejudices, devious manipulations, and most of all, the overwhelming might and overpowering influence of some in any establishment, the right path can still be chosen as long as the conscience is clear, the heart is brave, and the actions are justified.

It is an assertion of the fact that with the right amount of belief in oneself, and with enough courage in one's heart, every cloud can have a silver lining, and every story can have a fairy-tale ending.

It is a rebirth of our long-lost conviction that Sleeping Beauty will awaken, that Pinocchio will come to life, and that the frog will turn into a Prince.

It is a re-discovery within ourselves of the determination, the strength and the courage of David which lives in every one of us – and which has the power to fell a Goliath any day.

But, most notably, it is a reminder of the fact that it takes only one display of good intent from the "powers that be", to ignite a sense of purpose in those who serve, one act of sincerity to buy a lifetime of trust, one act of compassion to secure a wealth of commitment, one act of kindness to kindle the heart, one act of fairness to feed the flames of faith, and one act of tenderhearted tolerance to tide over tears and tragedies.

And at the same time, it is also a reminder that it takes only one insignificant and seemingly harmless matchstick to make a fiery, thunderous, and sometimes even a catastrophic explosion.

Chapter 10
EPILOGUE
The establishment today – Where is it?

The recollections of some of my experiences as a doctor in the forces span a period of fifteen years, which ended almost sixteen years ago.

Sixteen years is time enough for the evolutionary history of any establishment to be able to deliver changes capable of improving upon its infrastructure as well as its functional philosophy. Over such time, one expects changes within an establishment which truly embraces the needs of those who serve in it, and those who are served by it. It is a moral obligation for those who administer an organization as complex as the armed forces, and a functionary as demanding as the medical corps, to regularly examine its moving parts and constantly improve its machinery. But, when that does not happen, as is often the case, any organization is likely to be rendered redundant, where it fails to serve the purpose behind its creation and to uphold the concept behind its existence.

My reflections on the functional state of an organization as it existed more than sixteen years ago, as well as the working conditions therein, had been prompted by the realization that the moral and ethical practices of a handful few within it were not always quite proper or justified. It was also the outcome of my observation that the practices, principles and philosophies of such individuals were a distorted version of what should otherwise have been exemplary, virtuous, just and upright, being members of the kind of establishment they were a part of. But sadly, a bullet-proof hierarchical set-up and the immunity of seniority gave such people all the indemnity they ever needed in order to carry on with some of their covert intents and gainful aspirations. That most were able to get away with it was, in my opinion, simply because the juniors constantly feared the denial of deserved promotions, and the seniors the deprivation of coveted positions, in case they rocked the boat or belled the cat.

Sixteen years down the road, fate compelled me to re-enter the gates of the establishment, and interact with it from the perspective of one soliciting its services – more specifically the services of CMH Dhaka. I will certainly have to admit, however, that what one military hospital delivers – or does not – in terms of its capability and quality of service can, by no means, be considered a representation of the caliber of the entire establishment. It is nevertheless a smoking gun, well capable of pointing a finger of culpability, or of virtue, at the rest of the organizational entity.

On the face of it, the physical and outward appearance seemed to have undergone quite a bit of transformation, at least from what I saw of CMH Dhaka, the largest and the busiest military hospital in the country. Its edifices and corridors were now certainly more stately, and definitely more impressive and modern – almost futuristic. And yes, many of the sophisticated equipment and instruments within its four walls would certainly be the envy of those who didn't have those. Other installations too, seemed to have been transformed as well, quite nearly to the point of being glitzy.

This certainly did not look like the establishment I bade farewell to, almost sixteen years ago. It looked so much improved. Despite that, in some strange sort of way, there was a subtle hint that it perhaps was still the same, because the commonalities between the past and the present actually lay under the surface, and mostly out of sight. One needed only to get below the waterline to realize that only the tiny tip of the iceberg had been adorned and embellished, while the rest of it was perhaps still more or less the same. What some of the architects of the institution perhaps failed to realize is that an extravagant cosmetic overhaul is not always quite enough – that principles, practices and philosophies deep within the core need also to be resolved and rectified, before an organization can become a useful, productive and a proud part of the society and of the nation.

And so here I was again, at CMH Dhaka, standing on the same ground I had stomped almost twenty years ago.

Looking at all that was around me, one would begin to wonder as to who, or what, could have prompted such a breathtaking transformation, when it was known that things hadn't changed or improved to any appreciable degree in this hospital for years together. Obviously, neither the custodians of the corps nor the lofty offices ever seemed to bother. But, do not get me wrong. Some improvements did take place. And though they were few and far between, those took place only because the lofty offices, and not because the medical corps, wanted so.

And this time too, I did not have to dig too deep to discover that almost all of what had taken place was at the initiative of the high offices, and that the medical powerhouse had nothing much to do with it. There were hints, however, that some in the hierarchy of the corps had worked pretty hard in the transformation process and I sincerely congratulate and commend them for that. But, having served for fifteen long years I did not need to be told that all such changes had taken place only because the lofty offices had decided so.

It is not that it was never felt by the medical institution that a wholesale overhaul of the system was necessary in order to keep pace with the ever-changing scenario of the nature and quality of the delivery of medical services. In fact, a good number of medical officers and specialists of the corps had also spent a fair amount of time in various medical institutions abroad, doing post-graduate courses, and I am sure they were brimming with ideas of how to implement in our hospitals, the advancements they had seen. But unfortunately, either the lofty offices never took the suggestions of the medical institution seriously or perhaps because their proposals, to begin with, were not quite convincing or 'authoritative' enough.

To me, it always seemed that the medical corps was never taken seriously enough. And that was perhaps not as much a fault of the powers-that-be as it was of the powerbase of the corps itself. Amazingly, and for reasons beyond my comprehension, the custodians of the corps often seemed to adopt a posture of fear and subservience towards the higher offices, oftentimes at the expense of the corps itself. Expectedly, this conveyed the impression to those 'upstairs' that they had a free hand to impose at will upon the medical functionary. But, the final nail in the coffin that sealed the fate of the corps was the fact that anything enforced upon it was frequently accepted without a shade of dissention, even though it was sometimes not quite acceptable.

The handful few in the medical hierarchy who did protest and disagree, habitually fell out of favor with the mighty and the powerful, and eventually faded out of sight. Interestingly, since this did not bode well for future promotions and positions of power, most kept quiet. That, I remember, was the trend more than sixteen years ago and sadly, it seemed to be the trend even today. Whether this was more a consequence of an obstinate and arrogant mindset of some in the lofty offices, or the outcome of complacency and cowardice on the part of the medical hierarchy, I do not know. But unfortunately, that has always been the case, and that has always been the reason why the medical corps, including those who served in it – and those who were served by it – suffered.

At this point, I would like to begin the discourse by asking myself a most relevant question, and then work my way backwards to decide whether or not my answer to it had been accurate or even justified.

And that question is this:

Despite the outward structural magnificence and the sophistication within, had the services, their quality, or the means of delivering those services improved, at CMH Dhaka?

And after much deliberation, I have to say that the answer is a disappointing 'No'.

For one, the patient load had increased tremendously over the years, but the number of hospital personnel required to handle such a burden still remained well below what was required for the efficient functioning of a hospital as large and as busy as this. Most of the departments continued to remain under-staffed, just the way it had been in the past. Understandably, the balance between the numbers of hospital personnel versus the number of patients required to be dealt with is of critical importance, and is the basic element which decides how well a hospital is going to be able to function.

We have only to see the fatigue and the frustration in the eyes of Hawkeye Pierce and Trapper John from the famous TV serial MASH to understand what happens when doctors have to function beyond human capabilities and without the basic necessities. Interestingly, almost everyone working in this hospital looked like Hawkeye Pierce or Trapper John to me! But, just like the two of them, everyone here too kept their act together through sheer grit and gumption. Fancy equipment and superfluous sophistication were aplenty in this CMH of the twenty first century. But one needs to also understand that these can easily be rendered ineffective when the manpower is overtaken and overwhelmed by a deluge of patients.

I have to admit, nonetheless, that there was a noticeable increase in the number of medical officers and specialists now, when compared to the time when I was an active member of this establishment. But, unfortunately, there had also been a concomitant malignant and exponential explosion in the number of patients this hospital had to deal with, and which had clearly left the medical functionary struggling to contain the runaway wildfire. Here was a situation which was always going to be difficult to control – unless Nero was willing to stop playing his fiddle and douse the flames!

Another aspect which usually makes a hospital credible, viable, and most of all workable, is its handling efficiency of emergency cases. The swiftness and quality of response in such cases is what decides where, in the scale of efficiency and excellence, a hospital actually belongs. And, unfortunately, I felt that this hospital fell short here as well, particularly in the perspective of today's level of emergency response expected of a hospital at this level of national importance and critical value. Though this need not necessarily be taken as a representation of all that this hospital stood for, it was nevertheless significant enough to raise the question as to whether all that had been put into it had produced the desired outcome. And I could clearly see that there was an overall visible and palpable lack of vision, intent and content.

At this point, I would like to give my readers a brief background of what had brought me back to CMH Dhaka, and the events that had allowed me to get a glimpse of its capability of handling emergency medical situations.

During a recent visit to Dhaka my mother-in-law had a sudden attack of what is known as a heart block – which is when electrical impulses inherently generated within the heart fails to travel properly within it, thus failing to cause its different parts to contract at the moments that they should. The most grievous outcome of such an event is the failure of blood going to the brain, often leading to irreversible brain damage, with residual effects like paralysis or loss of speech.

The incident occurred at around 1 am in the morning, when my mother-in-law was suddenly felled by a fainting attack. Knowing it could be serious, I tried to get through to the army telephone exchange, which in turn would connect me to the MI Room at CMH Dhaka, where I could ask for an ambulance to be sent. The reason for choosing CMH Dhaka was because it was the nearest hospital from the defense officers' residential area where my mother-in-law was residing. Moreover, my mother-in-law, being the wife of a retired air force officer, was entitled treatment there. The phone kept ringing, but there was no response. I tried almost all the different numbers of the telephone exchange that would put me through to the MI Room, but to no avail.

I presumed there could have been two possible explanations for this.

Firstly, that the numbers at the telephone exchange had changed. But, truly speaking, the telephone numbers of an installation as vital as those of the forces is neither expected to change, nor should those be changed often, unless under extreme and extenuating circumstances. And even if they were, common sense dictates that it ought to be properly and adequately disseminated to those who were likely to need it often.

The other possibility was that at that time of the night, none at the telephone exchange were particularly willing to be disturbed by a phone call. And it didn't seem to matter that that one call could potentially save a life. If I were ever allowed to have it my way, I would have had something akin to a 'hotline' to the MI Room, something similar to the efficient and easily accessible 911 services found in North America. After all, where it concerns saving a life, seconds matter.

I eventually failed to get through to the MI Room, and the only other option for me was to drive over and ask for an ambulance to be sent – which I did. Thankfully, during the time that it took me to perform this needless and time-consuming exercise, my mother-in-law did not have any further episodes. But, there is no telling whether or not it could have been disabling, or even fatal, if she did.

Finally, my mother-in-law was admitted, and during the course of her hospital stay she was in the Intensive Care Unit and the Coronary Care Unit a couple of times over the next week or so, and finally taken to a cabin for recovery. For those of us at her side, it was a roller-coaster ride alternating between anxiety and despair on the one hand, and relief and hope on the other. Finally, both fortune and Providence smiled upon her – as it did on all of us – and my mother-in-law came out of this debacle with a permanent pacemaker in place.

For me, it was about two weeks of a series of whirlwind events that I had neither anticipated, nor was I prepared for. But as I moved through it, I realized that a part-and-parcel of what made this hospital function was what was actually being contributed to its performance through the tireless and unreserved efforts of those who worked in it – the specialists, the medical officers, the nurses and the medical assistants alike. And surprisingly, even after all these years, the hospital staff still seemed to be at odds with those who administered this institution, as much as the administrators themselves were at odds with the concept of what constituted a standard and seamless round-the-clock functional efficiency and setup of a hospital as central and as vital as this.

An inconspicuously-located and mosquito-infested blood bank, where the lone technician had to be roused from a deep slumber in the middle of the night, looked more like a scene from almost thirty years ago – and was certainly not an indication of functionality.

Surprisingly, the Coronary Care Unit (CCU) was a floor above the room for cardiac procedures. So, for anyone in the CCU requiring an emergency cardiac procedure, where minutes counted, it entailed a time-consuming trip on a trolley which would have made a Wal-Mart shopping cart look like a Mercedes Benz. This was followed by a trip in an elevator which would have lost a race to a tortoise any day. This was certainly no model of modernization or of efficiency!

A power failure in the Intensive Care Unit which took about fifteen minutes to be restored could, under no circumstances, be considered an ideal, acceptable or a safe setting for critically ill patients.

Visitors having to put on shoe-covers while entering a relatively sterile area where a good number of medical officers were walking in with only their army boots on – as if those were inherently bacteria-free – was an exhibition of the presumption that rank and status regularly outdid and out-smarted infective processes. To me, that seemed like a wanton disregard for the principles of medical practice and the safety of the patients.

To see that minivans converted to ambulances still existed, with stretchers reminiscent of World War I, was certainly not the high-point of modernization; nor was the fact that these ambulances had only a blood pressure machine and a tank of oxygen in them, in terms of patient care and monitoring, during the critical trip to the hospital. I wondered too, as to how many of the Medical Assistants who made that trip alongside the patient really knew how to properly conduct a CPR (Cardio-pulmonary Resuscitation) in case it was needed. And even if they did, I wondered whether or not their knowledge and expertise were being regularly assessed and upgraded.

However, not all that I saw around me implied doom-and-gloom. I did see a few rays of hope here and there but, regrettably, those were too few and far between to be able to bolster any confidence in me regarding the capabilities of this hospital. I saw certain improvements which made me proud to have been a part of this establishment once, but was sad to observe that most were no more than merely skin-deep.

I was happy to see that the MI Room now had an information desk which properly processed emergency cases. But at the same time, I was disappointed to observe that the process itself stumbled, because certain cumbersome and antiquated steps still existed.

I was impressed by the way elements of the field intelligence unit efficiently, yet quietly, descended upon the scene the next morning because I had inadvertently provided the information desk with a wrong retirement number – known as the TS number – of the patient's husband. This was communicated to me, and everything was back on course after I provided the correct one.

But, wouldn't it have been more efficient and convenient to have the computer at the reception desk at CMH Dhaka linked to relevant databases so that information such as this could have been verified in the blink of an eye? I do remember having seen a computer at the reception counter, but not much was being done with it by the person who was taking relevant patient information from me. At the very least, the computer at the reception desk, as well as those at every station at the hospital, ought to have been connected to the hospital database – provided there was one – so that both the present and the past medical histories of any admitted patient was readily available at any station in the hospital. And finally, any input made at any station ought to have been saved in a central hospital server, ready for retrieval whenever needed at any station within the hospital. All of that could certainly cut down on some time-consuming and cumbersome processes.

It was indeed a welcome sight to see specialists being brought in rather promptly, but disconcerting to be told there weren't enough of them. Almost every specialist I came across during those few days at CMH Dhaka seemed stooped and bent over – in a rather metaphorical sense – by the burden of their work-load and by the onus of their responsibilities. I heard frustration from the lips of disenchanted specialists and medical officers alike. I saw exhaustion in the eyes of overworked nurses, medical assistants, ward-helps and janitors.

I was pleasantly surprised to see that this hospital now had a qualified Intensive Care Specialist. But, at the same time, I was visibly dismayed by the fact that he seemed to be the only one in the entire hospital. Because during the two weeks or so that I frequented CMH Dhaka, both during regular and odd hours, his lone presence was a cause for surprise and concern. I was terrified by the fatigue and the almost-helpless desperation I saw in his eyes from having to work without respite, but being compelled to be at his judgmental best at the same time.

It took almost forty years for the medical institution to wake up to the fact that this hospital needed Intensive Care Specialists. Was it going to take them another forty to realize it needed many more of such, and not only at CMH Dhaka, but in all the other military hospitals of the country as well? Obviously, afflictions requiring critical care did not necessarily have a predilection only for those for whom CMH Dhaka was easily accessible. Understandably, evacuating such cases from far-flung CMHs to CMH Dhaka would, more often than not, amount to a one-way trip to the mortuary. The mountain, obviously, needed to come to Muhammad. But, to be able to move a mountain, it takes vision, resolve, intent and enterprise – all of which, unfortunately, seemed as elusive today as they were in the past.

But, above all, I was very disappointed to observe that even after sixteen long years, connections were still sometimes being exploited as much as justice and fairness were being denied to some; that rank and status were still being 'worshipped' by certain elements as much as merit and proficiency were being ignored by most; that achieving the near-impossible in the face of scarcity was still being regularly expected, as frequently as medical personnel were being abandoned by their custodians in the face of every expressed displeasure of the higher offices; that this medical institution was not yet quite free of interferences from 'above', and that it still smarted under the weight of a practice where rank sometimes came before sickness, and hospital deaths were being dealt with by a system that was skewed to a one-sided verdict.

But then, all these were naturally to be expected in a setting where those who held the helm of the medical institution did not quite hold it with enough authority. This, I was disappointed to learn, was still a fact today, as it had been almost three decades ago.

I never could make the time to visit every department, ward or procedure room of CMH Dhaka during this short and rather chaotic visit. So, whatever I observed concerned only a small, but nonetheless, essential and critical segments of it. Moreover, I cannot speak for the whole hospital by the same token that I cannot comment on the state of affairs at the other CMHs in the country, not knowing their present functional capabilities. What I observed over those few days at CMH Dhaka was nothing more than a scattered collection of snapshots in an on-going chain of events and activities.

However, where it concerns a hospital, all one requires to look at are its emergency and critical care services, including the Intensive Care and the Coronary Care Units, to be able to assess the overall functional efficiency of any medical machinery. I am not quite sure how many would agree with me, but personally speaking, I wasn't particularly impressed.

But, at the end of the day, I would like to commend those individuals – be they specialists or administrators – for their role in keeping the wheels of the medical machinery turning to the best of their abilities despite constraints of material and manpower as well as 'impediments' from both within and outside of the medical establishment. They have my respect.

As for the rest of the armed forces, whatever I say will be largely conjectural and basically speculative. Therefore, I shall refrain from venturing into a territory where I may not be able to do justice to what was beyond my knowledge and awareness. Yet, while I interacted with the men and the machinery of this establishment and dealt with its dynamics, I could not but ignore a good number of scattered, yet telling, acts and accounts of deception, deprivation, dejection and unjust denials. To me, these reverberated like echoes from the past, and served as a haunting reminder that the legendary ship was still as dilapidated, those deep within its hull still as damned, and some in its bridge perhaps still as devious.

If sensible and logical inference was anything to go by, I would give myself to believe that despite some overly-evident outward cosmetics, things were perhaps in no better shape than what it was, almost three decades ago. Yes, this organization is much bigger now. And yes, it has some rather fanciful toys in its arsenal today – toys which would make those from the yesteryear look like sling-shots and crossbows. Yet, those are in no way a measure of the vital, virtuous and essential qualities of wisdom, ingenuity, sincerity and empathy expected to reside within the core of an organization such as this – elements which provide the impetus for progress in the proper direction.

However, I am quite sure that embedded within the on-going daily affairs and activities of those who serve today are moments of successes, accomplishments and jubilations, as are emotions of despair, dejection, hopelessness and helplessness – one perhaps eclipsing the other. Which eclipses which, actually depends on who you are, and where you stand in the overall scheme of contributions, expectations and reciprocations.

It depends on what you gave without reservation, and what was given back to you – or perhaps taken away.

It depends on how much you valued your association with an entity and, in return, how much you were valued – or perhaps devalued.

It depends on how much, you toiled for a cause and, in return, how much of your dreams and aspirations were foiled.

It also depends on whether you are able to look back with a sense of pride and satisfaction at the yesteryears, or whether you would rather not – because certain things in life are better left behind, and also because you have reached a point where you would like to end your past, to be able to mend your future.

In the weighing scale of gains and losses, it is not the question of which side is supposed to be heavier or which side lighter. It is a question of which side you are on. Because in the event you come up short, you pick up your pieces, and move along. You do so because that's what's left of you. You do so because that is *who you are.*

And strangely enough, as I walked down the corridors of the present, the sights were somewhat reminiscent of a worn-out picture in black-and-white, and the sounds a haunting reverberation of an unfulfilled and, perhaps, an unsavory past. And as I wandered down memory lanes – both pleasant and painful – it seemed as if I was still stranded in the pages of a diary made yellow and brittle with age, and which I had written almost three decades ago.

And three decades later, it seemed to me as if some affairs and administrations were still somewhat *disorderly,* while a few deeds and doctrines still a lamentable representation of *misconduct.*